ACCLAIM FOR

THE
PRODUCTIVITY
PROJECT

"If you are a life hacker, this book is a keeper."

—*Forbes*

"So often we get stuck just doing what we have always done, even if it's not really working. This book helps you cut through all the productivity advice out there to find and test what really works for you."

—Shawn Achor, positive psychology researcher and
New York Times bestselling author of *The Happiness Advantage*

"Chris doesn't just want you to be more productive. He wants you to live a better life. This book is a two-hour ticket to not only becoming more productive but becoming genuinely happier."

—Neil Pasricha, author of *The Book of Awesome* and
The Happiness Equation

"Chris has written the ultimate guidebook for setting your life on fire. Read it, and you'll not only get more done, you'll feel better about it too."

—Laura Vanderkam, author of *I Know How She Does It*

"Because of [Bailey's] personal experiences, the book has a special appeal. . . . Although it's about his personal odyssey, it's really about you—and how you can accomplish more and be happier each day. . . . The year has started with a productivity bang, at least in books . . . All are excellent, but I would rate [*The Productivity Project*] the best if you had to read just one."

—*Globe and Mail*

"My initial reaction was 'A self-help book? Not for me.' But it turns out, this book is for me—and you. . . . This funny read . . . will really get you thinking about how to make the most of your time and energy."

—*Ottawa*

"Every entrepreneur and professional I've met in business wants and needs to be more productive, but finding the approach that works for them can be elusive. I think you will find the techniques presented here well worth adding to your work ethic."

—Martin Zwilling, *Forbes*

"Straightforward and packed with practical tips, it'll have you reevaluating how you spend your precious minutes."

—*Vitamin Daily*

"Bailey's commitment to long-form writing, analysis, and experimenting with different approaches attracted my attention. His willingness to track results, numbers, and share his findings reminds me of Tim Ferriss's earlier work on productivity. The world needs more experimentation and validation for productivity ideas, so I hope Bailey continues his work. . . . Bailey does us a service when he reminds us that 'common sense is not common practice.'"

—*Project Management Hacks*

"Chris [Bailey] writes in an engaging way that really captured my attention. . . . He gives a lot of good insights that I think many students, young adults, and any career-minded person should read. Highly recommend!"

—*Petite Christine*

THE PRODUCTIVITY PROJECT

Accomplishing More by Managing Your Time, Attention, and Energy

CHRIS BAILEY

CURRENCY
NEW YORK

CURRENCY and its colophon are trademarks of Penguin Random House LLC.

Originally published in hardcover in the United States by Crown Business, an
imprint of the Crown Publishing Group, a division of Penguin Random House LLC,
New York, in 2016. Subsequently published in softcover in the United States by
Crown Business, an imprint of the Crown Publishing Group, a division of
Penguin Random House LLC, New York, in 2017.

Currency books are available at special discounts for bulk purchases for sales
promotions or corporate use. Special editions, including personalized covers, excerpts
of existing books, or books with corporate logos, can be created in large quantities for
special needs. For more information, contact Premium Sales at (212) 572-2232 or
e-mail specialmarkets@penguinrandomhouse.com.

Library of Congress Cataloging-in-Publication Data
Bailey, Chris
The productivity project : accomplishing more by managing your time, attention, and
energy better / Chris Bailey.
    pages cm
1. Time management. 2. Distraction (Psychology) 3. Industrial productivity. I. Title.
BF637.T5B35 2016
650.1—dc23201502   2019

ISBN 978-1-101-90405-3
Ebook ISBN 978-1-101-90404-6

Printed in India

Book design by Lauren Dong
Cover design by Tal Goretsky

10

For everyone at Camp.

CONTENTS

THE
PRODUCTIVITY
PROJECT

INTRODUCTION

While some people have normal interests like sports, music, and cooking, as strange as it might sound, I have always been obsessed with becoming as productive as possible.

I can't remember when I was first bit by the productivity bug. It could have been when I picked up David Allen's canonical *Getting Things Done* book in high school, when I started diving deep into productivity blogs as a young teenager, or when I began exploring my parents' collection of psychology books around the same time—but I've been obsessed with productivity for the better part of a decade, and over that time I've brought that obsession to virtually every facet of my life.

In high school, I began to experiment with as many productivity techniques as I could find, which let me graduate with a 95 percent average while carving out huge swaths of time for myself. At Carleton University in Ottawa, I studied business where I did much the same thing, deploying my favorite productivity tactics to keep an A average while doing as little work as I possibly could.

While in school, I had the chance to experiment with productivity techniques at several real-world full-time co-op internships, including one yearlong job where I autonomously hired about two hundred students for a global telecommunications company, and another where I worked from home for a global marketing team, helping the team create marketing materials and coordinate video shoots around the world.

Because of my hard work (and productivity), my school awarded me their Co-op Student of the Year Award, and I graduated from the university with two full-time job offers.

THE POINT OF PRODUCTIVITY

I don't mention what I've accomplished to try to impress you, but rather to impress *upon* you how powerful of an idea productivity can be. As much as I'd sometimes like to think so, I wasn't offered two full-time jobs out of college because I'm particularly smart or gifted. I simply think I have a very firm grasp of what it takes to become more productive and get more done on a daily basis.

Although the jobs and school were fun, at the end of the day I was truthfully much more excited that I had a chance to use both contexts as sandboxes to filter out the productivity tactics that work from the ones that didn't.

To see the profound effects that investing in your productivity can have, look no further than to how the average American spends his or her day. According to the most recent American Time Use Survey, the average employed person aged twenty-five to fifty-four with kids spends:

- 8.7 hours a day working
- 7.7 hours a day sleeping
- 1.1 hours a day on household chores
- 1.0 hours a day eating and drinking
- 1.3 hours a day caring for others
- 1.7 hours a day on "Other"
- **2.5 hours a day on leisure activities**

Every day we get twenty-four hours to live our lives in a meaningful way. But once you account for all the obligations each of us has, there really isn't much time left; a paltry two and a half hours for most of us, to be exact. I've converted the numbers into a pie chart to illustrate just how little time in our day that is:

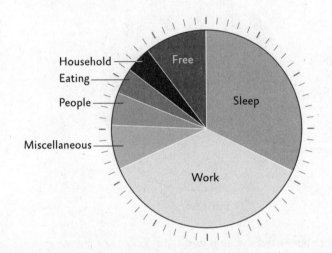

This is where productivity can come to the rescue. I think productivity tactics—like the ones that I discuss in this book—exist to help you accomplish everything you have to do in less time, so you can carve out more time for what's actually important and meaningful in your life. Productivity is what makes the difference between someone who runs a company and the employees who work for her. It is also the difference between having no time or energy left at the end of the day and having a ton of time and energy left over to invest however you want.

Obviously you can use the tactics in this book however you want; my approach has always been one of striking a balance between carving out more time and energy for the things that are meaningful to me, and accomplishing more. This approach simply fits with the way I think. I like to accomplish and do cool things, but I also love having the freedom to spend my time as I please.

When you take the time to invest in your productivity, and use what you learn to carve out more time for what matters most to you, I think it's entirely realistic that your average day could look a little more like this:

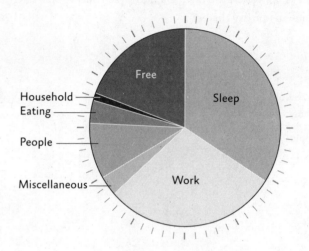

At least, that's what I've found during my decade of intense experimentation with productivity.

A YEAR OF PRODUCTIVITY

I was caught on the horns of a dilemma. Both job offers I had received had great starting salaries, promises of career advancement, and looked like a lot of fun on the surface. But as I began to think about each of them more deeply, I came to the realization that they weren't really what I wanted to do with my life.

Don't get me wrong, I'm not some spoiled dilettante obsessed with spouting eighteenth-century French poetry all day. I just didn't want to throw the limited time I had into a black hole that did nothing more than provide me with a paycheck every second Friday.

So I began to consider what other options I had—and suddenly everything fell into place.

During the 1960s and 1970s, the University of California at Irvine was one of a group of universities that decided to build their campuses without any paths. (I went to school in Canada, but I love this story.) Students and faculty simply walked in the grass around the campus buildings as they pleased, without following a walkway that was already paved for them. A year or so later, once the school could see where the grass was worn around the buildings, they paved over *those* paths instead. The sidewalks at UC Irvine don't simply connect the buildings to one another in a predetermined way—they're mapped to where people naturally want to walk. Landscape architects call these paths "desire paths."

In a similar fashion, as I began to question the two traditional paths I had before me, I thought about what paths I had already carved out in my life that I actually wanted to continue traveling on. It only took me a few seconds to see that the thing I was most passionate about was productivity.

I knew I couldn't explore the topic of productivity forever. When I graduated, I had about $10,000 saved up (Canadian dollars—equal to about $30 US dollars, or $1,500 in *Monopoly* money). After I ran the numbers, I figured it was enough money to continue traveling down my desire path for a year, or in other words, get me through one year of exploring the topic of productivity. I also had $19,000 in student loans, so it would be a gamble. I would have to eat a lot of beans and rice, but if there was a time in my life when it made sense to make a big bet on my future, it was then. Sure, the idea of a yearlong project was a bit of a cliché, but that was simply a function of how much financial runway I had to explore the topic.

Shortly after I graduated in May of 2013, I officially declined the two full-time job offers to start a project of my own that I named *A Year of Productivity* (or *AYOP*).

The idea behind the project was simple. For one entire year, I would devour everything I could get my hands on about productivity and write about what I learned on my website, ayearofproductivity.com.

For 365 days, I

- Read countless books and academic journal articles on productivity, delving deep into the prevailing research on the topic.

- Interviewed productivity gurus to see how they live productively every day.
- Conducted as many productivity experiments as I could, using myself as a guinea pig to explore what it takes to become as productive as possible.

Although much of my time was spent on research and interviews to get to the bottom of what it takes to become more productive, my productivity experiments quickly became the most noteworthy part of my project—in part because I learned so many unique lessons from them (and in part because so many of them were batshit crazy). My productivity experiments included

- Meditating for 35 hours a week.
- Working 90-hour weeks.
- Waking up at 5:30 every morning to see the impact on my productivity.
- Watching 70 hours of TED talks one week.
- Gaining 10 pounds of lean muscle mass.
- Living in total isolation.
- Drinking only water for a month.

And many more.

AYOP served as the perfect framework to experiment with all the productivity tactics I was curious about but hadn't had the time to research or experiment with. The purpose of my project was to dive as deeply as possible into productivity for a year, and then share everything I learned with the world.

ABOUT THIS BOOK

The Productivity Project is the crescendo for my year of intense research and experimentation. Over the last decade I've read about, researched, and tested thousands of productivity hacks to filter out the ones that work from the ones that don't. For *The Productivity Project* I have selected the *twenty-five* productivity tactics that, among the thousands I've encountered, I believe will make the biggest impact on your work on a daily basis. I have personally experimented with and use every tactic in this book regularly—and I'm confident they will help you, too.

I won't spoil too much of what's to come, but in the chapters ahead I will reveal my favorite productivity tactics so that you can

- Identify the integral tasks in your work.
- Work on those tasks more efficiently.
- Manage your time like a ninja.
- Quit procrastinating.
- Work smarter, not harder.
- Develop laserlike focus.
- Achieve zenlike mental clarity throughout the day.
- Have more energy than you have ever had before.
- And much more!

If that sounds like a daunting list, don't worry—it'll be a blast, and we'll tackle it all one page at a time.

You ready? Let's do this.

A NEW DEFINITION OF PRODUCTIVITY

Never one to back away from a weird experiment, I registered for four months' worth of yoga classes about seven years ago.

Yoga classes cost as much as $25 per lesson, so when my university advertised a four-month, $60 special, I instantly jumped on board. Yoga felt like nothing more than a passing fad to me at that point, but pretty much every cute girl I knew was signing up, so I decided to try it out to, you know, see what the fuss was about.

But as the semester marched on, I found myself becoming more and more excited for the Thursday night class (surprisingly less for the girls, and more for the class itself). The class was the antithesis of the busy, hurried life I was accustomed to living, and, if anything, it afforded me the ability to slow down and actually appreciate all the accomplishments my productivity had brought about.

One of my favorite elements of the class was how it ended. Before France (our instructor, not the country) allowed us to venture back into our busy university world, she ended the class with a simple breathing meditation, where she would guide us through mindfully observing our breath.

Those meditation sessions were only five minutes long, but I still remember how much they helped me feel calmer, more clear-headed, and more at ease than anything else I had done before.

A MEDITATION ON PRODUCTIVITY

As the years passed in college, my fondness for meditation deepened. As I dove deeper and deeper into the ritual, I went from meditating five minutes a day, to ten minutes, to fifteen minutes, to twenty minutes, and eventually, a few years ago, to thirty minutes every day. That's longer than most people meditate, but I chose to meditate instead of do other (more "productive") things simply because I loved it so much.

I think a lot of people make meditation out to be way more complicated than it actually is, but I won't get too technical here about the ritual (I talk about meditation more on page 201 if you're curious). Basically, I simply sit on a chair or a cushion—usually in my work clothes—and observe my breath. I'm not into rituals like chanting or focusing on my "third eye" (whatever that means). I simply focus on my breath for thirty minutes, and when my mind inevitably wanders away from my breath to focus on something more interesting, I gently bring my attention back to my breath. I continue to observe its natural ebbs and flows until my meditation timer rings after thirty minutes. It's frustrating at times, but over time the ritual grew to easily be the most calming part of my day.

Over the last several years, while exploring meditation further, I also delved more deeply into productivity. Whenever I wasn't working as efficiently as possible, I would research books on how to become more productive, catch up on the latest productivity hacks, and keep up with all the productivity blogs and websites I followed. After seeing both interests snowballing in tandem I made the decision to start *A Year of Productivity*.

Until that point, I hadn't given much thought as to how meditation and productivity were connected. But after examining how every element of my life either added to or subtracted from my productivity, I reached a devastating conclusion: my meditation ritual and newly launched yearlong productivity experiment could not have been more different.

The problem wasn't so much with the ritual itself—but rather with my understanding of the mindset behind it. I practiced meditation and mindfulness as a way of doing less, at a slower pace, and I saw productivity as a way of doing more, faster. After the first few months of my project, I even began to feel guilty about my meditation ritual. After all, shouldn't I be getting real work done during that time, instead of sitting in a meditative pose and doing nothing for half an hour?

When I had to choose between working for thirty minutes longer and meditating for thirty minutes, I would almost always choose to work longer and get more work done, and not meditate at all.

Eventually, a couple of months into my project, I stopped meditating entirely.

WORKING ON AUTOPILOT

In the weeks that followed I began to work completely differently. Instead of taking frequent breaks to step back from my project, I would work straight through my tiredness and fatigue to try to write and experiment as much as possible. As I began to work at a more hurried pace, I felt less calm and focused throughout the day. My head wasn't as clear, and I became less excited by the work I was doing—even though I was exploring my deepest passion. Worst of all, I began to work less deliberately, and a lot more often on autopilot. Because of all this, I became much *less* productive (I'll talk about how I measured my productivity during my project on page 28).

This is, of course, not a book about meditation. I know that not everyone will be attracted by the practice. In fact, my guess is that only a fraction of you will give it a shot. But I think there is something to be said for the *mindset* behind the practice, because it helps you slow down and work calmly and deliberately throughout the day.

Meditation didn't have a profound impact on my productivity because it helped me relax, clear my head, or relieve my stress after a long day—though it certainly did that. *Meditation had such a profound effect on my productivity because it allowed me to slow down enough so that I could work deliberately and not on autopilot.* I think one of the biggest mistakes people make when they invest effort in improving their productivity is that they continue to work automatically, in response to the work that comes their way. But I've found that when you work on autopilot, it's virtually impossible to step back from your work to determine what's important, how to think more creatively, how to work smarter instead of just harder, and how to take control over what you're working on instead of working on the tasks that other people throw (or in most cases, email) your way.

After I stopped meditating every day, I began to work more frantically and less deliberately, which prevented me from working smarter. And that wiped out the productivity gains I had made.

THE MONK AND THE COCAINE-FUELED STOCK TRADER

Naturally, not everyone approaches his or her work with the same degree of deliberateness. Take, for example, the world's most devout monk, who meditates all day, and takes an hour to do anything because he wants to do it slowly and mindfully. The monk does as little as possible, as deliberately as possible, and can do things so purposefully because he moves at a snail's pace.

The opposite of the monk is the cocaine-fueled stock trader, who works quickly, automatically, at the most frenzied pace imaginable. Unlike the monk, the stock trader doesn't often step back from what he works on to reflect on its value or meaning—he simply tries to do as much as possible, as quickly as possible. Because he works so fast, he doesn't have any spare time or attention to do things purposefully or with intention.

I've experimented with both paces (but never with cocaine) and have found that neither approach is ideal as far as productivity is concerned. Meditating all day may bring you inner peace, and working at a frenzied pace may be incredibly stimulating, but productivity has nothing to do with how much you *do*, and everything to do with how much you accomplish. As a monk or a cocaine-fueled stock trader, you won't accomplish much. When you work like a monk, you work too slowly to accomplish much of anything, and when you work like a stock trader, you're too hurried to step back from your work to identify what's important so that you work smarter instead of just harder.

The most productive people work at a pace somewhere between the monk and the stock trader—fast enough to get everything done, and slowly enough so they can identify what's important and then work deliberately and with intention.

THE THREE INGREDIENTS OF PRODUCTIVITY

Although it's impossible to become more productive when you work on autopilot today, this wasn't always the case.

Fifty years ago, about a third of all U.S. employees worked in factories. In a factory, or in a methodical, assembly-line kind of job, productivity was simpler: the more widgets you produced in the same amount of time, the more efficient and productive you were. Your work didn't change much, there was very little room to work smarter instead of harder, and you didn't have much of a say over what you worked on or when you worked on it.

Many people still work in factories or have factory-type jobs, but if you picked up this book, chances are you don't. Chances are your work involves more intellectual capital than in the past and is intricate and ever changing, and you have more freedom than ever before to work on what you want, when you want. You may not have *total* control over your work, but you have a lot more control than someone who worked in a factory or on an assembly line half a century ago.

In most jobs today—including in the ones I've had, and in the kinds of jobs every high-performing person I have interviewed for this book has—efficiency is no longer enough. When you have more to do than ever before, less time to do it, and unparalleled freedom and flexibility with how you get it done, productivity is no longer about how efficiently you work. **Productivity is about how much you *accomplish*.**

That requires you to work smarter instead and manage your time, attention, and energy better than ever before.

Somewhere toward the end of my project, I arrived at an epiphany: every lesson I learned fell into better management of one of three categories: my time, my attention, and my energy. Although many lessons or insights fit into more than one category, there was not a single thing I had explored that didn't have to do with some combination of the three—and I explored some crazy approaches over the course of my project.

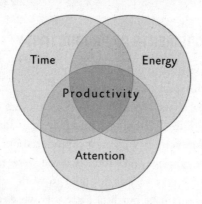

With factory-type jobs, managing your attention and energy wasn't as important, because simple, repetitive work didn't require a lot of either. Managing your time well was good enough, so if you showed up at nine, did your job well for eight hours, and left at five, you got paid reasonably well and lived a relatively happy life.

Today, things couldn't be more different. We have more demands than ever before on our time, an overwhelming number of distractions surrounding us, stress and pressure coming at us from every direction, work that comes home with us, beeps and notifications that follow us around all day and hijack our attention, and less time than ever before to cultivate our energy levels by doing things like exercising, eating well, or getting enough sleep.

In this new environment, the most productive people not only manage their time well—they also manage their attention and energy well.

Near the end of my project, I couldn't stop marveling at how interconnected and important all three of the ingredients of productivity are. For example, getting enough sleep requires more *time*, but it boosts your *energy* and ability to manage your *attention*. Eliminating noise and distractions also takes *time*, but helps you manage your *attention* better because it provides you with more focus and clarity throughout the day. Changing your mindset takes *energy* and *attention*, but will let you get more done in less *time*.

All three are vitally important. If you don't spend your time wisely, it doesn't matter how much energy and focus you have—you won't accomplish a lot at the end of the day. If you can't focus or bring a lot of attention to what you're doing, it doesn't matter if you know what your smartest tasks are or have a ton of energy—you won't be able to engage fully with your work and become more productive. And if you can't manage your energy well, it doesn't matter how well you can manage your time or attention—you're not going to have enough fuel in the tank to get everything done that you intend to.

Perhaps most important, if you can't manage all three—time, attention, energy—well, it is next to impossible to work deliberately and with intention throughout the day.

When we waste time, we're procrastinating. When we can't manage our attention well, we're distracted. And when we don't cultivate our energy levels, we're tired, or "burned out." (Interestingly, the construct of "burnout" is relatively new; it was first identified in the 1970s—somewhere in the middle of our transition from a factory mindset to a productivity mindset in the workplace.)

In the coming chapters, I'll talk about the most powerful time-management techniques I've encountered over my decade of experimenting with productivity, but I'll spend just as much time on the best ways to manage your attention and energy. Most of us no longer work in factories, and with productivity being less about how much we do and everything to do with how much we accomplish, all three ingredients could not be more important.

It is with this new mindset and definition of productivity that *The Productivity Project* begins.

With more control than ever before over what you work on, and with more to work on than ever before, the absolute best place to start is determining the right things to become more productive on. Your effort toward taking control of your time, attention, and energy will be fruitless when you don't first take stock of what tasks are the most valuable and meaningful to you.

Unfortunately, that's a lesson I had to learn the hard way.

Part One

LAYING THE GROUNDWORK

1

WHERE TO START

Takeaway: Everyone likes the idea of becoming more productive and making positive changes to his or her life. But in practice, both are tough, and having a deep, meaningful reason for becoming more productive will help you sustain your motivation in the long run.

Estimated Reading Time: 8 minutes, 40 seconds

A DREAM COME TRUE

Before each chapter, I've included a takeaway of what you'll get out of it, so you can prime your mind for what's to come. I've also included an estimate of how long it will take you to read each chapter, based on an average reading speed of 250 words per minute.

I have been enchanted with the idea of becoming an early riser since I can remember. Before starting my project, I would frequently daydream about waking up just a few minutes before my alarm clock sounded at 5:30, propelling myself out of bed to ritualistically prepare a coffee, catch up on the news that had taken place overnight, meditate, and go for a morning run before the rest of the world woke up. In my daydream I also woke up beside Mila Kunis, but that's for another book.

Suffice it to say, when I started *A Year of Productivity*, I was determined to wake up at 5:30 every morning—even if it took me all year.

Before my project, as obsessed as I was with productivity, my nighttime and morning routines couldn't have been less conducive to an early morning routine. After I would finish working for the day (as efficiently as possible, naturally), I would often lose track of time reading, hanging out with friends, or soaking in online cosmology lectures until I was either out of time or energy for the evening. As much as I was in love with the idea of rising early, becoming an early riser would have meant completely changing my nighttime rituals and morning routines, which felt like more than I could handle.

Of all the productivity experiments I conducted during my year of productivity, waking up at 5:30 was easily the most challenging. At first, I found that my 9:30 target bedtime snuck up faster and faster, and that I often had to make the choice: pack things in earlier in the day when I still had lots to do, or stay up late to get everything done and sleep in later. I sometimes found myself going to bed right when I had the most energy, focus, and creativity—I'm a natural late-night person—and so I decided to stay up later. I also wanted to hang out with my friends and my girlfriend when I was finished researching and writing for the day, which would have been impossible if I headed to bed early.

After about six months of chipping away at countless habits to integrate an early morning routine into my life, I settled into a new wake-up ritual, one where I rewarded myself for waking up early (page 132), shut off my devices from 8 p.m. to 8 a.m. (page 186), quit drinking caffeine at noon (page 228), and eased into the ritual by gradually moving my bedtime earlier over the course of a couple of months (page 248). I'll explain these tactics in detail later on, but needless to say, this was one of those experiments where I learned a lot of valuable lessons the hard way.

Nonetheless, six months in, I had done it: I had woken up at 5:30 every weekday morning for several weeks and settled into a new morning ritual. My morning routine was the stuff I imagined productivity dreams are made of:

- 5:30–6:00: Wake up; prepare and drink a coffee.
- 6:00–7:15: Walk to the gym; plan out my entire day while working out.
- 7:15–8:15: Make a big, healthy breakfast; shower; meditate.
- 8:15: Reconnect to the internet (after my daily shutoff ritual).
- 8:15–9:00: Read.
- 9:00–: Begin working.

I continued to follow the ritual for several months afterward, religiously powering down my devices every night at 8 p.m., heading to bed at 9:30, and waking up promptly at 5:30, feeling virtuous and pleased with my efforts until, one Monday morning, I realized something that stopped me cold in my tracks. I absolutely *hated* going to bed and waking up early.

After my initial excitement over my new routine wore off, I found myself growing tired of saying no to hanging out with my friends, simply because I had to head to bed early. I couldn't stand quitting work when I was "in the zone" late at night. Every morning I found I felt groggy for the first hour or two I was awake. And I discovered I much preferred to meditate, work out, read, and plan out my day later on in the day, when I had more energy and attention to bring to the tasks.

Worst of all, the ritual *didn't* make me more productive. With my new routine, I found I accomplished what I intended to a lot less often, wrote fewer words on average per day, and had less energy and focus throughout the day. And after doing the research, I discovered that there is absolutely no difference in socioeconomic standing between someone who is an early riser and someone who is a night owl—we are all wired differently, and one routine is not inherently better than another. It's what you do with your waking hours, I discovered, that makes the difference in how productive you are (I talk more about this on page 250).

As much as I adored the idea of waking up early, in practice I liked waking up later much more.

PRODUCTIVITY WITH A PURPOSE

I think the same is true of productivity itself. Everyone likes the *idea* of taking on more and making positive changes to their life. But in practice, becoming more productive is one of the toughest things you can undertake to do. If it were easy, I probably wouldn't have dedicated a year of my life to exploring the topic, and there would be no reason for this book to exist.

Though I learned a great many productivity lessons from this yearlong experiment, perhaps the biggest lesson I learned was just how important it is to deeply care about *why* you want to become more productive.

If I were reading this book instead of writing it, that last sentence is one I might have glossed over, so I think it's worth repeating: *perhaps the biggest lesson I learned from this experiment was just how important it is to deeply care about your productivity goals, about* why *you want to become more productive.*

When I committed to turning my morning and nighttime routines inside out to wake up at 5:30 every morning, I didn't think much about whether I deeply cared about waking up early. I was in love with the sepia-toned fantasy of being the "productivity guy" who rose while everyone else was still sleeping and got more done than everyone else. I didn't think much about what it would take to make that a reality, or about whether I actually cared about what was involved in making that change on a deeper level.

Working deliberately and purposefully throughout the day can make or break how productive you are. But having a purpose is just as important. The intention behind your actions is like the shaft behind an arrowhead—it's pretty difficult to become more productive day in and day out when you don't care about what you want to accomplish on a deeper level. This productivity insight is *by far* the least sexy tip in this book, but it may be the most important. Investing countless hours becoming more productive, or taking on new habits or routines, is a waste if you don't actually care about the changes you're trying to make. And you won't have the motivation to sustain these changes in the long term.

SEXY VALUES

The reason I have continued to research and explore productivity over the last decade is that productivity is connected with so many things I value at a deep level: efficiency, meaning, control, discipline, growth, freedom, learning, staying organized. These values are what motivate me to spend so much of my leisure time reading and seeking out online science lectures.

Waking up at 5:30 every morning? Not so much.

A long procession of people before me have written about "acting in accordance with your values," and to be honest, whenever I've read those kinds of statements about values, I have almost always tuned out, or simply read on. Unlike Mila Kunis, values are anything but sexy. But they are most definitely worth thinking about when you're planning on making major changes to your life. If I had taken just a few minutes to think about how waking up early was connected with what I deeply cared about—not at all—I could have saved myself months of willpower and sacrifice and done something much more productive with that time. Questioning *why* you want to make a change to your life can save you countless hours or even days of time, when you discover that you don't really want to make the change in the first place.

THE PRACTICAL PART

I know right now you're deep in "reading mode" and aren't eager to stop reading and perform a quick challenge, despite how much more productive doing so will make you.

But making the jump between knowing and doing is what productivity is all about.

Let's gently transition from "reading" into "doing" and try the first productivity challenge of the book. Don't worry, it's a lot easier than you think: most of the challenges in this book will take you less than ten minutes, and all you need for most of them is a pen and a sheet or two of paper. There isn't a challenge in every chapter, but I have added them when I think they will be worth your time. I know your time is the most valuable and limited resource you have, and I promise I won't waste any of it. For every minute you spend on these challenges, I promise you'll make that time back at least ten times over.

Ready to go?

Go ahead and grab yourself a pen and paper, and then read on.

THE VALUES CHALLENGE

Time required: 7 minutes
Energy/Focus Required: 6/10
Value: 8/10
Fun: 3/10
What you'll get out of it: Access to your deeper reasons for becoming more productive. If you're using the tactics in this book to take more on, you could potentially save countless hours by only focusing on the productivity goals you care about. The return on this challenge can be massive.

I know that if I simply suggested you make a list of your deepest-held values and then create a plan how to act in accordance with them, you'd either put down this book to write a negative review on Amazon, or skip ahead to see what other productivity tips I have up my sleeve.

For that reason, I've instead selected a few very simple questions for you to ask yourself that I've found helpful when examining new routines and habits. I've personally done every single one of the challenges in this book and can vouch for their efficacy. They work. I'm not just pulling them out of the ether to waste your time. To start with:

- Imagine this: As a result of implementing the tactics in this book, you have **two more hours** of leisure time every day. How will you use that time? What new things will you take on? What will you spend more time on?

- When you picked up this book, what productivity goals, or new habits, routines, or rituals did you have in mind that you wanted to take on?

Here are some important questions regarding your values and goals to think about.

- **Go deep.** Ask yourself: What deep-rooted values are associated with your productivity goals? Why do you want to become more productive? If you find yourself coming up with a lot of values you deeply care about (like meaning, community, relationships, freedom, learning, etc.), chances are you care about the goal on a deep personal level, and the change you have in mind is probably worth making. If you find yourself blustering your way through this exercise, maybe a particular change or goal isn't in tune with your values and is not really all that important to you. (Google "list of values" for a few great lists to start with.)

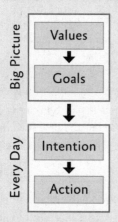

- **If thinking about values is too daunting to you,** fill in this blank with each change you want to make: I *deeply* care about this because _____. Spin off as many reasons as you can to determine whether you care about each change on a deeper level.

- **Another quick shortcut** to determine if a change is meaningful to you: fast-forward to when you're on your deathbed. Ask yourself: Would I regret doing more or less of this?

I believe the point of greater productivity is to carve out more time for the things that are actually meaningful to you.

But tasks and commitments aren't valuable only because they are meaningful to you. They can also be valuable because they have a significant impact in your work.

NOT ALL TASKS ARE CREATED EQUAL

Takeaway: Not all tasks are created equal; there are certain tasks in your work that, for every minute you spend on them, let you accomplish more than your other tasks. Taking a step back from your work to identify your highest-impact tasks will let you invest your time, attention, and energy in the right things.

Estimated Reading Time: 9 minutes, 47 seconds

MEDITATING FOR THIRTY-FIVE HOURS

I learned the hard way how important it was to slow down and work more deliberately when I abandoned my meditation practice. So I decided to conduct an experiment to get to the bottom of just how much meditation and slowing down impacted my productivity—and designed an experiment to meditate for thirty-five hours over six days.

As a seasoned meditator I was no stranger to meditating for long stretches of time. Before the experiment, I had meditated for thirty minutes every day for several years, practiced meditation with my Buddhist meditation group every week, and attended an occasional meditation retreat, where I lived in total silence for days at a time while meditating with other attendees for five or six hours every day.

Thirty-five hours of meditation in a week would be a lot for even our old friend the seasoned monk, who takes an hour to do anything. But I was too curious not to do it. To spice things up, throughout the week I also performed the same simple chores and tasks I would usually undertake, but in a mindful state.

While running the experiment, I tried my best to remain as productive as possible during the time when I wasn't meditating, so I could observe the day-to-day effects of meditation on my energy levels, focus, and productivity.

Over six days—after live-streaming a tally of how long I meditated for each day—I performed:

- 14.3 hours of sitting meditation
- 8.5 hours of walking meditation
- 6.2 hours of mindfully doing chores
- 6 hours of mindful eating

MEASURING PRODUCTIVITY

One of the most interesting parts of this project was how circular it was by design. Being productive about studying productivity is, in a way, like writing about writing. But first and foremost, *A Year of Productivity* was a research project, and to me, having a productive day meant learning as much as possible, and sharing what I learned with readers of my blog to help them become more productive, too.

When I started *A Year of Productivity*, I created a fancy landing page on my website that contained live-updating charts of exactly how many words I wrote, pages I read, and hours I worked each day (it's still live at http://alifeofproductivity.com/statistics). My thought behind the graphs was simple: the more I wrote and read, the more productive I would be.

The problem with these metrics, as you might have guessed, is they only tell a part of the story. If I worked all day long and wrote 1,000 words, I would be considered productive under these metrics. But what if I intended to write *2,000* words and wrote only 1,000? What if I couldn't focus all day long and wasted hours watching cooking shows on Netflix? What if I felt totally burned out at the end of the day? What if those 1,000 words were worthless? The entire Gettysburg Address, after all, was only 272 words!

A month or two into my project, I realized my mistake in designing my website's Stats page—a mistake I think people make all too often with productivity. I had essentially reverted to a factory mindset and equated productivity with efficiency, instead of looking at how much I accomplished. Once I set aside that mindset, and instead focused on how much I accomplished, my productivity skyrocketed.

I think the best way to measure productivity is to ask yourself a very simple question at the end of every day: **Did I get done what I intended to?** When you accomplish what you intend to, and you're realistic and deliberate about the productivity goals you set, in my opinion you are productive.

If at the beginning of the day you intend to write a thousand great words, and you do, you were productive.

If you intend to finish a report at work, ace a job interview, and spend quality time with your family, and you do, again, you are perfectly productive.

If you intend to relax for a day, and you have the most relaxing day you've had all year, you were perfectly productive.

Intention and deliberateness are two sides of the same coin, and I think both are essential if you want to live more productively. Asking myself whether I accomplished what I intended to was the first of two ways I measured how productive I was over the course of my project.

The second was observing how each new experiment or productivity technique affected my ability to manage the three ingredients of productivity:

- **Time:** I observed how intelligently I used my time, how much I got done throughout the day, how many words and pages I wrote/ read, and how often I procrastinated.

- **Attention:** I noted what I focused on, how well I focused, and how easily I was distracted.

- **Energy:** I scrutinized how much drive, motivation, and overall energy I had, tracking how my energy levels fluctuated over the course of an experiment.

Naturally, these variables are more subjective than whether I accomplished what I had intended to accomplish. My productivity experiments triggered me to study the research when I noticed how a topic affected how I spent my time, attention, or energy. I'm skeptical by nature, so I leaned on science as much as possible to explain my results. Plus, the science behind this stuff is fascinating.

WORKING SMARTER

While my meditation experiment helped me to improve my focus more than anything I had tried up to that point, the experiment had another effect I hadn't anticipated: it let me manage my *time* better, because it made it much easier for me to identify what was important, which let me work smarter instead of just harder.

The reason I found it easier to work smarter during this experiment wasn't because of the meditation practice itself. It was simply because I had so little time to get work done that week. During the experiment, I continued to write articles and read as much as possible. But since I had so little time to do it in, I frequently had to step back from my work to reflect on whether the writing I was doing was important and worth doing. With so little time, it was my only option. (A similar thing happened during my experiment on ninety-hour workweeks.)

This led me to one of my most obvious-in-hindsight epiphanies: **not all tasks are created equal.** Put another way, there are certain tasks in your work that, minute for minute, lead you to accomplish more. This is true regardless of where you work or what you do.

Take, for example, tasks like:

- Planning out your week
- Mentoring new employees
- Investing in your learning
- Pushing back on meetings without an agenda
- Saying no to as much busywork as possible
- Automating repetitive tasks

- Looking at pictures of baby animals (more on cute baby animals on page 260)

Minute for minute, you accomplish more doing these tasks than you do through tasks like:

- Attending pointless meetings
- Keeping up-to-date with social media
- Checking your email repeatedly
- Reading news websites
- Participating in idle chitchat

The more time, energy, and attention you invest in your most significant tasks, the more you accomplish in the same amount of time, and the more productive you become.

When meditating for thirty-five hours a week, I had about twenty hours outside of the experiment to get real work done, which meant that if I didn't determine what my smartest tasks were, I wouldn't have accomplished what I intended to that week. That forced me to step back from my work to carefully plan my week so I could make the most use of the limited time I had.

At some level, everyone knows that not all tasks are equal—most people can see that they will accomplish more working on doing their taxes for an hour than watching a movie. But as the cliché goes, common sense isn't always common action. Just because you know something to be true, doesn't mean you'll act on it—even though acting on what you know is exactly what you have to do in order to become more productive.

YOUR MOST IMPORTANT TASKS

A task, project, or commitment is important for one of two reasons: because it's meaningful to you (it's connected with your values) or because it makes a large impact in your work. Activities that are connected with your deepest-held values will lead you to be happier and more motivated, and activities that are primary to your work will let you become more productive in the same amount of time. If you're lucky, you'll have tasks in your job that are both meaningful and effective. How close or how far your job is from working in a factory or an assembly line will determine how much control you have over this. Whereas a factory worker has to work on whatever he's assigned, an entrepreneur can work on whatever she wants.*

As I began to think hard about how I spent my time, I quickly realized how much productivity I was leaving on the table every day—not because I wasn't working hard, but because I wasn't working hard on the best possible tasks. I wasn't as productive as I could have been because I had never sat down, determined the highest-impact tasks in my work, and deliberately worked on those tasks. Instead, I had been spending my time on the items that happened to fall onto my to-do list.

I think this realization speaks volumes to how valuable this project became for me, and for many of my readers. When we're hunkered down in our work, we often aren't able to step back to observe how smart we're working. Keeping productivity in mind for an entire year led me to many realizations like this one—despite how obvious some of those insights are in hindsight.

You may already be familiar with the "Pareto Principle," often referred to as the 80-20 rule. The rule says that 80 percent of [some result] comes from 20 percent of [some cause]. For example, 80 percent of your sales come from 20 percent of your customers, or 80 percent of all income is earned by 20 percent of the people. I think this rule can be applied to productivity as well: a very small number of tasks lead to the majority of what you accomplish.

Productivity isn't about doing more things—it's about doing the right things.

After my meditation experiment, I took the time to step back from my project, make a list of everything I was responsible for, and pick my

---

* As a quick aside, I don't consider either type of task better or worse, since everyone values meaningful work and money differently.

most important tasks. That's when I discovered something fascinating: I accomplished the most through just *three* main tasks. In order, they were:

1. Writing articles about what I learned during my project
2. Conducting productivity experiments on myself
3. Reading and researching about productivity

Naturally, I had other things I was responsible for as well—like website maintenance, sending email newsletters, interviewing experts, managing my social media accounts, answering email, and coaching people on becoming more productive—but it was through the preceding three activities that I accomplished the most by a long shot. All my other commitments led me to accomplish less in the same amount of time, and most of them could be eliminated or compressed (see Part Four).

THE IMPACT CHALLENGE

Estimated time to do the challenge: 10 minutes
Energy/Focus Required: 8/10
Value: 10/10
Fun: 8/10
What you'll get out of it: You will discover the highest-impact tasks in your work, which will show you where you should invest the majority of your time, attention, and energy. Before you invest in increasing your productivity, it's crucial you determine which areas you want to become more productive in. This simple activity will help you do that. This challenge also lays the groundwork for the rest of this book.

Thankfully, you don't have to meditate for thirty-five hours in a week to determine your highest-impact tasks.

I have experimented with innumerable techniques to help me organize and prioritize my tasks, and while some systems worked well, most quickly fell by the wayside. Prioritizing everything you're responsible for might sound like a pain, but people make it out to be much more complicated than it actually is.

Of all the challenges in this book, this is one of the most important. After all, it is difficult to become more productive when you don't first take stock of what you should actually be productive on.

My absolute favorite technique for prioritizing what's important comes from Brian Tracy, who wrote the book *Eat That Frog*. Brian, who has a similar view on high-impact tasks, says in his book that "90 percent of the value that you contribute to your company is contained in [just] three tasks."

Brian recommends a linear process to identify your highest-impact tasks, projects, and commitments. His method is quite simple, and I have modified and expanded on it a bit to make it more helpful:

1. Make a list of everything you're responsible for in your work. This part of the activity takes the longest, but it feels incredible to get everything you're responsible for onto a sheet of paper in front of you (or into whatever your preferred digital equivalent is). There's a good chance you haven't taken a moment to step back and think about everything you're responsible for in your work on a weekly or monthly basis.

2. After you've collected a list of everything you're responsible for, ask yourself: If you could just do *one item* on that list all day, every day, what item would you do that would allow you to accomplish the most with the same amount of time? Put another way, what item on the list is the most valuable to your boss or yourself (if you're self-employed, like I am)?

3. Finally, ask yourself: If you could do only *two more items on* that list all day, what second and third tasks let you accomplish the most in the same amount of time?

These three tasks (or four, if you have a fourth that's as important as your top three) are the 20 percent of your tasks through which you contribute *at least* 80 percent of your value. *Value* is the operative word here; unlike your most meaningful tasks, your most purposeful tasks may not necessarily contribute a lot of value or meaning to *you*, but they contribute an incredible amount of value to your productivity.

As I began to deliberately and intentionally invest more time, attention, and energy into my highest-return tasks, my productivity shot through the roof. Working smarter instead of just harder is impossible without first stepping back from your work, and that's what this first section of the book—*Laying the Groundwork*—is all about.

After you've begun to lay the groundwork by determining your smartest tasks to work on, what comes next?

Working on them, of course.

3

THREE DAILY TASKS

Takeaway: The absolute best technique I've found to work deliberately and with intention every day is the Rule of 3. The rule is simple: at the beginning of each day, before you start working, decide what three things you want to accomplish by the end of the day. Do the same at the start of every week.

Estimated Reading Time: 8 minutes, 1 second

THE RULE OF 3

Knowing your most valuable tasks is important, but as G.I. Joe would say, knowing is only half the battle. When you sit in front of your computer tomorrow morning and open up your inbox, it is far too easy to forget about what's important to work on when more urgent (but less important) tasks come your way.

So while working deliberately is good in theory, what does it actually look like in practice?

I have experimented with dozens of systems to manage everything on my plate—everything from the GTD (Getting Things Done) system, to "kanban," to keeping sticky notes everywhere, to trying out more productivity apps than I can count. Most of them worked well for capturing and organizing everything I had to get done—and I'll talk about the ones that will help you the most later on. But every single one of them also had a rather large downside: they didn't help me slow down and work more deliberately.

Having a great system for managing what you need to get done is important, but it's just as important to work on the tasks you organize in your system deliberately, with intention. That's what this chapter is about. Before you invest in better managing your time, attention, and energy, it's important you continue laying the groundwork by deciding what to focus on every day.

And that's where the Rule of 3 comes in.

About halfway into my project I picked up a productivity book named *Getting Results the Agile Way*, written by J. D. Meier, Microsoft's director of business programs. On the surface, the book looks more like a textbook than it does a general interest book—it's typeset in Papyrus, which is among my least favorite typefaces on the planet. But the content is incredibly powerful because of the way it focuses on productivity through a lens of simplicity. One of my favorite nuggets from the book is "the Rule of 3." Though the concept behind the idea is nothing new—and has been talked about before by productivity bloggers like Leo Babauta of *Zen Habits* and Gina Trapani of *Lifehacker*—it was new to me, and too intriguing not to try.

Although you can download all the productivity apps in the world (and I have), no app will make you care about what you have to do like the Rule of 3.

The rule is dead simple:

1. At the beginning of every day, mentally fast-forward to the end of the day, and ask yourself: *When the day is over, what three things will I want to have accomplished?* Write those three things down.
2. Do the same at the beginning of every week.

The three things you identify then become your focus for the day and the week ahead.

That's it.

WHAT IT LOOKS LIKE IN PRACTICE

When I first started experimenting with the rule, it took me a couple of weeks to adjust. At first, I made my three daily accomplishments too small and way overshot them. Then I started to make them too ambitious—sometimes intimidatingly so—and felt much less motivated throughout the day as I fell short. About a week and a half into experimenting with the ritual, I finally settled into the right balance: one where I became aware of how much time, attention, and energy I had to get stuff done every day.

To give you an idea of what the rule looks like in practice, here are three things I defined this morning that I'm aiming to accomplish today:

1. Finish the Rule of 3 chapter of book
2. Clear out my email inbox—and only check email twice throughout the day
3. Organize everything I need to get a U.S. tax number

When I sat down this morning and thought ahead to the end of the day, these are the three things I wanted to accomplish—and so far I'm on pace to do so.

Just for fun, here are the three things I'm aiming to accomplish this week:

1. Finalize the "Laying the Groundwork" section of book and send to my editor
2. Write and load blog posts for the month
3. Create mind maps (a graphical way of thinking out ideas and concepts) for two speaking engagements in January

At the start of every day and week, I also define three *personal* things I want to accomplish. I don't always come up with three (and the same is true for my work items), but I find that the ritual lets me feel much more in control of my week ahead and also get excited about the things I have coming up. In case you're curious, here are my three goals for today and for this week:

Today:

1. Have fun at tea tasting with Ardyn (my girlfriend)
2. Read twenty-five pages for fun
3. Finalize Christmas shopping list

And for this week:

1. Plan for and buy all Christmas presents
2. Completely disconnect from work for birthday plans
3. Pack; travel home for Christmas

These goals are simple, but they're aligned to what I value and find meaningful, and you can bet I'll feel connected and engaged after I accomplish them.

Determine the foremost meaningful tasks in your work and life. Use the Rule of 3 on a daily and weekly basis.

THINKING IN THREES

When I asked J. D. Meier why choosing just three daily and weekly accomplishments works best—why not two? or one? or four or five?—he had an intriguing answer. "I originally focused on the Rule of 3 because when my manager asked me what the team achieved for the week, he didn't want a laundry list. He was willing to listen to three compelling outcomes."

When J.D. later asked his own team members what they were focused on for the day, he similarly found himself not wanting to hear more than three outcomes, or three meaningful things: "And for myself, I found that three things was very easy to keep top of mind, without having to write it down or look it up. I could rattle off my three outcomes in the hall. This especially helped when doing prioritization on the fly or to really keep myself on track."

Three may seem like an arbitrary number on the surface, but it's large enough to fit the main things you want to accomplish, and small enough to make you think hard about what's important. The rule also helps you work smarter because by deciding what you intend to accomplish, you consequently decide what you *don't* intend to accomplish. And since the rule focuses on the goals you want to accomplish instead of how much you get done, it's much more in line with what productivity is all about.

You don't have to look far to see evidence that we like to think in threes. According to J.D., "the simplest reason [three accomplishments work so well] is because our brains are trained from early on to think in threes: the beginning, the middle, the end." For example, "the military uses threes to help people remember survival information: You can go three minutes without air, three days without water, three weeks without food."

When you look around, there are also countless examples of sets of threes embedded everywhere: the three bears, three blind mice, three little pigs, and three musketeers; phrases like "blood, sweat, and tears" and "the good, the bad, and the ugly"; and ideas like gold, silver, and bronze medals, and "life, liberty, and the pursuit of happiness." Our mind is wired to think in groups of three.

It also works well because, well, despite your best intentions, emergencies come up, more urgent tasks come your way, and crises will erupt. Defining three things to accomplish will give you a guiding light when you're in the trenches, as opposed to tackling a laundry list of things you want to get done, and the dissatisfied feeling of not accomplishing any of it. While later I'll dive into the best ways I've found to deflect unimportant work, shrink low-impact tasks, and minimize the noise around you, having just three items to focus on throughout the day and week will help you stay centered and accomplish more even on days where everything hits the fan. I think J.D. put it well when he said, "Simplicity makes it easier to evolve and innovate and deal with complexity."

THE RULE OF 3 CHALLENGE

Estimated time to do challenge: 5 minutes
Energy/Focus Required: 6/10
Value: 8/10
Fun: 9/10
What you'll get out of it: You'll be able to step back to determine what your most productive tasks are at the beginning of the day, the tasks where you should be investing the predominance of your time, attention, and energy. This will give you something to focus on throughout the day, so you can work smarter instead of just harder.

The challenge here is simple: try the Rule of 3 tomorrow morning.

To accomplish more and spend time on your highest-impact tasks, you have to act on them on a daily basis.

Before you open up your inbox or start your day tomorrow, simply sit down with a pen and paper, mentally fast-forward to the end of the day, and write down the three main things you want to have accomplished when the day is done. Fighting the urge to check your email is tough, but it's worth resisting so you can step back to have a clear mind while you think about what's important to you. If you have trouble thinking in terms of things you will achieve, J.D. Meier recommends you think in terms of "wins, achievements, or highlights," like achieving a milestone on a project, clearing out your backlog of things to do, or winning over a customer.

I also find it helpful to look through my calendar to see what meetings and commitments I have coming up, so I can get a good handle on how much time, attention, and energy I'll have to work with. Becoming more productive is a process of understanding your constraints, and observing how much time, attention, and energy you have will help you adjust accordingly. (In the very next chapter, I'll guide you through accounting for all three ingredients of productivity in more detail.)

If you want to ramp up the rule even further, here are a few simple suggestions:

- Think about when, where, and how you're going to accomplish each item throughout the day. Studies show this makes acting out the goal easier and more automatic, and that it's especially helpful for carrying out unpleasant tasks.

- In addition to deciding on the three main things you want to accomplish, select other small tasks you intend to accomplish over the course of the day. The three things you intend to accomplish may be your primary focuses for the day, but there will almost definitely be other smaller tasks you need to accomplish, too. Keep in mind your constraints.

- Start with just the daily ritual. Once you feel how effective the Rule of 3 is over the course of the day, you'll jump at the chance to use it on a weekly basis, too. Trust me on this one.

- When planning, keep your highest-impact tasks in the back of your mind. And if you decide to try the rule in your personal life (which is worth a shot, especially when you have a lot of personal goals), keep in mind how connected your three accomplishments are with your values.

- Set two alarms during your workday. When they go off ask yourself: *Do you remember what your three daily goals are? Do you remember your three weekly goals? If you do, are you on track to achieve them?*

- At the end of the day and week, reflect on how realistic your three accomplishments were. Were they too small and did you overshoot them? Or were they too large and intimidating? Did you have a good understanding of how much time, attention, and energy you would have to accomplish the three items? Reflecting on how realistic you were will let the rule help you more and more over time.

When your aim is to work more deliberately and accomplish more over the course of the day, the Rule of 3 is in a league of its own.

4

READY FOR PRIME TIME

Takeaway: When you take the time to observe how your energy fluctuates over the course of the day, you can work on your highest-impact tasks during your Biological Prime Time—when you are able to bring the most energy and focus to them. In a similar way, tracking how you spend your time over a week will let you see how intelligently you use your time, and how well you focus throughout the day.

Estimated Reading Time: 11 minutes, 3 seconds

If identifying your highest-impact tasks and your daily focus were enough to become perfectly productive, this book could end right here. But our story is just getting started—and not only because I have an eighty thousand word count to hit. It's because, despite our best intentions to work on the right things, we don't, for countless reasons.

All these reasons involve either how you spend your time, attention, or energy. And I definitely don't count myself out of this group: almost every day I waste time, become distracted, have trouble focusing, and feel low on energy. Thanks to my research and practice, I may be better than most, but I would be lying if I said I was perfectly productive—and so would any other productivity expert out there.

Chances are you're in the same boat. Despite your best intentions, you don't have as much time, energy, or attention as you would like. Or perhaps you procrastinate (Part Two of the book), spend too much time on low-impact tasks that get thrown your way (Part Three), don't spend your time intelligently (Part Four), feel overwhelmed (Part Five), are constantly distracted and can't focus (Part Six), or don't properly cultivate how much energy you have (Part Seven). From what I've experienced, that is perfectly normal.

Throughout the rest of the book, I'll provide you with the absolute best ways I've uncovered to better manage your time, attention, and energy. But before you learn to better manage the three ingredients of productivity, it's essential that you establish one final, important piece of groundwork, and take stock of how well you manage your time, attention, and energy already.

The following two productivity experiments measured how I managed my time, attention, and energy; they produced valuable intel into how I was doing: one experiment measured my energy over the course of the day, and another diligently tracked how I spent my time and attention.

YOUR BIOLOGICAL PRIME TIME

As you may already be aware, your energy levels can fluctuate quite a bit over the course of the day.

If you're an early bird, you have more energy early in the morning. If you're a night owl, you have more energy late at night. After you drink a coffee, you may feel a sudden energy boost, and then an energy crash later on. And if you're like many people, your energy levels may crash in the early afternoon, after your energy levels spike after a large lunch.

I see energy as the fuel that you burn over the course of the day to become productive. As such, it's critically important that you manage your energy well. If you have no fuel in the tank to do good work, or you're burned out because you don't cultivate your energy levels throughout the day by eating well or getting enough sleep, your productivity will plummet, regardless of how well you manage your time or attention.

To get to the bottom of how my energy levels fluctuated over the course of a typical day during my project, I designed an experiment where I kept a log every hour of the day to assess how much energy I had, for three weeks. During those weeks I also did the following:

- Cut out all caffeine and alcohol from my diet
- Ate as little sugar as possible
- Ate small, frequent meals throughout the day for fuel
- Woke up and fell asleep naturally, without setting an alarm

The reasoning behind this productivity experiment was simple: by tracking the natural ebbs and flows of my energy over the course of a few weeks, with as few stimulants as possible, I would get an accurate picture of how much energy I naturally had throughout the day. I would then be able to take steps to become more productive. For example, I would be able to work on my most important tasks when I naturally had the most energy, or take steps to increase my body's and brain's energy when my energy naturally dipped. Everyone is wired differently, and everyone has different energy patterns throughout the day, depending on how their biological clock is set. I wanted to get to the bottom of how my clock was set in this experiment.

After three weeks of inputting how much energy I had every hour, an interesting pattern emerged.

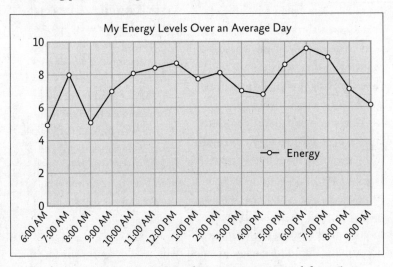

Every day between the hours of 10 a.m. to noon and from 5 p.m. to 8 p.m., I had more energy than any other time of the day.

Different experts refer to this high peak time period by different names, but my favorite is your Biological Prime Time (BPT), a phrase coined by Sam Carpenter in his book *Work the System*.

Taking the time to observe how your energy fluctuates over the course of the day, you can work on your highest-impact tasks during your BPT—when you are able to bring the most energy and focus to them—and work on your lower-impact tasks when your energy levels dip.

The most productive people don't just manage their time well, they also manage their energy and attention well. Rearranging your day around when you have the most energy is one simple way to work smarter instead of just harder.

After determining my BPT, I began to rearrange what I worked on over the course of the day, accordingly. Every day, between the hours of 10 a.m. and noon, and 5 and 8 p.m., I worked on my highest-impact and most meaningful tasks. Conversely, when my energy dipped throughout the day, I worked on my lowest-impact tasks, or invested in a lasting energy boost (like drinking a cup of green tea), and took time to recharge.

You may not have complete control over what you work on and when you work on it, but whenever you do, choosing the smartest time to work on high- and low-impact tasks can make a huge difference in your productivity. For example,

Research shows that your brain's prefrontal cortex—the part of your brain responsible for creative thinking—is the most active immediately after you wake up. That means that even if you're low on energy after you wake up, if you do a lot of creative work, you may want to consider working in the morning instead of when you have the most energy, focus, and motivation. To me, it also feels incredible to tackle your important tasks at the beginning of the day—you'll feel like you're unstoppable for the rest of the day.

if you have the most energy at noon, why would you break for lunch then, instead of waiting until you actually need to refuel?

We'll do a deep dive into how to take advantage of when you have the most energy later on, but getting a handle on your body's natural rhythm is one of the best ways I've found to work smarter instead of just harder.

Of course, your energy is just one of the three ingredients of productivity. Becoming aware of how intelligently you spend your time and attention is just as important.

A DAY IN YOUR LIFE

Although I've never been much of a procrastinator, I've always been a dawdler.

Before taking a shower in the morning, I dawdle and tidy up things around the house. Before heading out the door to run errands, I often open up a book to read a few pages, snack a bit, or get lost in my thoughts.

I don't waste a ton of time in general, and I almost always get done what I intend to get done, but I love punctuating my productivity with short bursts of dawdling throughout the day. Dawdling helps me decompress, transition from one activity to the next, and even come up with better ideas (Chapter 17). Sure, it frustrates the hell out of the people around me—virtually every woman in my life, including my mom, sister, and girlfriend, has at some point told me to "quit my dawdling"—but I love it.

Much like calculating my BPT, tracking how I spent my time every hour for a week was simple in theory, but quite tedious in practice. To do so, I printed out a sheet of paper that looked much like an Excel spreadsheet, with a grid with the hours of the day in rows, and the days of the week as columns. Before getting to the results of my time log, it's worth talking briefly about why keeping a time log is so powerful.

I personally don't maintain a time log very often, largely because doing so takes so much effort. But every few months or so I make an effort to track how I spend my time to see how intelligently I'm using what limited time I have. Of the three ingredients every day that will make you more productive, your time is the most limited. While there are a multitude of ways to get more focus and energy, there's no way to get more time.

To spend your time more intelligently—on your highest-impact and most meaningful tasks—you have to be aware of how you're already spending your time, so you can make adjustments. For example, you might value personal fitness and spirituality and yet spend zero minutes over the course of a week on either one. Or you might decide that training your team is one of your most important work tasks and, again, spend no time on the task throughout the week. Without becoming aware of how you currently spend your time, it's hard to reflect on whether you're acting in ways that match up with what your values and highest-impact tasks are. Keeping a time log is a great way to find your starting point, your base level, to better access how often you work on your highest-impact and most meaningful tasks.

A time log is also a great way to determine how well you focus throughout the day. If you check in every hour to jot down what you're doing and find that you consistently put important things off, you may need to invest in battling procrastination (Chapter 5), working out your attention muscle (Chapter 18), or reducing the number of distractions around you (Chapter 19).

Laura Vanderkam, the time-taming author of *I Know How She Does It* and *168 Hours: You Have More Time Than You Think*, says that keeping a time log is a very useful tool to get a map of how you're *actually* spending your time.

"It can seem like a tedious and boring task, but it can free up literally hours in your week," she told me. "The key is to find a system that works for you."

Naturally, since you're logging how you spend your time every hour (or half hour, or fifteen minutes), keeping a time log also makes you accountable to yourself every hour, instead of holding yourself accountable at the end of the day when you reflect back on whether you accomplished what you intended to. Studies show that when you keep a food log you double the amount of weight you lose. A similar effect occurs after you begin to maintain a time log.

Vanderkam usually records her time in thirty-minute chunks each quarter, for about a week each time. She says it's important to pick a typical week to record, and to use the method you're most comfortable with, whether it's a simple notebook, a spreadsheet on your computer, or a productivity app.

"Even though this is a good tool for finding out where you're wasting time, it can also help you see that dreaded tasks you've been putting off actually don't take as long as you think," she says. "This is good for getting past procrastination."

I conducted my first time log halfway through my project, and I think you may be a bit surprised by the results. But before getting to that, it's time for one final challenge to help you lay the groundwork while you read the rest of *The Productivity Project*.

THE PRIME-TIME CHALLENGE

Estimated time to do challenge: About one minute every hour for at least one week
Energy/Focus Required: 1/10
Value: 9/10
Fun: 3/10
What you'll get out of it: An understanding of how well you manage the three ingredients of productivity, so you know your starting point and can make adjustments to get more done every day.

The fourth challenge I have for you will pay for itself many times over: track your energy to determine your BPT, and keep a time log to evaluate how well you manage your time and attention.

Energy

If you want to truly observe your body's natural rhythms, before keeping a log of how much energy you have, you should:

- Cut out caffeine, alcohol, sugar, and as many other stimulants as possible from your diet. If it takes you a few days to adjust, you may want to consider throwing out your first few days' worth of data, because they may skew your results.

- Eat small, frequent meals throughout the day.

- If you can, wake up and fall asleep naturally, without the aid of an alarm clock or smartphone.

Cutting out caffeine and alcohol is probably the most difficult thing I'll ask you to do in one of these challenges, but to get a good measurement of when you naturally have the most energy, it's almost essential. I see drinking alcohol as a way of borrowing energy from tomorrow; and because you invariably crash after a caffeine high, drinking caffeine is a way of borrowing energy from later on in the day. To get a consistent reading on when you're naturally the most productive, you should cut out both for your measurements. And though sugar can serve as a temporary boost every once in a while, from an energy and productivity standpoint, it's not helpful in the long run.

I personally recommend cutting out all three starting a week before you track your energy levels. Your BPT doesn't change much over time, and the knowledge of when you naturally have the most energy will pay dividends for years to come.

To track your energy levels, as well as your time, you simply need a sheet of paper that lists the hours of the day and the days of the week. To save you some time, I've put together a chart that has everything you need to track your time and energy levels for one week. Just head on over to the website for this book—productivityprojectbook .com—to download and print off the chart!

Time

Every hour, on the hour, in addition to noting how much energy you have (on a scale of 1 to 10), make a note of

- What you are doing.

- How many minutes you procrastinated over the hour (an estimate).

Here are a few tips I think you will find helpful for this challenge:

- In addition to tracking how you spend your time with a pen and paper, if you work a lot of time on the computer, there are some great apps that will let you track how you spend time there, too. If you have the freedom to install programs on your work computer, I highly recommend RescueTime (Rescuetime.com—free; PC, Mac, and Android), and Toggl (Toggl.com—free; PC, Mac, iPhone, Android). RescueTime tracks your time for you automatically in the background, and Toggl lets you track your time manually.

- If you find yourself procrastinating, don't worry—that's normal. According to the procrastination researchers I have interviewed, everyone procrastinates at times—including some of the most renowned procrastination researchers from around the world. Don't be too hard on yourself when you write down how long you procrastinate—and don't be afraid to be honest.

- If the thought of tracking your time and energy for a week or more puts you off, try tracking your time and energy for just a few days. Once you begin to observe some patterns, I think you'll be encouraged to pursue both further. Personally, I recommend tracking your time for a week, and your energy levels for two to three weeks if you can.

- Tracking your time and energy is tedious, I'll grant you. But the return on both activities is huge—so much so that I still track both my time and energy every few months, even though, compared to my initial reading, the return is much smaller. I believe there is incredible value in this activity.

This exercise might be, in itself, enough to motivate you to reduce the amount of time that you waste on low-impact tasks. But if it isn't, don't worry—the rest of this book will guide you through some of the best ways I've discovered to better manage your time, attention, and energy.

Now that we've laid the groundwork to becoming more productive, let me get to the one thing I've swept under the rug thus far in this book: the results of my first time tracking experiment.

Part Two

WASTING TIME

COZYING UP TO UGLY TASKS

Takeaway: Procrastination is human. The biggest reason your highest-impact tasks are so valuable is that they are often more intimidating; they almost always require more time, attention, and energy than your lower-impact tasks. They're typically also more boring, frustrating, difficult, unstructured, and lacking in intrinsic rewards—which all act as triggers for procrastination.

Estimated Reading Time: 16 minutes, 54 seconds

WASTING TIME

In October of 2013, after I conducted a productivity experiment around watching 296 TED Talks in a week, a staff member of the prestigious TED organization invited me to participate in an interview for its official blog.* I was over the moon. I was about halfway into my yearlong experiment, people were starting to discover my website, and the interview was a huge coup. Along with other TED luminaries like Bill Clinton, Malcolm Gladwell, Jane Goodall, and Bill Gates, I would be on the front page of TED.com!

When my interview was posted a week later, I was excited all over again. My favorite part of it was the opening line, which read, "Chris Bailey might be the most productive man you'd ever hope to meet."

---

* TED, which stands for Technology, Entertainment, and Design, is a worldwide series of conferences where leaders in all three fields gather together to talk about their "ideas worth spreading."

TED thought I was the most productive man *ever*! That should go on the cover of my book, right?

That same week, I tracked how I spent my time as an experiment. What I discovered was humbling. Over the course of the week, after tracking how I spent every hour of every day (including how much time I spent procrastinating), I discovered that I spent:*

- 19 hours on reading and research
- 16.5 hours writing
- 4 hours conducting and participating in interviews
- 8.5 hours doing maintenance-type tasks
- *6 hours procrastinating*

By pretty much any measure, my week was extraordinarily productive. TED organizers published their interview with me, I wrote 4,683 words, finished reading two books, and read countless articles on productivity. I also invested 37.5 hours into two of my highest-impact tasks. And there were no gaps between what I intended to accomplish and what I actually accomplished. As the icing on the cake, I had a ton of energy and focus throughout the week.

Yet I spent *six hours* putting off what I had intended to do—which didn't include the time I spent taking breaks.

While I was excited to share what I learned in tracking my time, I ultimately decided against putting the results up on my blog. I'm revealing them for the first time in this book. I didn't often shy away from being vulnerable during my project, and always wrote about the times I failed, but this time my pride got in the way. It stubbornly prevented me from saying anything that would take away from my newfound identify as the world's most productive person.

But as it turns out, procrastinating isn't something to be ashamed of. And here's why.

---

* If you're curious, over those five days I also spent 39.5 hours sleeping, 9 hours on household and personal tasks, 6 hours working out, 2.5 hours meditating, and 10.5 hours on leisure activities (mostly reading and spending time with friends).

"EVERYONE PROCRASTINATES"

One of the smartest decisions I made when I started *A Year of Productivity* was blogging every day about what I learned from my research and experiments. As more and more people began to follow my approach to exploring productivity, I was able to use this growing attention to dive even deeper into what it takes to become more productive—such as interviewing experts like Tim Pychyl.

Tim Pychyl wrote the bestselling book *Solving the Procrastination Puzzle*. He has been researching procrastination for more than twenty years. Tim walks with a spring in his step, exuding a zenlike calmness that's not unlike the meditators I have interviewed for this book. His personality and demeanor, on the surface, seem incongruous with what one might expect of one of the world's foremost authorities on procrastination.

What Tim said during our first conversation set me more at ease than anything I had heard in a long time: "Everyone procrastinates." Procrastination is simply human nature. Piers Steel, the author of *The Procrastination Equation*, backs that up, explaining that "across scores of surveys, about 95 percent of people admit to procrastinating." (The other 5 percent are lying.)

Naturally, different people procrastinate in different ways and amounts every day. Research shows that about 20 percent of people procrastinate chronically. But whether or not you're a chronic procrastinator, you probably put things off more than you realize. My six hours over the course of a week may even be on the low end of the spectrum. According to a recent Salary.com survey, 31 percent of people openly admitted to wasting at least an hour every day, and 26 percent of people admitted to wasting two or more hours *every day*. And that's only the time employees consciously wasted. Depending on your work, you may procrastinate for more than two hours every day. Pychyl found in one of his studies that the average student procrastinates for *a third of his or her waking hours.*

THE SIX TRIGGERS OF PROCRASTINATION

The science behind why we procrastinate is simple. One of my favorite pieces of research on the topic, which Tim Pychyl also participated in, found that there are a handful of attributes a task can have that make you more likely to procrastinate on it. (There are also personality traits that make you more likely to procrastinate, but I'll get to those in a bit. I personally prefer to focus on the tasks themselves, since a task is way easier to change than your personality. Plus, you're great. Don't ever change.)

It's actually relatively straightforward: personality aside, the more aversive (unattractive) a task or project is to you, the more likely you are to put it off. And there are six main task attributes that make procrastination more likely. Those are whether a task is one or more of the following:

- Boring
- Frustrating
- Difficult
- Unstructured or ambiguous
- Lacking in personal meaning
- Lacking in intrinsic rewards (i.e., it's not fun or engaging)

The more of these attributes a task has, and the more intense these attributes are, the less attractive a task will be to you, and the more likely you'll procrastinate on it. This is why you put off some tasks to the very last moment, like doing your taxes, in favor of doing other tasks, like watching Netflix, which don't set off nearly as many triggers.

Doing your taxes is one of the most boring, frustrating, difficult, and unstructured tasks there is, and if you're like me, you probably don't find it all that meaningful or fun. For most people, doing your taxes has all six procrastination triggers. Other commitments like visiting the doctor for a checkup, calling your mother, working from home, running a marathon, and writing a book also set off multiple procrastination triggers, which makes you more likely to put them off.

It's important to think about *why* you're procrastinating. As Tim put it, "sometimes procrastination is just a symptom that your life just doesn't match what you're interested in and . . . maybe you should do something else."

The reason you feel so much less mental resistance to watching Netflix than you do with doing your taxes is Netflix is far less boring, frustrating, and difficult, and it's more stimulating and structured. Netflix even shows a link to play the next episode of a series as you finish watching the current one! Because watching Netflix has almost no procrastination triggers, we don't put it off.

The biggest reason your highest-impact tasks are so valuable is that they too are aversive; they almost always require more time, attention, and energy than your lower-impact tasks, and they're usually more boring, frustrating, difficult, unstructured, and lacking in intrinsic rewards. They're valuable and meaningful because they're hard, and that's why you get paid more than minimum wage to do them. This is a simple reality of not working in a factory: the more valuable your work, the more aversive it will be. This is also why becoming more productive can be so challenging; although every single person on Earth wants to get more done, accomplishing more involves taking on tasks that are more aversive.

By the way, are you interested in gaining back 13.6 years of your life in an instant? Quit watching TV. According to Nielsen, the average American adult watches 5 hours and 4 minutes of television every single day. Assuming you live until eighty and start watching TV at ten, that adds up to 13.6 *years* of your life.

Procrastination gets in the way of accomplishing more since it is, in its simplest form, a gap between your intention and action.

NERDING OUT

Let's look at what happens inside your brain as you procrastinate.

As you consider procrastinating on a task, a fascinating internal war rages on in your brain. Often, you go from justifying why it is okay to watch one more episode of *House of Cards* to thinking about the fact that you need to do your taxes; from being tempted to check Facebook or Twitter one more time to thinking about how you really need to get started on your report that's due next Friday.

This back-and-forth is the result of two parts of your brain—your "limbic system" and "prefrontal cortex"—going to war with each other.

Your limbic system is the emotional, instinctual part of your brain that includes, among other things, your pleasure center. Evolutionarily speaking, the limbic is an old part of your brain—like an animal, it's what makes you instinctual and pushes you to give in to emotions and temptations. This is the part of your brain that tries to tempt you to put off doing your taxes to watch a few episodes of *House of Cards*.

Your prefrontal cortex is the logical part of your brain that's fighting to get you to do your taxes. It's responsible for, among other things, logic, reason, and keeping your longer-term goals in mind. It's also what motivated you to pick up this book. If you've done the productivity experiments I've mentioned so far, it's because your prefrontal cortex won out; if you've put them off and simply read on, your limbic system won out.

This back-and-forth between your emotional limbic system and logical prefrontal cortex is what leads to the decisions you make throughout the day. It's also what makes you human. If your prefrontal cortex won out 100 percent of the time, all your decisions would be perfectly logical, and you would be akin to a Vulcan from the *Star Trek* franchise; basing your decisions on pure logic and reason, without consideration of your emotions or the emotions of others. If your limbic system won out 100 percent of the time, you would be no different from an animal who makes every decision on instinct.

In every decision we make, either our limbic system or prefrontal cortex gains the upper hand. Our limbic system wins out when we go home with the cute girl at the bar, don't resist ordering a donut with our morning coffee, or when we procrastinate. Tim often refers to procrastination as "giving in to feel good," and if you look at a brain scan of someone who is procrastinating, you'll see that on a neurological level, that's exactly what happens. The prefrontal cortex surrenders to the limbic system so that we can feel good in the short term.

But our prefrontal cortex wins out a lot of the time, too. It is the reason we set aside money for retirement, hit the gym after work to get into shape, overcome the six triggers of procrastination, and read about productivity. It's the part of your brain that is constantly fighting for you to achieve your long-term goals, instead of the goals that are only pleasurable in the short term. And it is nearly impossible to become more productive without a strong prefrontal cortex.

Whenever we think about whether we should work on an ugly task, our limbic system and prefrontal cortex battle it out, and then we either procrastinate or we tackle the dreaded task.*

But there's just one issue with this battle between the limbic system and prefrontal cortex: the deck is stacked.

REGAINING CONTROL OVER YOUR BRAIN

So far, I have painted a picture in which your limbic system and prefrontal cortex are in constant battle with each other. Although that's true as far as procrastination is concerned, the rest of the time the two systems work together in incredible ways. Since the two systems are responsible for both logic and emotion, they're jointly responsible for some of the most remarkable innovations known to humankind—including language, the printing press, the lightbulb, the wheel, and the internet. Logic created the wheel, but out of a desire to create a better and more modern world. Plus, the first inventor of the wheel probably got some mad props from his bros and scored well with the ladies afterward. But that is just my subjective guess (not based on any evolutionary psychology whatsoever).

---

* I'm simplifying things a tad here—the brain is an intricate system that we're only beginning to understand, and any generalized statement of how the brain works won't account for its complexity and beauty. For example, the frontal cortex handles some emotional processing, and according to Jonathan Haidt, the author of *The Happiness Hypothesis*, has "enabled a great expansion of emotionality in humans." In a very general sense, though, your limbic system is emotional, and your prefrontal cortex is logical.

The interplay of your prefrontal cortex and limbic system is also what lets you pursue things that are pleasurable, engaging, and meaningful, like learning to play the cello, saving up to hike the Inca Trail, climbing a mountain, volunteering, building strong relationships, pursuing long-term goals, and following your passion.

While our limbic system is essential, much of productivity has to do with building up a strong prefrontal cortex, one that can show your limbic system who's boss when it needs to and smack down impulses like checking your email or Facebook one more time in favor of working on higher-impact tasks. While we need to keep our limbic system happy, it is impossible to invest in our achievements, relationships, and values without a strong prefrontal cortex.

The part of studying the brain that I find fascinating is that even though these types of battles occur in our brain thousands of times every day, we usually aren't aware of them. Just as 90 percent of an iceberg sits underwater, our mind is only able to consciously observe a fraction of what's going on in our brain—the rest is hidden within the depths of our unconsciousness. This is why productivity can be so powerful, because you can harness this power by combining the science of how you think and act with the intention of learning how to accomplish more.

But that's easier said than done. While the interplay between our prefrontal cortex and limbic system is what makes us human, our prefrontal cortex is also much weaker than our limbic system. The limbic system has evolved over millions of years, while the prefrontal cortex has been around for thousands.

In the exact same way that the most productive people learn to step back from working on autopilot, the most productive people learn to use their prefrontal cortexes more than their limbic systems.

TILTING THE SCALE

I've designed this chapter to be a bit longer than the others for a very specific reason: to ignite your prefrontal cortex. As you're reading these words, your prefrontal cortex is on fire, processing the meaning behind the words you're reading right now, while connecting these words to what you already know. Igniting your prefrontal cortex is, conveniently, what you have to do to defeat your limbic system and work on your highest-impact tasks.

For me, although procrastinating for six hours in a given week is probably on the low end of the procrastination spectrum, I wanted to squeeze every ounce of productivity out of my time. I wanted to get that number as low as I possibly could. After I discovered the source of procrastination—my limbic system bullying my prefrontal cortex—I did all I could to give my prefrontal cortex the advantage the next time my limbic system tempted me to give in to feeling good.

After you have identified your most important tasks and have formed an intention to work on them, you *will* procrastinate on them, even though you likely have a stronger prefrontal cortex than most.

But there are several strategies that work wonders for turning the tables on procrastination. In fact, with enough forethought, it's entirely possible to make doing your taxes as sexy a task as watching an entire season of *House of Cards*.

EXTREME MAKEOVER: TAXES EDITION

Oh @#%*@#!, look at the calendar! Your taxes are due in a month! And you haven't even thought about getting started on them!

But they can wait until tomorrow, right?

The moment you notice your mind having an internal debate about whether or not to work on a task, or you begin to notice yourself saying things like "I'll do them later," "I just don't feel like it right now," or worst of all, "I'll do them when I have more time," it's a signal that the task before you is an aversive task, and that you need to make doing it much more attractive.*

Because doing taxes is such an aversive task, it has created the entire tax preparation industry, which in the United States alone employs an estimated 320,000 people. And it's no wonder: if completing your taxes were as simple as clicking a button, the industry wouldn't exist. According to Intuit—the makers of TurboTax, the software program that, among many others, makes doing your taxes less boring, frustrating, difficult, and so on—"nearly 1/3 of taxpayers procrastinate on filing their taxes."

My method of choice for making my tax task less ugly is to hire someone to do them for me. Every year I hire a business to do my taxes, and for a couple hundred bucks I basically buy back hours of my time and attention so I can level up and focus on higher-impact tasks and projects. It's tax season right now, and instead of collecting receipts, crunching numbers, and figuring out what I can and can't write off under my business, I'm writing these words. But let's assume that hiring a business to do them for you is out, and you have to file them yourself, on paper.

Just thinking about doing your taxes, maybe your limbic system is resisting reading on, or dreading these next few paragraphs. So let's make over doing your taxes so they're just as attractive as watching Netflix.

By seeing what triggers procrastination, and then making a plan to flip those triggers, doing your taxes becomes more attractive. If I found myself putting off doing my taxes, I might sit down and make a plan to change those triggers. For example, if the trigger is:

- **Boring:** I go to my favorite café for an afternoon on Saturday to do my taxes over a fancy drink while doing some people watching.

- **Frustrating:** I bring a book to the same café, and set a timer on my phone to limit myself to working on my taxes for thirty minutes— and only work for longer if I'm on a roll and feel like going on.

---

* By the way, I have something quick to get off my chest: "I don't have time for that" is the biggest excuse out there. When someone says they "don't have time" for something, what they're really saying is that a task isn't as important or attractive as whatever else they have on their plate. Every person gets twenty-four hours of time every day and gets to spend those twenty-four hours however he or she chooses. But I digress.

- **Difficult:** I research the tax process to see what steps I need to follow, and what paperwork I need to gather. And I visit the café during my Biological Prime Time, when I'll naturally have more energy.

- **Unstructured or Ambiguous:** I make a detailed plan from my research that has the *very next steps* I need to take to do them.

- **Lacking in Personal Meaning:** If I expect to get a refund, think about how much money I will get back, and make a list of the meaningful things I'll spend that money on.

- **Lacking in Intrinsic Rewards:** For every fifteen minutes I spend on my taxes, I set aside $2.50 to treat myself or reward myself in some meaningful way for reaching milestones.

Okay, maybe doing your taxes will never be as sexy as watching Netflix. But I think we came close, right?

THREE MORE WAYS TO REGAIN CONTROL OVER YOUR BRAIN

Flipping a task's triggers tackles two birds with one stone: it simultaneously makes a task less aversive by disabling its procrastination triggers, while it readies your prefrontal cortex to battle your brain's limbic system. If you need to give your prefrontal cortex an even bigger shove, here are three more ways to regain control and work on your most aversive tasks.

I. Create a procrastination list

It's actually possible to procrastinate productively. When you make a list of meaningful and high-impact tasks to do the next time you procrastinate, you can remain productive while your prefrontal cortex warms up. During my project, I often found myself putting off reading long, tedious research papers. So I made a procrastination list that included items like writing and sending important emails, organizing folders on my computer, and tracking expenses related to my project. I think it's also helpful to give yourself a choice between working on only two tasks: the task that you're tempted to procrastinate on, and another task that's high return.

2. List the costs

Listing every single cost of putting something off is one of my favorite ways to get my prefrontal cortex fired up. It's a simple tactic, but it gives you a much better shot at winning out.

3. Just get started

Note that I didn't write "just do it." If you have a big, aversive task like cleaning your basement, simply get *started* on it. Try setting a timer for just fifteen minutes, after which you will stop cleaning and begin to work on something else. If you feel like going on after you get started, by all means do, but if you don't, don't worry about it. Every single time I have simply got started on something, even if just for a few minutes, tasks have rarely been as aversive as I had imagined. Rita Emmett, the author of *The Procrastinator's Handbook*, summed this up well in what she labeled Emmett's law: "The dread of doing a task uses up more time and energy than doing the task itself."

PROGRESS

Over the ensuing months, whenever I noticed myself trying to justify my way out of a task, I used that as a trigger to fire up my prefrontal cortex. According to Tim Pychyl, procrastination is at its most fundamental level, "a visceral, emotional reaction" to a task that sets off multiple procrastination triggers.

Firing up your prefrontal cortex is the best way out.

Since my first time log, I wanted to get to the bottom of how to waste less time every day—a tumultuous journey, but one that taught me a lot along the way. At the time of my most recent time log, I was in the middle of writing this book. Writing a book is a task that, for me, sets off even more procrastination triggers than my project did; it's one of the least structured and intrinsically rewarding tasks out there (especially for a business-minded guy like myself), and it can be insanely boring, frustrating, and difficult at times. But whenever I have been tempted to procrastinate writing this over the last several months, the first thing I did was fire up my prefrontal cortex.

And it worked. Here's what my most recent time log looked like:

- 17.5 hours reading and research
- 15 hours writing
- 5.5 hours conducting and participating in interviews
- 2.5 hours doing maintenance-type tasks
- *1 hour procrastinating*

Much better, to my relief.

A part of me was tempted to write that I didn't procrastinate at all, and though that may have made for a better story to end this chapter with, it simply wouldn't be true.

Sometimes our prefrontal cortex wins out.

THE FLIPPING CHALLENGE

Time required: 6 minutes
Energy/Focus Required: 8/10
Value: 8/10
Fun: 7/10
What you'll get out of it: The ugliest tasks in your work and personal life will become much more appealing, and you will waste less time when you work on them. This will help you free up even more time for your highest-impact and most meaningful tasks.

If you want to become more productive, you simply have to work on your highest-impact tasks more often. But when you do, you're also going to procrastinate more often because the more aversive a task is to you, the more likely you'll put it off. The next time you notice yourself putting off a task, use that as a trigger to think hard about what procrastination triggers set you off.

Then, write those triggers down and make a plan to flip them. And if you need to fire up your prefrontal cortex even further, create a procrastination list, list the costs of putting off the task, or simply get started on it.

Ironically, the tasks that will make you the most productive are also the most aversive. Fighting the emotional urge you have to put them off can go a long way toward making you more productive.

Working on more aversive tasks is essential if you want to become more productive. Of course, if you constantly find yourself procrastinating, that may be a strong signal that you need to seek out a different job. Who wants to only work on stuff that is boring, frustrating, difficult, ambiguous, unstructured, and lacking in pleasure and meaning every day?

6

MEET YOURSELF . . . FROM THE FUTURE

Takeaway: The more you see your "future self" (you, only in the future) as a stranger, the more likely you are to give your future self the same workload that you would give a stranger, and put things off to tomorrow. It's important to get in touch with your future self, by doing things like sending a letter to future you, creating a "future memory," or even downloading an app that will show you what you look like in the future.

Estimated Reading Time: 7 minutes, 5 seconds

AN AWKWARD LETTER

About one week ago, I received a letter in the mail. Receiving an actual letter is odd itself, but to make things even odder, it was from myself.

Here is the letter in its entirety, which I sent to myself eight months ago:

Hi man,

Right now you're kind of at a crossroads—unsure of what career, money, life, and other choices to make. I'd like to fast-forward several months to see how things turn out, I'm not going to lie.

But right now, you're surrounded by eight brand-new friends, and you're happy—in the fray of uncertainty. Everything is good, because you're surrounded by people you care for, and that care for you.

I'm not sure how things will be with Ardyn (my guess: pretty good at this rate), but you were happy to hear her voice today. I'm not sure how healthy you'll be, but right now you're in the best shape of your life. I'm also not sure (sense a common theme here?) how happy, positive, mindful, or anything else you'll be, but I guess that's the beauty of it all. It's a cliché, but you believe this: happiness is nothing more than coming to terms with how things change. I hope you're happy and doing great. At this rate, I know you are.

Love,
Chris

For the last five years I've volunteered for an organization named Camp Quality. Camp Quality is a worldwide charity that puts on week-long summer camps designed to help kids who suffer from cancer feel like kids again. Volunteers are paired up with a camper, and we hang out with them for the week, and every once in a while throughout the year.

In addition to the weeklong camps, the organization puts on a yearly four-day leadership camp for teenagers who suffered from cancer when they were kids. The camp lets people like myself share what we've learned so the campers can navigate some of the teen experiences we've already gone through.

One of the activities at last year's leadership camp—whether you were a camper or a volunteer—was to write a letter to your future self. Even though my letter is a little awkward to look back on, I still remember the activity being valuable, for a very specific reason: we hardly ever think about our future selves.

THE DIFFERENCE BETWEEN YOU AND TAYLOR SWIFT

If you were to lie down in an fMRI machine—a machine that measures your brain activity by looking at changes in blood flow—and you thought about your future self and then thought about a total stranger (like Taylor Swift), you would notice something peculiar when you looked at the two scans: they wouldn't be all that different.

Hal Hershfield, a professor at UCLA's Anderson School of Management, has conducted this exact study and found that while the average participant's brain scan of his or her *present* self and a stranger's scan varied quite a bit, the participant's brain scan of his or her *future* self and a total stranger's scan were almost identical.

This has a huge impact on your productivity: the more you see yourself like a stranger, the more likely you are to give your future self the same workload that you would give a stranger, and the more likely you are to put things off to tomorrow—for your future self to do.

Since you see yourself from the future as no different from a stranger, you also see her or him as less tired, busy, and more focused and disciplined than the version of you that's reading this book. And while in some ways that will be true—particularly as you begin to implement the tactics in this book—you will obviously have a lot more in common with yourself today than with a total stranger.

The more disconnected you are from your future self, the more likely you are to do things like:

✔ Give your future self more work than you would give your present self
✔ Agree to unproductive or pointless meetings far off in the future
✔ Keep ten uninspiring documentaries around on your PVR that you'll "get around to watching"
✔ Continually transfer aversive tasks to tomorrow's to-do list
✔ Save less money for retirement

If I asked if you wanted to sign up for a marathon that's ten weeks from now, chances are you wouldn't agree to it; that would require a ton of work over the next several months to build up to running 26.2 miles. But if I asked you if you wanted to sign up for a marathon that's two and a half *years* from now, though you still may not agree, chances are you'll feel a lot less resistance to the idea. You're a lot more likely to be attracted to the grand idea of running a marathon than you are to think about what your future self will have to do to get there.

Surprisingly, though our limbic system takes over when we procrastinate, the prefrontal cortex is responsible for us not taking our future selves into account when we make decisions.

GETTING IN TOUCH

To understand how we think about our future selves, Hal Hershfield conducted a fascinating experiment: he teamed up with professional animators to set up a simulator that showed participants a live 3-D model of what they will look like when they retire. If a student moved even slightly, opened her or his mouth to speak, or turned one way or another, the model did the exact same thing, in real time.

After Hershfield asked students a bunch of questions in the simulator, he gave them a task: allocate $1,000 between their present-day selves, and for themselves at retirement. After the experiment, he discovered something remarkable: students who stepped into the simulator saved *more than twice as much* for retirement than those who didn't.

"It's so easy to commit your future self to things your current self wouldn't want to do," he says. "We call this a 'planning fallacy.'"

He explains that you have the best of intentions when you make commitments for your future self, but that your future self usually gets the short end of the stick. But it's part of our biological makeup.

"Evolutionarily speaking, when you could be eaten by a lion at any moment, saving for the future doesn't make much sense," he says.

But, it's easier to travel through time and get in touch with your future self than you think.*

I've already revealed my favorite way to get in touch with my future self: through the Rule of 3. In the Rule of 3, your future self takes center stage. By mentally fast-forwarding to the end of the day and thinking about what you want to accomplish, you activate the planning centers in your prefrontal cortex, *while* you also step into the shoes of your future

---

* By the way, I see you're reading this from the future! What's it like?

self. And you do the same when you plan out your three accomplishments at the start of every week.

After coming across Hershfield's research, I conducted a number of experiments to get in touch with my future self. Here are my favorite three:

- **Fire up AgingBooth.** While hiring a programmer to create a 3-D virtual reality simulator is probably out of your price range, I personally love an app called AgingBooth, which transforms a picture of your face into what you will look like in several decades. There are also other apps like it, like Merrill Edge's web app that shows you a live avatar of what you'll look like at retirement (face retirement.merrilledge.com). AgingBooth is my favorite of them all, and it's available for both Android and iOS, and it's free. On the website for this book (productivityprojectbook.com), you can see what to expect out of the app—I've framed a picture of myself that hangs above my computer in my office, where I see it every day. Visitors are usually freaked out.

- **Send a letter to your future self.** Like the letter I wrote at camp, writing and sending a letter to yourself in the future is a great way to bridge the gap between you and your future self. I frequently use FutureMe.org to send emails to myself in the future, particularly when I see myself being unfair to future me.

- **Create a future memory.** I'm not a fan of hocus-pocus visualizations, so I hope this doesn't sound like one. In her brilliant book *The Willpower Instinct*, Kelly McGonigal recommends creating a memory of yourself in the future—like one where you don't put off a report you're procrastinating on, or one where you read ten interesting books because you staved off the temptation of binge-watching three seasons of *House of Cards* on Netflix. Simply imagining a better, more productive version of yourself down the line has been shown to be enough to motivate you to act in ways that are helpful for your future self.

At the end of most winters, I leave a $20 bill in my pocket, which I completely forget about until I reach into my winter coat pocket the next year. While it's important to not be unfair to your future self, one of the awesome things you can do is treat your future self—whether that means saving for the future, saying no to eating pizza tonight, working out, learning calculus, putting on sunscreen, flossing, reading more—or leaving some money in your coat pocket to find six months later. You'll feel incredible later on.

THE TIME-TRAVELING CHALLENGE

Time required: 10 minutes
Energy/Focus Required: 4/10
Value: 7/10
Fun: 9/10
What you'll get out of it: You'll become less likely to put things off until tomorrow, foisting them on your future self, because you no longer see your future self as a stranger.

When you put something off or waste time, you're almost always being unfair to your future self.

Before you get in touch with your future self, it's worth pausing for a few seconds to think about how tight you two are in the first place. According to Hershfield, everyone identifies with their future self differently. He calls how closely you identify with future you your "future-self continuity." Before getting in touch with your future self, ask yourself: Where do you sit on the chart below?

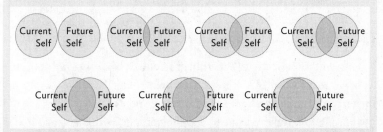

After you have identified where you fall, if you find yourself a bit estranged from your future self, invest in connecting with future you, either by downloading an app like AgingBooth, sending a letter to future you through a site like FutureMe.org, or if you're feeling adventurous, by imagining your future self and creating a future memory.

Trust me: You'll thank yourself later.

WHY THE INTERNET IS KILLING YOUR PRODUCTIVITY

Takeaway: The internet can destroy your productivity if you're not careful. The best way I have found to prevent the internet from wasting my time has been to simply disconnect from it when working on a high-impact or ugly task, and to disconnect as much as possible throughout the day. After getting over the initial withdrawal, the calm and productivity you'll experience will be unlike anything else.

Estimated Reading Time: 9 minutes, 40 seconds

TECHNOLOGY IS FREAKING AWESOME

The very first productivity experiment I conducted during my project—which was also one of the most memorable ones—involved using my smartphone for just an hour a day, for three months.

Throughout the experiment, traveling around with a notepad in one pocket and my iPhone in the other, I meticulously noted whenever I used my phone (which usually happened in fifteen-minute chunks of time) so I wouldn't go over the hour limit. I love running experiments like this—where I remove an element from my work and observe how my routines, habits, and rituals are affected—because I can observe how certain aspects of my work, like using my smartphone and constantly being connected, either help or hinder my productivity.

While humans have evolved at quite a consistent rate over the last 2.5 million years, in the last couple of centuries technology has progressed at a hugely accelerated rate. Moore's law, which says that the number of transistors on a chip will double every two years, has held true for more than fifty years, and today's run-of-the-mill smartphone packs more punch into 200 grams than an entire multiroom supercomputer did just a few decades ago. And humanity has, of course, advanced alongside this revolution. While the average life expectancy throughout the world hovered at twenty-five years from 5000 BCE through 1820, after the industrial revolution, our life expectancy began accelerating. It now sits at eighty years in the United States.

But I would argue that of all the technology we have, the internet has changed our life the most. The internet, along with the technology it has inspired, has flattened the world and connected more people than anything that came before it. Plus, when you tap your smartphone a very specific way, a pizza man shows up at your door twenty minutes later. Wrap your head about this: if you were to send today's iPhone back in time to two decades ago, people would think you were a witch, because the device would be indistinguishable from magic. Try to imagine what internet device will exist ten or twenty years from now that is so advanced that if we brought it back to today, you would think the same.

(This is the kind of stuff that goes on in my head all day long. Please send help.)

As far as human history is concerned, the internet and the technologies it spawned are a godsend. But because humans—and the newer parts of our brain, like the prefrontal cortex—have continued to evolve in a linear fashion alongside these technologies, at least as far as productivity is concerned, it's made us unprepared to deal with how disruptive those technologies can be to our work.

The internet can absolutely obliterate your productivity if you're not careful.

THE ZEN OF DISCONNECTING

A huge part of me is relieved that I didn't keep a time log before my smartphone experiment. Working deliberately is hard enough without the internet, and if I had to wager a guess, I would say I procrastinated ten hours or more each week before actively disconnecting every day. And that wouldn't be above the norm. Once you account for how much time you spend online, how often your work gets interrupted when you're online (Chapter 19), and the inefficiencies that come along with multitasking online (Chapter 20), it's safe to say that the internet is one of the biggest disruptions of our productivity.

The internet is so distracting that I've dedicated an entire part of this book to dealing with the distractions it sends our way (page 184). Our brains simply aren't equipped to deal with how distracting it is; if they were, we wouldn't be drowning in a sea of emails, notifications, phone calls, and buzzes, vibrations, and sounds. But the internet also impacts your productivity in a second way that's, on the surface, pretty easy to overlook: every day, it leads you to waste an insane amount of time.

Although the first few weeks of my smartphone experiment were admittedly quite rough—I would often habitually reach for my phone in my pocket when it wasn't there, or feel a phantom vibration on my leg even when my phone was turned off—I quickly settled into a new equilibrium and got accustomed to how peaceful I felt when I disconnected. I still used my laptop to write, do research, and conduct interviews, but every day I felt progressively more liberated from the shiny, black rectangle that used to be attached at my hip throughout the day. After I survived the first few weeks of the experiment, I felt as though I had cleared a bend; a whole new expanse of focus and clarity opened up for me, and I was able to dive much deeper into what I had to get done every day.

While the internet is fun and stimulating, it will almost always try to tempt you away from working on the highest-impact tasks you identified in Part One. Compared to your high-impact tasks, the internet is drop-dead sexy: it's one of the least boring, frustrating, and difficult things out there, and it's also insanely rewarding, and in an immediate way—a deadly combination for fostering addiction and procrastination. Oh, and structure! The internet has seeped into almost every area of our life, so much so that it's almost impossible to go a day without it. Despite how good your intentions at the beginning of the day, next to the internet, your high-impact tasks often don't stand a chance.

The best way I have found to prevent the internet from wasting my time has been to simply disconnect from it when working on a demanding or unappealing task. Although that isn't always realistic, every person I know has periods of time every day when he or she can disconnect. After getting over the withdrawal that will set in over the first few weeks, the calm and productivity you'll experience will be unlike anything else.

As I write these words, my smartphone is in another room, and the computer I'm writing these very words on is totally disconnected from the internet. It's just past 11 a.m. I woke up naturally just before 7 this morning, and over the last four hours I've been connected to the internet for a total of an hour. It's not that I dislike the internet—just the opposite, the internet is one of my favorite things on the planet. I simply value my productivity too much to stay connected all the time, especially when I'm working on something important.

A recent study from IDC, a U.S. market research company, found that 80 percent of eighteen- to forty-four-year-olds check their smartphones within the first fifteen minutes of waking up. I used to do this, too, except I took the ritual up several notches. After I woke up, I would immediately reach for my phone and then mindlessly bounce around between my favorite apps in a stimulation-fueled feedback loop for about thirty minutes, continuously bouncing around between Twitter, email, Facebook, Instagram, and several news websites until I snapped out of my trance.

Today, my morning couldn't be more different, or more productive. Every day I shut my smartphone completely off between 8 p.m. and 8 a.m.—one of my favorite daily rituals—so I can ease into and out of each day without wasting valuable time. This is especially powerful at the end of the day, when I have less willpower to resist distractions. And whenever I can, I switch my smartphone and laptop into airplane mode to hunker down on my most unattractive and high-impact tasks.

The internet is arguably the most powerful thing we have ever invented, and in the coming years and decades it will continue to shape the way we live and work in ways we can't imagine. But despite its power, and its ability to serve you a never-ending stream of kitten pictures at your beck and call, as far as productivity is concerned it's a dish that's best served in small doses.

THE WORLD'S LARGEST CANDY STORE

In the same Salary.com survey where 26 percent of people surveyed openly admitted to wasting at least two hours every day, participants named the internet as their biggest overall time waster by a massive margin. (The runners-up: too many meetings and conference calls; dealing with annoying coworkers; and returning pointless emails.) But while this figure may not surprise you, maybe the most damning stat comes from another study Tim Pychyl conducted, where he discovered that participants spent an average of *47 percent* of their time online procrastinating. In his book, he calls that figure a "conservative estimate."

It's easy to see why we waste so much time online: the internet is basically the world's largest candy store for your limbic system. With every tap and click, your limbic system receives a steady stream of stimulation. As Nicholas Carr put it in his eye-opening book *The Shallows: What the Internet Is Doing to Our Brains*, "The net engages all of our senses," and to make matters worse, "it engages them simultaneously." Our hands are engaged as we tap our smartphones, or as we type and move our mouse across our desk. Our ears are engaged with the sounds of our keyboard and mouse, and with the sounds that come out of the speakers in front of us. And our eyes are continually stimulated as brand-new text, images, and videos appear on screen. The internet hijacks your limbic system by overwhelming it. Take it from me: I've been meditating every day for the past six years, and even I find it hard to be mindful against the mind-numbing allure of the internet.

LEVELING UP

Though studies like Tim's show us how much time we waste every day on the internet, they don't account for one more huge impact on your productivity: the internet tempts us to work on lower-impact tasks. Though we are technically *working* when we do things like continually check our email, we're not as productive, because we don't accomplish as much through those tasks. Disconnecting doesn't only prevent you from wasting time; it also prevents you from being tempted to work on lower-impact tasks that live on the internet, like email, instant messaging, and checking social media.

This makes disconnecting from the internet doubly important: disconnecting not only lets you reclaim the time (and attention) you waste mindlessly, it also makes it easier to focus on your higher-impact tasks.

As I stepped away from the internet candy store, I discovered that without the constant temptations I automatically worked more on my higher-impact tasks. While I wasted less time and was distracted a lot less, I also stopped checking my email so often, quit refreshing Twitter, and found myself doing things like picking up a book, planning for an interview, or writing articles for my site. When I finished work for the day, whenever I stayed disconnected, I found myself doing things like meditating or making tea for my girlfriend, to fill the hole in my schedule where previously I had been mindlessly wasting time online. And if I found I was tired after work, I actually took steps to cultivate my energy levels (Part Seven), instead of switching into autopilot mode.

Disconnecting made my work and home lives more boring at first—my limbic system was accustomed to the constant sugar rush of the internet candy store. It took me a few weeks to adjust to the new, lower level of stimulation. But after I adjusted, I had a lot more time and attention for what was actually important.

WHAT TO DO ABOUT IT

Unless you're a cocaine-fueled stock trader, the internet is probably the most stimulating element of your workday. At the risk of sounding like a broken record, of the three ingredients of productivity—time, attention, and energy—your time is the most limited—there is no way to get more of it. Disconnecting from the internet might sound dismaying—and I'll be honest, at first it is—but it's also one of the best things you can do for your productivity. Disconnecting won't only lead you to waste less time; it will also let you focus on the highest-return and most meaningful tasks in your work and life.

Research shows that of all the character traits we have, impulsiveness is the one that is most highly correlated with procrastination. The more impulsive you are, the more you procrastinate, because your limbic system is that much stronger than your prefrontal cortex. (Piers Steel, who wrote *The Procrastination Equation*, calls impulsiveness the "cornerstone of procrastination" and mentions that "without impulsiveness, there wouldn't be such a thing as chronic procrastination.") Although firing up your prefrontal cortex—either by breaking down an aversive task or connecting with your future self—is a great way to overcome procrastination, an equally great way to quit wasting so much time is to eliminate time wasters in the first place. Disconnecting from the internet is my favorite way to do that, and it will make you more productive than you think.

From my experience, to become more productive, it's important to see the internet as a nicety—not a necessity.

THE DISCONNECTING CHALLENGE

Time required: 30 minutes
Energy/Focus Required: 1/10
Value: 10/10
Fun: 4/10
What you'll get out of it: You'll waste much less time and find your-self working on your higher-impact and meaningful tasks more often, both at work and at home.

Here is my simple challenge for you for this chapter: disconnect from the internet for thirty minutes tomorrow. Whether that means put-ting your phone on airplane mode as you eat dinner with your sig-nificant other, disconnecting from Wi-Fi as you work on one of your three daily tasks, or disconnecting when you have less energy so you're not tempted to waste time—disconnect, and observe how much work you get done. After you observe how much work you get done when you disconnect, my guess is you'll use this strategy a ton. You may even be tempted to implement a nightly shutoff ritual.

It's not always easy to observe when you're surfing the internet on autopilot, but at some point—when you snap back to attention as you find yourself staring at someone's twenty-seventh profile picture on Facebook—you will realize that you are. When you notice yourself surfing on autopilot, I've found it helpful to use that as a trigger to disconnect. This will prevent you from wasting more time, and let you ease back into work mode, and step back from what you're doing to work more deliberately.

A word to the wise, though: when you disconnect, you may feel a bit bored as your brain adjusts to the new lower level of stimulation. That's simply your limbic system begging for the internet high that being online used to give you.

To waste less time, don't listen to it.

Part Three

THE END OF TIME MANAGEMENT

8

THE TIME ECONOMY

Takeaway: When time was "created" by the Big Bang 13.8 billion years ago, the universe had a past, present, and future for the first time. Measuring time first became important during the industrial revolution, when factory owners needed their workers to arrive on time. Today, in the knowledge economy, if you want to become more productive, managing your time should take a backseat to how you manage your energy and attention.

Estimated Reading Time: 7 minutes, 2 seconds

THE BEGINNING OF TIME

Since the Big Bang, the universe has had a very distinct past, present, and future. It gave birth to, in sequence, the first nuclei, atoms, galaxies, and stars, and then closest to home, our own solar system.

Today, an inconceivably large number of galaxies exist in the known universe—approximately 100 billion of them, by most estimates—many of which are similar in size and shape to our own Milky Way galaxy.

To me, the most fascinating part of our cosmic story isn't the sheer number of galaxies, though. It's that these galaxies are not standing still—as time marches forward, the galaxies are expanding farther and farther away from one another.

Time is a way of cataloging and labeling exactly when something happens relative to other things. As long as there are sequences of events to order, there will be time. Or to put it another way, without a sequence of events that have a distinct past, present, and future, time wouldn't exist.

WHEN TIME BECAME IMPORTANT

If you were around before the industrial revolution ended in the early 1800s, you wouldn't have measured time down to the minute, not only because you didn't have the technology to do so, but also because you didn't need to. Before the industrial revolution, measuring time wasn't as important, and most of us worked on the farm, where we had way fewer deadlines, meetings, and events to sequence than we have today. In fact, until the first mass-market, machine-made watches were produced in the 1850s, timepieces were unobtainable by pretty much anyone except for the super rich, and most of us charted the day's progression by looking at the sun. Because we didn't measure time with a clock, we would speak about events relative to other events. In the Malay language, there is even the phrase *pisan zapra*, which roughly translates to "about the time it takes to eat a banana."

But by the mid-1800s, technology continued to accelerate, and a pivotal shift began to take place that made time a lot more relevant: railroads began to expand across the United States and Canada, as well as across many other parts of the world. As they expanded, an interesting conundrum arose: no two cities kept the same time. After all, why would they? Time was consistent within each individual city, and since cities weren't connected to one another, there was no reason for two cities to sync up.

As railroads continued to connect individual cities, though, there were often dozens of time zones in a single state, which led to all sorts of problems for the railroad companies. After several accidents and near misses, the railroads had finally had it and decided that the sun was no longer cutting it as a timekeeper. That's when, in 1883, railroad operators teamed up to define four simple time zones across the United States and Canada. These time zones were originally created for the railroads to use internally. To make matters even more complicated, up until 1883 the railroads *themselves* had fifty-three different time zones they used to track their trains. Across the United States and Canada, railroads switched to using just four time zones at exactly noon on November 18, 1883.

Thirty-five years later, in 1918, the United States officially went from using hundreds of time zones to using just four, and time zones were codified into federal law.

I find this fascinating. Even though humans have been around for two hundred thousand years, we have only been living by the clock for the last 175.

It's a good thing for time zones, too; try to imagine how difficult it would be to coordinate a meeting or get everyone in one place for an event if each city kept different time.

In the early 1900s, around the same time that time zones were codified into law, we were in the midst of two other crucial shifts in North America: more and more people began working in factories, and labor unions across the United States began fighting for (and winning) shorter, eight-hour workdays.

Within the span of a few decades, we went from selling goods we produced ourselves to helping create mass-produced goods in factories, which also meant we began to trade our time for a paycheck. While time has been ticking on for billions of years, we only began measuring it down to the minute after the industrial revolution because we finally had a reason to: time was money, and there was a direct connection between how many minutes and hours we worked and how much we produced. We had always worked for money, but it was in the factory era that how long we worked began to be exactly measured.

Almost overnight, time management had become an essential part of living in a postindustrial world and the time economy was born.

TODAY

Of course, you're already familiar with what comes next. In the same way that we went from working on farms to working in factories, since the 1950s many of us have gone from working in factories to working in offices.

Over the last sixty years, manufacturing in the United States went from accounting for 28 percent of the country's GDP to just 12 percent—and this shrinkage happened in the face of more and more automation. Over the same time period, the sector of the U.S. economy that has grown the most *by far* has been the Professional and Business Services sector, a fancy name for the chunk of the economy that includes every single high-tech, engineering, legal, consulting, and accounting company—companies like Apple, Google, Boeing, General Electric, McKinsey & Company, and Deloitte. As the manufacturing industry has wilted over the last six decades, this sector has *tripled* in size.

When we transitioned into the time economy, we began to trade our time for a paycheck. But as we have transitioned into the knowledge economy, we've begun to trade so much more than just our time. Most people who work nonfactory jobs trade some combination of their time, attention, energy, skills, knowledge, social intelligence, network, and ultimately their productivity, for a paycheck.

Today, time is no longer money. *Productivity* is money.

A CRAZY IDEA

This begs the question: What does time management look like in the knowledge economy?

I'm going to present you with a crazy idea that will begin to make more and more sense the deeper you dive into this section of the book: **if you want to become more productive, managing your time should take a backseat to how you manage your energy and attention.**

Don't get me wrong: time is still important—we don't live in some hocus-pocus world where time doesn't exist—but it's simply not *as* important as it once was when the majority of us worked in factories, where our traditional views of managing our time arose.

Ever since there have been events to chronicle, time has ticked on, and there has been no way to stop it. For as long as we can predict, time will continue to tick on at the same rate, but what *actually fluctuates* on a day-to-day basis is how much energy and attention you have. In the knowledge economy, that's what makes or breaks how productive you are, and more important, it's something you can actually control. Time is a necessity of work and of nature, but as far as productivity is concerned, it should merely be the backdrop against which you work.

Take, for example, the largest relic from the time economy: the nine-to-five workday. In the time economy, the whole nine-to-five idea made a lot of sense: we had a lot of machines and people to coordinate, time was money, and running an efficient factory meant getting machines and employees in the same place at once. It made sense to pay people to work by the hour because the work performed by employees was not all that different from the work performed by machines.

Today, when productivity is about what you accomplish and not how much you produce, a nine-to-five workday makes as much sense as diligently tracking your time out on the farm. After all, what if your Biological Prime Time falls when you're not working, and you have the most energy from 6 to 9 a.m., or from 7 to 11 p.m.? Or what if you have trouble focusing because you're trying to multitask on a million things at once? Or what if you're constantly bombarded by distractions and interruptions?

Time is still important—and we likely won't go back to comparing how long something takes to eating a banana anytime soon—but today, time is just one part of three in the productivity equation.

WORKING SMARTER

I find it fascinating that it's impossible to talk about managing your time without also talking about how you manage your attention and energy. If it sounds to you like I'm hitting the crack pipe, consider this notion: when we schedule time for something, what we're actually doing is simply deciding when we will invest our attention and energy into the task. That's where time management should fit into the productivity equation. Scheduling time for something is really just a way of creating attentional and energy boundaries around a task—and for that reason, your time, attention, and energy are inseparable.

Managing your time becomes important only after you understand how much energy and focus you will have throughout the day and define what you want to accomplish.

Unless you're an entrepreneur or a CEO, you likely don't have *complete* control over your time. If you work with more than one person, meetings are inevitable, and so is having to manage your time, at least to some extent. Since you don't have complete control over the sequence of events that make up your workday—and few do—it's essential that you carve out time for coordinating with other people. But unless you work in a factory, you at least have *some* modicum of control over your time, and over what you work on.

Some days, I schedule my entire day, and I've found that doing so makes me incredibly productive—especially when I form a strong intention about what I'm going to get done. But I only ever plan out my day after I account for how much attention and energy I will have, and most important, what I intend to accomplish.

During my project, I learned to work smarter instead of just harder. It has helped me accomplish things like writing the very book you're holding in your hands. It's not that I'm smarter or more talented—it's that I learned the hard way how to step out of the time economy and into the knowledge economy to become more productive.

Here are a few of the best ways I discovered to do that.

9

WORKING LESS

Takeaway: When you work consistently long hours, or spend too much time on tasks, that's usually not a sign that you have too much to do—it's a sign that you're not spending your energy and attention wisely. As one example, during my experiment to work ninety-hour workweeks, I found I accomplished *only a bit more* than when I worked twenty-hour workweeks.

Estimated Reading Time: 9 minutes, 29 seconds

WORKING NINETY-HOUR WEEKS

One of the most exciting parts of my project was that because I spent most of my time reading, researching, conducting interviews and experiments, and writing, technically speaking, I could work 168 hours every week (24 x 7) if I really wanted to. My work could expand to accommodate how much or how little time I had for it. Aside from the pressure I put on myself to get a lot done every day, I had total freedom and flexibility for how long I worked, which made productivity experiments like working ninety-hour weeks possible. (By comparison, for most of my project I worked an average of forty-six hours a week.)

Before I started *AYOP*, whenever I had more work to do than I had time to do it in—which was pretty much all the time—I would usually put in longer hours so I could finish my tasks.

When you feel like your to-do list is expanding faster than the universe is, working longer hours almost always feels like the best option to getting everything done. On the surface, it makes total sense: the longer you work, the more time you have to do everything in.

But in practice, working longer hours means having less time to refocus and recharge, which leads to more stress and lower energy.

That's what got me curious, especially as my work quickly began to pile up during my project: Is there a better and smarter way to get everything done? Or is working longer hours simply the only option?

Fortunately, I had created the perfect test environment to find out.

To get to the bottom of the link between the number of hours spent working and productivity, I designed a productivity experiment to test out how my productivity was affected by working both insane hours and relaxed hours. For four weeks I alternated between working ninety hours one week, and twenty the next to see how working both extreme hours and shorter hours affected how much I got done every day.

During the experiment, at the end of each day and week, I asked myself the same three questions:

- How much energy and focus did I have left?
- How easily was I distracted?
- Did I accomplish what I intended to?

Every day and week I also made a list of everything I accomplished so I could compare how my hours affected my productivity.

As a science nerd I have to say that this experiment was anything but scientific. But I quickly began to discover two big, surprising lessons from it.

TWO HUGE LESSONS

After slogging through one ninety-hour week and one twenty-hour week, I quickly discovered something breathtaking when I was looking through my experiment logs: I accomplished *only a bit more* working ninety-hour weeks than I did in my twenty-hour weeks.

This was easily one of the more surprising findings I made during my project. It went against everything I knew about productivity; I had always assumed that working longer hours gave you more time to accomplish everything you need to get done.

On the surface, it made little sense—until I looked beyond how much *time* I invested in my work, and instead looked at how much *energy and attention* I invested in it.

When I invested more time in my work during my insane weeks, my work became a lot less urgent; on a minute-by-minute basis, I invested less energy and focus into everything I intended to get done. But when I had a limited amount of time in my twenty-hour weeks, I forced myself to expend significantly *more* energy and focus over that shorter period of time so I could get everything done I had to do. Of course, all the pressure I felt during this experiment came from me—I didn't have a boss, team, or any large, looming deadlines around the corner. But the lesson is just as potent:

By controlling how much time you spend on a task, you control how much energy and attention you spend on it.

The second invaluable lesson I discovered from the experiment was that *even though on paper I accomplished about the same in both long and short weeks, I felt* twice *as productive working longer hours.* Even though I wasn't spending my attention or energy wisely, I sure as hell *felt* productive.

It's hard not to feel productive when you're busy all day long. But busyness does not translate into productivity if it doesn't lead you to accomplish anything.

Before I started my project, when I reflected on how productive I was at the end of each day and each week I usually made a critical mistake: I looked at how busy I was instead of how much I accomplished. Productivity is an elusive idea; because it's hard to get a handle on just how much you accomplish every day, looking at how busy you are is a quick, down and dirty, and usually inaccurate shortcut to seeing how productive you are.

In the middle of my twenty-hour weeks, I couldn't help but feel guilty that I wasn't as busy as I thought I should be. Because I was working a shorter amount of time, I perceived myself as less productive, and I became unnecessarily hard on myself because of it—even though I was spending a ton of energy and focus on what I had to get done, and I was accomplishing about the same amount of work.

This is a trap almost all of us fall into. When you have more work to do than you have time to do it in, it's easy to trick yourself into thinking you have only two options: keep working a standard workweek and fall behind, or begin putting in more hours to get everything done.

But as I discovered during this experiment, there is a third, less obvious option that is much more powerful than spending more time on your work: learn to invest more energy and attention into your work, so you can get the same amount done in a fraction of the time.

FOR IMPORTANT THINGS, SPEND *LESS* TIME

When I worked twenty-hour weeks, something magical began to happen: I forced myself to expend more energy over a shorter period of time so I could get my work done more quickly.

When you limit how much time you spend on an important task, these things happen:

- You set an artificial deadline, which motivates you to expend more energy and focus over a shorter period of time.
- You create urgency around the task, because you have a limited amount of time to get it done.
- You flip some of the task's procrastination triggers, because limiting the time you'll spend on a task makes it more structured, and less boring, frustrating, and difficult.

And when you also work on the task during your prime productive time? Ahhh . . . That's the sweet spot on your productivity racket.

By the way, shrinking how long you'll work on the task is also a great way to warm up to difficult tasks that you are more likely to procrastinate on. For example, on days when I really don't feel like exercising or meditating, I simply shrink how long I'll meditate or exercise for in my head until I no longer feel resistance to it. For example: *Can I work out for an hour? Naw, I feel a lot of resistance to that. Thirty minutes? Better, but still too much. How about twenty minutes? Perfect, I'll work out for twenty minutes!* Shrinking a task works wonders every time—and the hack is helpful for forming new daily habits, too. Plus, once you get started, chances are you'll want to keep going beyond your original point of resistance.

After conducting this experiment, whenever I had an important article to write, speech to prepare, or project to crank out throughout the rest of the project, instead of scheduling an entire afternoon to work on the task, I scheduled just two or three hours for the task, usually smackdab in the middle of my Biological Prime Time. And whenever I had a good handle on how much time, attention, and energy a task would take, I got it done.

With a limited amount of time, I had no other choice.

THE EXACT NUMBER OF HOURS YOU SHOULD WORK EVERY WEEK

If limiting how much time you spend on a task lets you get it done more efficiently, does the same rule apply to working fewer hours in general?

Intriguingly, several studies suggest that it does.

If you were to work just one hour a week, no matter how well you managed your energy and attention over that hour, you wouldn't be all that productive. One hour of work a week simply isn't enough time to accomplish much of anything important.

But your productivity also becomes shot when you work for too long. Working ninety hours a week for any longer than one week is a recipe for burnout. Doing so leaves you with hardly any time to recharge your energy levels and focus. Just as you can work too few hours, you can also simply work too much.

So where is the sweet spot for how many hours you should work every week?

Over the course of my project, I settled into a nice equilibrium of working forty-six hours a week, which was enough time for me to get everything done, while taking needed breaks to recharge my energy levels and attention over the course of the day. But studies show that the ideal number of hours to work every week is even lower than that. They suggest that optimal number is roughly thirty-five to forty hours.

On the surface, thirty-five to forty hours seems low. When your to-do list is always longer than the number of hours you have in the day, you might feel guilty if you began working forty hours a week, especially if the people around you continued to work fifty, sixty, or even more.

But studies show that after roughly thirty-five or forty hours, your productivity begins to plummet.

In the short term, there are huge productivity gains to be had by working extra hours, particularly when deadlines are fast approaching. Sometimes there is simply a ton of work to do, and you need to dedicate more time to do that work. But in the long term, working longer hours is a recipe for disaster—especially when they lead you to have less time to cultivate your attention and energy, as I'll discuss in the next chapters. After thirty-five to forty hours of work, studies show that your marginal productivity begins to drop, until "at approximately eight 60-hour weeks, the total work done is the same as what would have been done in eight 40-hour weeks." The same study found that with seventy- and eighty-hour weeks, you reach the same breakeven point in just three weeks. In working ninety hours a week, I stumbled upon that breakeven point in just two weeks, even though the two weeks were separated by a luxurious twenty-hour week.

But often even in the *short* term, working longer hours can decrease your productivity. One study found that when you work sixty-hour weeks, in order to accomplish one more hour of work, you need to work *two* hours of overtime. Yet another study found that your productivity "falls off a cliff after 55 hours—so much so that someone who puts in 70 hours produces nothing more with those extra 15 hours."

Beyond a certain point, you simply begin to do more busywork than important or meaningful work. You'll feel a lot less guilty, like I did when working ninety hours a week, but you'll also be a lot less productive.

In the time economy, when work required a lot less energy and attention, and there was a direct correlation between how many hours you worked and how much you produced, working insane hours would have made you much more productive. Today, though, the equation has changed. Since your time, attention, and energy all contribute to your productivity, working long hours can destroy your productivity because doing so compromises your energy and focus.

In the knowledge economy, the most productive people don't only manage their time well—they also manage their energy and attention well. Limiting how much time you spend on your work—whether on an important task or on your work in general—is a great way to spend your time, attention, and energy wisely. Depending on how much control you have over when you work, setting limits for how long you work in general—even reasonable limits like working for thirty-five hours—may not be realistic. But whenever possible, it's worth setting limits for how long you work so you spend more energy on what you have to get done, not more valuable time.

THE "SHRINK YOUR WORK" CHALLENGE

Time required: 1 minute
Energy/Focus Required: 4/10
Value: 8/10
Fun: 8.5/10
What you'll get out of it: You'll learn to expend more energy and attention on your work to get things done in a fraction of the time.

The challenge for this chapter is simple: tomorrow, limit how much time you'll spend on an important task, and stick to that limit.

My favorite way to limit how much time I spend on something is to simply set a countdown timer on my phone for about half of the amount of time I think a task will take. If I think I need four hours to crank out an important presentation, I'll schedule just two—during my Biological Prime Time if I can.

This tactic won't work for every single item on your task list, but it works wonders on tasks that are important and that have a deadline that's fast approaching.

Once you start limiting how much time you'll spend on specific tasks, my bet is that you'll also begin to limit how long you work *in general*. Consistently working for more than thirty-five or forty hours a week makes you less productive over time, because it leads you to make more mistakes and poorer decisions, both of which can take a lot of time to fix. It also causes you to miss new ideas, opportunities, shortcuts, and opportunities to work smarter instead of just harder.

When you work consistently long hours, or spend too much time on tasks, that's usually not a sign that you have too much to do—it's a sign that you're not spending your energy and attention wisely.

10

ENERGY ENLIGHTENMENT

Takeaway: Some time management is inevitable, but you'll accomplish a lot more when you work on your most important and meaningful tasks when you have the most energy—not when you have the most time. Figure out when your prime time is; it's sacred, and it's worth spending wisely.

Estimated Reading Time: 10 minutes, 0 seconds

YOUR PRIME TIME IN ACTION

After my project found its legs around the time TED published my interview, more folks wanted to chat with me about productivity. In almost every instance, I was asked what my typical day looked like. At first, I didn't expect to get that question that often, but once I did, it made total sense: I had been experimenting with my daily routine for about a decade until I settled on the one that was the most productive for me.*

After experimenting with quite a few routines over the course of my project—including my wretched one of waking up at 5:30 every morning—I settled into one that let me accomplish the most:†

---

*   Plus, daily routines are "productivity porn" in the purest sense of the term: they're easy to read, entertaining, and forgettable. Don't worry: I'll do my best to make this chapter as practical as possible! Plus, I need to redeem myself for writing about the cosmic origin of time earlier on.

†   My daily routine as I write this a year later is virtually identical.

- 6:30–7 a.m.: Wake up naturally.
- 7 a.m.–9 a.m.: Eat breakfast, work out, meditate, shower.
- 9 a.m.–1 p.m.: Write.
- 1 p.m.–3 p.m.: Break.
- 3 p.m.–8 p.m.: Read, conduct/participate in interviews and meetings.
- 8 p.m.–11 p.m.: Leisure time, bed.

Although this routine is pretty simple on the surface, a lot of consideration stands behind it.

Tracking your time and energy levels for a few weeks is admittedly a pain in the ass—especially when you cut out caffeine, alcohol, and sugar during the process—but the insights that the challenge I suggest in Chapter 4 will give you are incredible and will last decades. If you absolutely cannot stomach the experiment, at the very least set an hourly chime on your phone, and observe how your energy levels fluctuate over the day.

After I finished up my meditation experiment, I realized I mainly had three high-impact tasks that produced the most value for my project: writing articles, conducting productivity experiments, and reading about and researching productivity.

The best time of day by far to work on your highest-impact tasks is during your Biological Prime Time. The reason for this goes without saying: during your BPT, you bring at least double the energy and focus to whatever it is you're working on. When you work on your highest-impact tasks during your prime time, you complete them faster, get more engrossed in them, do a noticeably better job on them, work on them with more resilience, and begin to work smarter instead of just harder.

My BPT is between 10 to noon and 5 to 8 p.m., and every day during the project I predominately did two things with that time: wrote articles for my site and researched productivity. I designed some productivity experiments to simply exist in the background as I worked (like using my smartphone for an hour a day), and others to be my main focus for a week or two (like my meditation experiment). Whenever I was conducting one, I integrated the experiment into my schedule, too.

After calculating when I had the most energy, I made sure to block off my BPT in my calendar every day, not only to set that time aside for high-impact tasks, but also to keep that time open in case another vital task came my way. Whenever I interviewed a productivity expert, had an important interview myself, gave a talk, hunkered down on one of my three daily tasks, or wanted to bring as much of myself as possible to a commitment that was meaningful, like having dinner with my girlfriend, I did all I could to schedule the event during my prime time.

Though interruptions always come up—no one has perfect control over how they spend their time—I quickly realized that my BPT was worth spending intelligently, and defending religiously.

This connection is simple, but incredibly profound: the more important and meaningful tasks and commitments you schedule during your BPT, the more influential and meaningful your work and life will become.

IN THE MOMENT

You likely already have some days when you effortlessly breeze through your task list, and get more done than on any other day. And you likely also have others where, despite doing everything according to plan, you simply aren't able to focus or get stuff done. That's one of the strangest aspects of productivity, and another thing that makes it elusive: some days you'll do everything right, and yet you won't have enough energy or focus to do good work.

Quick productivity win: Right now, jump into Outlook, iCal, Google Calendar, or whatever your calendar of choice is, and block off your BPTs for the next several weeks. Make sure you set a reminder thirty and fifteen minutes before your prime time is about to start, and use that as a cue that you're about to hunker down on one of your most important and highest-impact tasks.

With the daily routine I settled into by the end of my project (and still have today), I would meditate, disconnect from the internet, work deliberately, work out, get enough sleep, and unwind after work. Yet some days the stars would align and I found myself writing thousands of words and reading hundreds of pages, while on others I would sit at my desk staring at a blank screen, with no energy or will or focus to do either.

Knowing your BPT is important, but at the same time, your energy and focus levels will fluctuate in ways you don't expect. Maybe a co-worker will run to Starbucks and pick you up a surprise coffee, or you'll receive a promotion and feel like you're unstoppable for the rest of the day. Or maybe your team takes you out for a big birthday lunch, and your energy levels crash for the rest of the afternoon. Regardless of the reason, things happen, and your energy levels and focus aren't 100 percent predictable.

Yesterday I had my day planned out to a T, but when it came time to quit working for the day, I found that I was on a roll, cranking out a steady stream of words for this book. I didn't want to stop—so I didn't. I had more energy than I expected to, so I decided to stay up later, writing late into the night, and sleep in this morning. If you're up on a roll on a project, with a ton of energy and focus and it's 10 p.m., why *wouldn't* you work a bit longer to become more productive when you have the flexibility to do so?

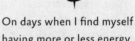

On the other hand, if it's 10 p.m. and you have no energy or focus left, your time would likely be best spent heading to bed early so you can continue working when you have more energy and focus in the morning. This is common sense, of course, but again, common sense isn't always common action. To work more deliberately, awareness is key. It's essential that you become aware of your energy levels so you

> On days when I find myself having more or less energy than I usually do, I simply write out how much energy (on a scale of 1–10) each of my three daily tasks will take. This makes it easier to adapt what I'm working on to the amount of energy and focus I have at the moment.

can spend your energy wisely throughout the day. (If having zenlike awareness doesn't come naturally to you, don't worry: I dedicate an entire section later in the book to awareness and productivity, page 190.)

As a rule, I try to manage my time as little as possible, and because I take on as few commitments as possible (page 134), this lets me adjust as the day goes on. That way I can work on my highest-impact tasks when I have the most energy, and my lowest-impact tasks when I have the least energy.

Over time, I've discovered that while most days follow the natural ebbs and flows of my daily energy cycle, many days don't. On those days, the more I adapt what I'm working on to mesh with my energy levels, the more productive I become.

Managing your time becomes important only after you define what you want to accomplish and understand how much energy and focus you have throughout the day.

> Just as your energy levels fluctuate over the course of the day, so does how much attention you have. While I've found that how well you can focus rises and falls in tandem with your energy, there are also periods of the day when you have more or less attention to dedicate to your work, such as when fewer people are in the office, or when you find you aren't interrupted or distracted by a deluge of meetings and phone calls. It's worth being mindful of how much attention you have throughout the day, particularly if it fluctuates quite a bit, if you have kids at home, or if you have team projects at work.

THE PERFECT AMOUNT OF STRUCTURE

In the productivity project, I had control not only over how long I would work every week but also over how I structured each day. Unlike the more rigid nine-to-five jobs I worked, in my project I was free to schedule my days however I wanted, as well as experiment with how the structure made me more or less productive.

As with the number of hours you work, there is a zone where your day has the perfect balance of structure and free time, where you have enough structure to guide you to being productive, but not so much structure that your day feels rigid and out of your control.

According to Paul Graham, who cofounded the venture capital firm Y Combinator, people in the knowledge economy have two types of schedules: a "maker's" schedule and a "manager's" schedule. As Paul put it in an article on his blog, "[t]he manager's schedule is for bosses. It's embodied in the traditional appointment book, with each day cut into one-hour intervals. You can block off several hours for a single task if you need to, but by default you change what you're doing every hour." The manager's schedule is mostly made up of meetings, appointments, calls, and email. But if you're a maker, the opposite is true—your days are naturally far less structured because you don't have people or projects to manage.

Asking yourself whether you're a maker or manager will show you your baseline; that is, the amount of structure that you should come to expect based on the nature of your job. You may fall somewhere in between; during my project I both created a lot of content and had a lot of meetings, so I kept a maker's schedule in the morning and scheduled all my meetings and interviews in the afternoon around my BPT. Knowing where you sit will help you discover how essential time management is in your work, and how much structure you should expect to have each day.

Regardless of whether you're a maker or manager, some structure is essential. Structure helps you accommodate for your BPT, guides you to work on what you intend to accomplish, and helps you nurture your attention and your energy so you can run on a full tank throughout the day. But beyond accounting for your prime time, intentions, and nature of your job, any additional structure will tend to make your day more rigid and will make you feel less in control of your day. And the more structure you have, the more difficult it becomes to adapt to how you work throughout the day.

The same holds true for structuring your downtime and weekends. It might sound counterintuitive (and not very fun) to structure your time away from work, but research says that doing so makes you more focused, creative, active, motivated, happy, involved in what you're doing, and a lot more likely to achieve "flow," that magical state where time seems to pass so quickly it's as if it doesn't exist at all. I don't believe in strictly structuring work or free time (where's the fun in that?), but some structure is helpful. For example, during my project I discovered that I always had more energy when I sat down and created a rough schedule of how I was going to spend my time over the weekend, even if that included scheduling time for putting my feet up and doing nothing at all.

THE "WORKING IN PRIME TIME" CHALLENGE

Time required: 5 minutes
Energy/Focus Required: 4/10
Value: 8/10
Fun: 7/10
What you'll get out of it: You'll get your highest-impact and most important daily tasks done more efficiently, because you'll work on them when you actually have the most energy—instead of when they become urgent or feel more important.

One of the most powerful ways I found to get more done in less time in my year of experimentation has been to manage my time as little as possible, and strategically work on tasks when I have the most energy and focus—both of which roughly rise and fall in tandem with each other over the course of the day.

Planning out how you'll work only takes five minutes of planning at the start of the day, but you'll make that time back tenfold.

Tomorrow, try letting your Biological Prime Time and energy levels dictate what you work on.[*] Here are a few extra pointers that you may find helpful:

---

[*] I've personally disabled the clock on my computer. My calendar notifies me when it's time to switch modes before meetings start so I can prep for them, and I always review my day when I plan out what I want to accomplish.

- During your BPT, schedule time in your calendar to work on your three most important tasks—particularly the ones that require the most energy and focus.

- Be defensive of your BPT—that time is yours to use to be crazy productive.

- Block off your BPT in your calendar so no one books you during that time, to remind yourself when it's time to hunker down, and to keep that time open for the high-impact tasks and projects that will come your way.

- Adapt on the fly. While your BPT shows you how your energy fluctuates over the average day, you're bound to have some days that are outliers, too, days when you have higher or lower amounts of energy. Run with it. Don't be afraid to shake up what you're working on when you find yourself having more or less energy than usual.

- If you're on a maker's schedule, chunk your meetings and appointments together so when you switch gears, you can tackle them all at once.

Your productivity per hour will not be consistent—it hinges on how much energy and attention you have. Just as not all tasks are created equal, not all hours of the day are created equal.

Some time management is inevitable, but you'll accomplish a lot more when you work on your most meaningful tasks when you have the most energy—not when you have the most time.

Your prime time is sacred; use it wisely.

CLEANING HOUSE

Takeaway: Gathering your maintenance tasks together and tackling them all at once is the perfect antidote to being a perfectionist about the wrong things. Nonetheless, maintenance tasks, or Maintenance Days, are essential if you want to have a life that's healthy and productive.

Estimated Reading Time: 8 minutes, 8 seconds

THE WORST KIND OF TASK

For years I've been fed up with maintenance tasks—tasks like watering your plants, clearing out your inbox, cutting your nails, sorting through mail, preparing lunches, and buying groceries. Maintenance tasks are essential, because they support your personal life and work, but minute for minute they provide you an abysmal return compared to your most important and meaningful tasks.

Because maintenance tasks are an essential part of life, they're usually pretty difficult to shrink, outsource, or eliminate, like the low-return tasks in your work (Part Four). But it's also impossible to be a functioning member of society when you don't do basic things like tidy up your house, prepare food, take out the trash, do the dishes, and do the laundry. I think that's a shame, because these tasks use up a lot of what limited time you have.

But they are essential in supporting what you want to accomplish. It's hard to eat healthfully when you don't prepare healthy food; it's hard to look great if you don't shave or wash and dry your hair every few days;

and it's hard to feel great about coming home if your house or apartment is a mess.

In one of my weirder experiments during my project, for a week I became a total slob. I ordered takeout for every meal, showered only three times throughout the week, wore sweatpants or pajamas every day, and of course still tried to be as productive as I could within these conditions. In the middle of the experiment, I started to feel terrible as I began to remove as many maintenance tasks as possible from my life. And I realized maintenance tasks are essential if you want to live a healthy, happy, socially engaged, and productive life.

MAINTENANCE DAY

As I first set up my own household when I went away to college, my maintenance tasks began to pile up quickly. Suddenly my laundry wasn't magically done for me, fresh groceries didn't appear in the kitchen, and my plants weren't magically watered once a week. I had a lot more maintenance tasks to do every day. But at the same time I didn't want to use up what little, valuable time I had every day on tasks that did nothing more for me than help me maintain the life I had.

One Sunday morning, when I was racking my brain about how I could do these newfangled tasks more efficiently, a lightbulb went off: What if instead of doing these menial tasks throughout the week, I lumped them all together and did as many of them as I could at once?

As an experiment, in the week that followed I purposely didn't tackle my maintenance tasks throughout the week. Instead, I made a list of the ones that popped up, and I tackled them all the next Sunday morning. And it worked. I got more done in less time.

I've used the same ritual ever since. I call it my "Maintenance Day."

My Maintenance Day ritual is incredibly simple, and incredibly powerful: throughout the week, I simply collect all of my low-return maintenance tasks on a list—everything from going grocery shopping to cutting my nails—and instead of doing them throughout the week, I do them all at once.

I finally felt like I was no longer treading water by working on tasks throughout the week that didn't move my life forward. And I had much more time, attention, and energy for tasks that were actually important and meaningful throughout the week.

WHAT I DO ON MAINTENANCE DAY

If you're curious, here's a complete list of everything I wait to tackle until Sunday morning—all of which takes me, at a leisurely pace, four to six hours:

- Grocery shopping
- Clean house and office
- Create a meal and workout plan
- Trim beard and shave
- Do laundry
- Prepare lunches in Tupperware containers for the week
- Water plants
- Read articles I've saved up throughout the week
- Review my projects, and define next steps (page 153)
- Review my "Waiting For" list (page 152)
- Define three outcomes for the week ahead (page 36)
- Clear out all my inboxes (page 155)
- Review my hot spots (page 162)
- Review my Accomplishments List (page 260)

Naturally, your own Maintenance Day ritual will vary. If you have kids, for example, it probably isn't realistic to only clean up around the house on Sunday morning. But perhaps you can relegate cleaning to two or three days a week, leaving the majority of your days free for high-priority tasks. Regardless of your lifestyle—whether you're a bachelor entrepreneur or an office worker with a family—you undoubtedly have maintenance tasks that you can chunk together and tackle all at once.

Your maintenance tasks, by their very nature, have to be kept up with. You can't always shrink, delegate, outsource, or eliminate them the way you can other low-return tasks, but you do have control over *when* you do them. By chunking them together and changing up when you work on maintenance tasks, you create the space to focus on bigger things throughout the week.

> **If scheduling a Maintenance Day is simply too unrealistic for you,** try gathering a list of the maintenance tasks you do throughout the week and create a maintenance *list*. This will help you chunk together some of your maintenance tasks so you can get many of them out of the way when you are low on energy and can't focus on more impactful or meaningful tasks.

Here's the curious thing about maintenance tasks: although they require a good amount of time to complete, most of them use *almost none* of your focused energy or attention. In fact, you can do most of your maintenance tasks automatically, without much thought.

While multitasking will make you less productive as you try to focus on two things that require a lot of attention, it's possible to multitask and become more productive with maintenance tasks simply because they require almost none of your attention and your energy. When you do maintenance tasks, you have attention and energy to spare.

Here are my favorite ways to use my time wisely when undertaking the tasks on my Maintenance Day list:

- Do them with someone else, like my girlfriend, to make the tasks more interesting and meaningful.
- Listen to a podcast or audiobook while completing them. I plow through so many tasks on my Maintenance Day, I can usually get through half of a book by the time I'm finished.
- Call someone or Skype someone so you can have a meaningful conversation while doing the tasks.
- Do the tasks mindfully to work out my "attention muscle" (page 190).

- Deliberately think about nothing while doing maintenance tasks, to give my mind a chance to rest and wander (page 168).

Want to accomplish more while completing your Maintenance Day tasks? The possibilities are endless; you can download a podcast to learn a new language, or plan for a vacation, do body weight exercises, or practice a new skill.

Although it's not possible to eliminate all the pesky maintenance tasks from your life, it is possible to spend your time on them much more intelligently and fruitfully.

Try setting a time limit for how long you'll work on your maintenance tasks, to get more done in less time. Just make sure you don't work on them during your BPT—that time is sacred.

STRIVING FOR IMPERFECTION

In the years following my first Maintenance Day ritual, I've noticed a ton of benefits that extend beyond having more time for important and meaningful tasks throughout the week. Having a Maintenance Day helps you eliminate both physical and mental clutter, so you can approach each new week with more clarity and energy. Plus, it feels freaking amazing to accomplish ten or fifteen things at once, and check them off your to-do list.

Over time, one of the biggest hidden benefits I've realized is that it causes me to waste less time. By their very nature, maintenance tasks shouldn't be done to perfection. They are low return. They support your work, but they aren't as essential as the high-return and meaningful tasks they support.

Many people—myself included—are perfectionists. We have the tendency to continue to work on tasks beyond the point where they're "good enough," where the return on investing more time into them diminishes rapidly. Picasso spent a lifetime mastering the art of painting; every small improvement made his work that much richer.

But low-return maintenance tasks don't offer the same return on investment. Past a certain point, overattending to more menial tasks simply cuts into time you would have otherwise spent on more meaningful or higher-return activities.

Lumping together your maintenance tasks—whether on a Maintenance Day or with a maintenance list—helps you eliminate spending too much time on them. And it gives you fewer lower-return tasks to waste time on throughout the week, which gives you the time to focus on what's actually important.

There is a time and a place for perfection—but your maintenance tasks aren't it. The extra time you spend on them is simply wasted. You can always make your house 10 percent cleaner, but does anyone really care?

Chunking your maintenance tasks together is the perfect antidote to being a perfectionist about the wrong things.

THE END OF TIME MANAGEMENT

In a book about productivity, it may seem strange that I've only dedicated three chapters to time-management techniques. But, as I've discussed, time management simply isn't as important in the knowledge economy as it was in the time economy.

In the knowledge economy, the most productive people see time as the backdrop against which they work. Some coordination is essential for managing your time around the work of other people, and for working smarter instead of harder. But whenever possible, the most productive people let time management take the backseat to how they manage their energy and attention. It used to be that time was the only resource we had to manage. Today, your time, attention, and energy are more interconnected than they ever have been, and the most productive people manage all three.

Time management is impossible. It's possible to manage when you work on things. You can't manage or control time—it's been ticking on for 13.8 billion years, and it shows no signs of stopping.

THE MAINTENANCE CHALLENGE

Time required: 10 minutes throughout the week; a few hours for the ritual, depending on how many tasks you chunk together
Energy/Focus Required: 2/10
Value: 7/10
Fun: 8/10
What you'll get out of it: You'll carve out more attention and energy to work on important things throughout the week. You'll also procrastinate less, experience more mental clarity, and feel great when you tackle a dozen of your maintenance tasks at once.

Establishing a Maintenance Day ritual is one of the most powerful things you can do to free up attention and energy throughout the week.

Here's the challenge for this chapter: next week, continue to do your maintenance tasks throughout the week, but as you do them, write them down on your Maintenance Day list, if you think you can safely do them later on in the week. (Watering plants, for example, or emptying the kitty litter may not wait.) If you're like me, you'll be surprised by how many tasks you don't have to do throughout the week but can group them together on a Maintenance Day or on a maintenance list.

Then, the next week, schedule a Maintenance Day, or half day, to tackle the tasks all at once. To use that time even more productively, use the spare energy and attention you have during your tasks for something even more important and meaningful, like learning a language, or listening to a favorite NPR podcast. Just make sure you don't tackle maintenance tasks during your BPT—that time is sacred!

If you're like me, once you start, you won't go back.

Part Four

THE ZEN OF PRODUCTIVITY

12

THE ZEN OF PRODUCTIVITY

Takeaway: Support tasks like checking email are likely a necessary evil for your workday, but shrinking how much time, attention, and energy you spend on them is one key to increasing your productivity. By creating more time and space around your highest-return activities, you become more creative, focused, and productive.

Estimated Reading Time: 4 minutes, 43 seconds

ZEN IN MAY

If you ever find yourself in Ottawa in May with an hour or two to spare, head down to Dows Lake, a man-made lake that sits smack-dab in the middle of the city. While the lake itself is pretty—especially in the wintertime when it freezes over and becomes one of the longest skating rinks in the world—what's even more attractive are the tulips that surround the lake in May. Every May, some three hundred thousand tulips planted around the Rideau Canal—which Dows Lake flows into—come into full bloom. Whether you're into flowers or not, it's a great place to unwind with friends, your significant other, or to take a bunch of appreciative tourists.

The other day, while looking through the pictures I took during my project, I stopped on one that I took on Sunday, May 5, just four days after I started my project. The picture looks up at a couple of leafy green trees, but it is focused on a book I'm holding up in the foreground: *Rapt*, by Winifred Gallagher—the first book I read for my project.

The picture perfectly embodies my emotions at the beginning of my project: a zenlike calm, an engaged curiosity, while being incredibly focused on the subject of productivity.

Before the explosion of interest in my project months later, the simple prospect of experimenting with productivity in a calm, curious, and focused way for a year was more alluring to me than even a lucrative job offer (or two).

OPPORTUNITY KNOCKS

But as my project progressed, its nature began to change very quickly.

Eight short months after I started my project—five months after my productivity experiment to meditate for thirty-five hours, and just two months after TED organizers published their interview with me—my project suddenly started to get, well, a lot *bigger*. Seemingly overnight, it gained momentum, and my site went from receiving a few hundred hits a day to a several thousand. My blog went from receiving a handful of comments every week to receiving dozens. I went from receiving about thirty emails every day to receiving a few *hundred* emails a day, and I quickly began to field requests for more media interviews, meetings, and productivity coaching calls than I knew what to do with.

The zenlike nature of my project quickly became disrupted—but in the best way possible. Since I designed my project from the ground up to experiment with productivity, it was a pretty sweet problem to have.

Oddly enough, the tasks in my project that began to balloon were all tasks that supported my work. Answering email, attending meetings, and keeping up with social media are the "maintenance tasks" of work; they support the most fruitful tasks in your job, and just like doing the laundry and paying your bills, they're very hard to get rid of. For me, support tasks are almost as pesky as maintenance tasks, because like your maintenance tasks, they can eat up a ton of your valuable time, attention, and energy—which you would have otherwise spent on more valuable and meaningful things.

But there's a more nuanced cost to spending too much time on low-return tasks: they're much *easier* to work on. They're the "watching Netflixes" of the work world; your limbic system puts up less of a fight against checking your email one more time, arranging one more phone call, or attending one more meeting. It's pretty easy to convince yourself in the moment that your low-impact tasks are more important than your real work, even though they provide you with a much smaller return on your time in the long run.

As with maintenance tasks, I've found that the answer to dealing with the low-return tasks in your work isn't to work faster or harder, or put in insanely long hours to get everything done. It's to shrink how much time, attention, and energy you spend on them in the first place.

THE ZEN OF LESS

The reason simplifying the low-impact tasks in your work can be so powerful is simple: the less time and attention you spend on them, the more time and attention you can invest in what's important. Your goal should be to simplify your work, so you spend most of your time on your most productive tasks.

Remember those sixteen-piece, four-by-four sliding puzzles you played with as a kid, where one square was empty and you slid the other pieces around to unscramble the puzzle? That's what your time is like. The more open space you have in your schedule, the more flexibility you have for when you work on tasks, and since your focus and energy fluctuate so much over the day, the more productive you can become. Simplifying what you take on lets you become more responsive to the tasks and projects that come your way that are your highest-return tasks. At the same time, things happen. A crisis erupts at work. Your kid comes down with the flu. Your boss calls an urgent meeting. Or your girlfriend is nagging you to go for a run with her, which is actually happening to me as I write this sentence.

Simplifying and creating more space around your high-return tasks gives you the wiggle room to react and then deal with whatever unexpected task comes along.

In addition, simplifying what you take on provides you with a beautiful zenlike mental clarity throughout the day—which feels absolutely incredible. According to urban planners—maybe even the same urban planners who came up with the idea of desire paths—what allows traffic to flow on the highway isn't how many cars there are, or how fast the cars move. It's how much space exists *between* the cars. The same is true for the tasks you work on throughout the day. It's difficult to be productive when you try to cram as much into your day as possible, because you'll inevitably create a mental logjam as unexpected tasks crop up. By simplifying how much you take on, you create more attentional space around your high-return activities, so you can focus on them much more deeply. Tasks are the cars on the productivity superhighway.*

Creating more attentional space around your highest-return activities will also help you come up with better ideas. The reason we tend to come up with a lot more great ideas in the shower compared to when we're on a smartphone is simple: when we're taking a shower, we create enough attentional space for our mind to wander and for new ideas and thoughts to bubble up to the surface. Simplifying your life of low-return tasks has a similar effect. Doing so not only allows you to dedicate more time and attention to your highest-return tasks; it also helps you generate more great ideas for them.

By creating more space between your high-return tasks and commitments, you can immerse yourself in them more completely, work smarter, and give them the time and attention they deserve.

The next two chapters contain the very best ways I discovered during my project to do that.

---

* That might be one of the corniest things I've ever written, but I'm going to leave it in so I can poke fun at myself later.

SHRINKING THE UNIMPORTANT

Takeaway: Every single support task in your work can be either shrunk, delegated, or even, in a few rare cases, eliminated entirely. After you have a better grip on how much time and attention you spend on your problem tasks, the maintenance tasks in your work are a lot easier to deal with.

Estimated Reading Time: 11 minutes, 22 seconds

THE UNIMPORTANT

Despite taking the time to figure out my highest-impact tasks at the beginning of my project, I didn't do anything about the lower-return tasks in my work until it was almost too late, until I was so overwhelmed by my support tasks that my productivity plummeted.

Something had to give.

One surprising discovery I made after looking at my first time log—in addition to how much time I spent procrastinating—was how much time I spent working on low-return maintenance tasks throughout the week. Even though I *felt* productive because I was so busy working on them, they didn't lead me to accomplish anything meaningful.

"Parkinson's law" states that your work expands to fit the amount of time you have available for it. In my project, I found this law to be especially true with tasks that are low return. Because your limbic system puts up such a fight against working on your more challenging, highest-return tasks, the low-impact tasks that support your work almost serve as work "crack" or work candy. You *feel* productive when you work on them—after all, you're incredibly busy. But they lead you to accomplish less.

Looking through my list of work tasks in my time log, I pinpointed the problem tasks in my work that ate up the most time; the ones that expanded to fit how much time I had available. They were, in order of how much time and attention they consumed:

- Answering email
- Attending meetings
- Loading blog articles and newsletters
- Managing my calendar
- Coaching people and businesses on productivity
- Researching and scheduling travel
- Coordinating and participating in conference calls
- Doing website maintenance
- Managing my social media accounts

Chances are that you have similar maintenance-type tasks that support your real work—pretty much every knowledge worker on the planet is inundated with email and gets invited to too many meetings and events.

But as I discovered, there's good news: every single support task can be shrunk, delegated, or perhaps eliminated entirely.

YOUR LOW-HANGING FRUIT

Depending on how defensive or protective you are of your time, you may discover that you have a few low-impact tasks that you can eliminate entirely. In my experience, though, it's very difficult to eliminate all these tasks. In the jobs I've worked in the past, I was paid to work on a lot of tasks that weren't always the best use of my time. And though pushing back against many of them would have made me more productive, doing so would have also made me look like a jerk or would have gotten me fired.

However, you may find that there are tasks and responsibilities that you can eliminate entirely. Tasks like:

- Recurring, low-return meetings
- Low-return phone calls, and the productivity porn of social media and news websites and other time wasters
- Tasks and projects that make little use of your time or unique talents or skills
- Tasks and projects in which you contribute little value, but which take up a lot of time

I've found that the tasks that support your work will almost always outnumber the tasks that you can safely eliminate. But if you do have low-hanging fruit on your list of low-leverage tasks that you can pluck and eliminate, it's worth making an effort to do so, to free up valuable time and attention that you can better spend on your most important tasks.

In my productivity project, I found I could only completely eliminate one item from my list—coaching people and businesses. Although the work paid decent money, it didn't directly contribute to my project, or let me reach out to more people with my work.

Alas, the rest I had to shrink the hard way.

SEVERE SHRINKAGE

I was in the pool!! I was in the pool!!
—George Costanza

After being stuck in email and meeting hell for a solid month or two, I finally decided to experiment with how I could shrink my support tasks to carve out more time and attentional space to get more actual, real work done. After a lot of trial, error, and late nights, I found that the most effective answer to shrinking low-return support tasks was to

- become aware of how much time and attention I spent on support tasks, and
- shrink the tasks by setting limits.

The simple act of keeping a time log makes you more aware of what you're working on daily. But time is only one part of the story. Low-return tasks also take up a boatload of your attention.

Take email, for example. After becoming inundated with email during my project, I asked several friends, in an informal survey, to keep a tally of how often they checked for new email messages at work every day for a week. The average between them? An astounding **forty-one times.** Another (more scientific) study found that most people check email about every fifteen minutes—which adds up to thirty-two times over an eight-hour day. When you check for new email thirty-two times a day, that's thirty-two times your attention is derailed from what you're supposed to be working on. It's pretty hard to maintain any mental clarity in those conditions. Email may be a vital support task, but you also don't have to check it thirty-two times a day. (I didn't fare any better—even while trying to work as deliberately as possible, I checked for new messages thirty-six times a day.)

After you identify your problem tasks, think about how frequently you focus on them throughout the day, by keeping a formal tally for a day or two.

After you have a grip on how much time and attention you spend on problem tasks, you'll find they are a lot easier to deal with. The best solution I have found to shrinking mine has been to set limits, both for how much time I spend on the task, and for how often I focus on the task.

ATTENTION HOGS

Some support tasks in your work take up a disproportionate amount of your attention rather than your time. For example, most emails only take a minute or two to respond to, but when you check your email dozens of times a day, that's countless times you have to transition from focusing on something important to focusing on email. (The switching costs associated with multitasking can be so enormous that I've devoted an entire later chapter to them.) There's also, of course, the uncertainty that comes with not knowing whether you have new messages, which costs you even more attentional space, not to mention how often email alerts interrupt you (page 185) when you're trying to work on something more productive.

For tasks like email, the best way I've found to shrink their impact on time and productivity is to limit how often I focus on them throughout the day. I turn off my email alerts, and only check emails at a few specific times—in the morning, before lunch, and at the end of the day. And I've found similar limits can work wonders for tasks like checking social media, making phone calls, and sending and responding to instant messages.

That said, some emails are worth spending more time on. Forcing yourself to wait before responding gives your mind time to collect and form a thoughtful reply. And you might save yourself from sending a bunch of emails back and forth in the end.

The following are a few examples of the limits I set during my project:

- Scheduled just three thirty-minute chunks of time every day to deal with email
- Limited myself to checking social media five times a day
- Lumped similar tasks together so I could focus on them less frequently (e.g., by making all my phone calls at once)
- Limited myself to starting just five new IM conversations a day
- Only checked for new email when I had the time, focus, and energy to respond to everything that might have come in

Determining ahead of time when you'll tackle a task like email—as opposed to whenever it comes in, or when you get the urge to do so—does a number of things at once. It helps you carve out more attentional space; it helps you work more deliberately; and it helps you stop thinking about your support tasks throughout the day because you've decided ahead of time when you'll focus on them.

It took me a few weeks to settle into a routine where I checked messages less frequently. But as with connecting to the internet less during the workday, after I settled into a new routine where I focused on my low-impact tasks less often, I had more mental clarity to devote to my real work than I had in a long, long time.

TIME HOGS

Many support tasks suck up more of your time than they do your attention. Take meetings, as an example. Although some meetings are important, the average person wastes an incredible amount of time in them: *37 percent* of the average office worker's time is spent in meetings. A survey of 150 senior executives found that they think 28 percent of meetings are an unnecessary waste of time. (I'd argue that number is north of 50 percent for most workers, because senior executives aren't invited to the most pointless ones.) Unproductive meetings are the opposite of support tasks like email: they use up a ton of your time, but hardly any of your attention or energy.

Here are a couple examples of how I put time limits on meetings during my project (granted, I am more in control of my day than most office workers and managers):

- Limited myself to attending four hours of meetings a week—and pushed back on or canceled any meetings beyond that
- Took "vacations" away from support tasks (e.g., took a holiday from email for a day or two by setting up a temporary autoresponder so I could work on a project that was high impact)

These limits not only motivated me to get tasks done faster, they also forced me to come up with clever ideas to work smarter, because I only had so much time. For support tasks that take up a lot of time *and* attention, I think it's helpful to set a time and attention limit for the task. During the productivity project, I found that email was sucking up a ton of my time, so in addition to blocking off three periods throughout the day to focus on emptying my inbox, I also made a rule that every single email I sent would be five sentences or less. I simply made a note of my actions in my email signature ("For your benefit and mine, I keep every email I send to 5 sentences or less"), to be as transparent as possible. My email recipients seemed to understand, and I instantly felt able to blow through my inbox like never before. When I found it hard to make a response shorter than five sentences, I discovered it was a cue that a phone call was usually a more productive way to handle the matter, anyway.

Some "time hogs," like idle office chitchat, are inherently harder to tame. Although forming deeper office friendships can help your productivity quite a bit (page 267), it's also worth reflecting on whether idle office chitchat is costing you valuable time. If it is, making a plan to avoid the banter—like by wearing headphones when working on critical tasks, avoiding gossip like the plague, finding another place to take a break besides in your office, asking the person interrupting you to help out with your work, or closing your office door during your BPT—will help you free up even more time for your highest-impact tasks.

Just as a Maintenance Day creates structure around the support tasks in your life, setting limits for support tasks in your work makes it much harder for them to expand and take up more of your time or attention than they need to.

> **You can also shrink** the distractions of email by installing a send-it-later email plugin. My favorites at the time of writing for Gmail: Boomerang (BoomerangGmail.com), Right Inbox (RightInbox.com); Apple Mail: SendLater (ChungwaSoft.com/sendlater); Outlook: SendLater (SendLaterEmail.com); Android: Boomerang (BoomerangGmail.com).

RETURNING TO ZEN

Since my project found its legs, instead of checking my email countless times a day as I did when I began to receive boatloads of email, I've slowly chipped away at how frequently I check for new messages. Today, I check my email three times every *week*.

Every Monday, Wednesday, and Friday afternoon at 3 p.m.—the time of the day I switch from a maker's schedule into a manager's schedule, when I have less energy—I fire up my email inbox, and go through it. And I've stuck to that schedule now for a long time. I value my time and want to spend it on the tasks that let me accomplish the most. I have a second priority inbox that only about ten people know about that I check a few times a day, so the people I care the most about and work the closest with can reach me more quickly. Like most people, I still receive a lot of email, but changing the way I've dealt with it has let me carve out more time and attention for what's actually important every day.

Although you probably don't have the flexibility to check your email only three times a week, it's worth respecting your attention and checking your inbox less than you do today. If you want to accomplish more, having additional attentional space is crucial. When you respond to every email within a few minutes of receiving it, chances are you're not using your attention wisely.

By the end of my yearlong productivity project, I gradually became more ruthless about defending my time from meetings, though that change was a bit tougher to make. When a meeting didn't have a clear purpose or agenda, or I wasn't needed, I began to push back to reclaim the time I would have otherwise wasted. That isn't always easy. But whenever I've given a reason for not attending,

One illuminating study found that "in the majority of [email sessions,] users were simply checking their email without acting on it." Don't check your email unless you have enough time, focus, and energy to respond to whatever might come in.

people are typically understanding. When I absolutely have to attend a meeting, I'll often also suggest shortening the meeting a little—which motivates everyone to expend more energy and focus over that shorter time to move through the meeting's agenda quicker. Because the default options in Outlook are to end a meeting on the :15, :30, :45, or :00 of every hour, people default to those limits. Why not end ten minutes early? And if you can ask a meeting participant for a one-minute recap after a meeting, it's probably not worth your time to attend. When you're nice about it and give a good reason, people are usually understanding.

Although it's impossible to completely eliminate email and meetings, it's possible to control how intelligently you spend your time and attention on them. Shrinking your low-return support tasks is the best way I've found to do that.

(Well, one of the two best ways, but I'll get to that in a bit.)

THE "ZENNING OUT" CHALLENGE

Time required: 15 minutes
Energy/Focus Required: 7/10, though it will vary depending on how strong your limbic system is
Value: 8/10
Fun: 4.5/10
What you'll get out of it: You'll spend considerably more time on your highest-impact and most meaningful tasks every week, instead of treading water while working on support tasks.

The challenge for this chapter, once again, is simple: choose one or two low-impact support tasks in your work that you have trouble taming, and shrink them, by setting a limit for how much time you spend on them, how frequently you focus on them, or both.

But just a quick warning. When you shrink your low-impact maintenance tasks, something will happen that you may be familiar with by this point: your limbic system will kick into full drive. When you simplify your work to focus on bigger and more challenging things throughout the week, your limbic system will act up; you'll feel guilty wondering if you've received any important emails, as well as about pushing back against unimportant meetings or fighting the urge to check social media one more time. Resist the urge! Like disconnecting from the internet initially, that sense of misplaced guilt goes away with time—after which you'll be able to focus more easily on what's actually important.

> **Don't be afraid to treat yourself after you successfully shrink your low-return tasks!** When I chatted with Charles Duhigg (the author of the bestselling and acclaimed book *The Power of Habit*) during my project, he stressed the importance of rewarding yourself as you form new habits. According to

Charles, "[when a habit] and a reward become neurologically intertwined, what's actually happening is a neural pathway is developing that links those [things] together in our head." When you successfully shrink your low-return support tasks, don't be afraid to treat yourself with something you find genuinely rewarding to make the challenge more fun. It will probably help you out in the long run.

14

REMOVING THE UNIMPORTANT

Takeaway: The word *no* is a powerful tool in your productivity tool kit. While time is no longer money in the knowledge economy, money can buy you time when you spend it intelligently. For every low-impact task, project, and commitment you say no to, you say yes to working on your most valuable tasks.

Estimated Reading Time: 13 minutes, 22 seconds

By eliminating and shrinking what I could—including coaching people and businesses, emailing, attending meetings, following social media, and accepting speaking gigs—I freed up a ton of time and attention to focus on bigger things. But as usual, I still wasn't satisfied.

I still had a number of pesky low-return tasks that needed to get done that I couldn't seem to shake off. Those included:

- Managing my calendar
- Arranging conference calls with multiple people
- Loading blog articles and newsletters
- Researching and scheduling travel
- Doing website maintenance

These tasks all took a good amount of time and attention, and that was time taken away from what I figured were more vital or meaningful tasks.

Thankfully, since we all deliver limited value through our low-impact tasks, we often also don't bring anything unique to them. These tasks are prime candidates to be delegated to other people. And that's the third and final way to handle the lowest-return tasks in your work.

Delegating tasks admittedly isn't a realistic option for everyone, but it's a lot more accessible than you might think.

WHAT'S YOUR TIME WORTH?

One of the most illuminating calculations you can make is how much your time is worth to you—not just in general, but in precise dollars and cents.

This is a calculation I've made periodically over the last few years, whenever my life conditions have changed. The way I calculate it usually requires a bit of thought. But it's quite simple. Every so often I ask myself: **How much would I be willing to pay in order to buy back one hour of my life?**

When I was a student and made almost no money, I was willing to pay very little. Since I had hardly any money to buy back my time with, I didn't have the financial freedom to hire people to do work for me. Back then, I figured my time was worth about $5/hour. Because of this, I filed my own taxes and was willing to work for minimum wage because my time wasn't worth any more than that. At the beginning of the year of my productivity project, I was willing to buy back an hour of my life for about $10.

Toward the end of my project, though, my time began to be worth significantly more—about $50 an hour. By then I had established a small business that began to earn a sustainable income, and I began thinking about building up a team to whom I could delegate my lowest-impact tasks.

Depending on how you value your time, it's possible to delegate tasks in your home, as well. Tasks like mowing your lawn, shoveling snow, or cleaning your house are tasks that are relatively easy to delegate and will let you buy back hours of your life. (Or just teach your kids to do them.)

Like with most of the tactics in this book, buying back time isn't about doing less; it's about working smarter to do more of the things you find meaningful.

I found that the value of my time has orbited around four things:

- How much money I earn
- How valuable my time is to me
- How valuable money is to me
- How overwhelmed I feel

I think if you're considering hiring an assistant, a virtual assistant (a part-time assistant who will work for you remotely), an intern, or a team, calculating the value of your time is essential. You may find that you don't value your time that much, and that you should work on your low-impact tasks yourself. Or perhaps you'll see the value in getting someone to do your low-return tasks for you. Regardless of where you stand, calculating the value of your time is worth the effort.

> If you've run the numbers and decide hiring someone to delegate tasks to is out of your budget, skip on down to "The Most Productive Word in Your Vocabulary"; you won't miss a beat. You can always revisit this section when you become so productive that you need to hire someone to help you out.

MY FIRST ASSISTANT

As an experiment, toward the end of my project I hired a virtual assistant. On the surface, the experiment was perfect: by delegating the low-impact tasks I had remaining, I would be able to hit several birds with one stone.

At once, I'd be able to

- eliminate my remaining low-return tasks by delegating them to someone else, and

- free up valuable time and attention to spend on more important things.

Not everyone has the freedom to hire an assistant. But when I looked at the rates of virtual assistants, I began to get pretty excited. I would be able to delegate my low-impact tasks to whomever I chose—as well as any low-impact tasks that came in over the course of the week—and the average hourly rate for the assistants I considered hiring was around $5 to $10 an hour; way below the $50/hour I valued my time at. Some folks charged much more, of course, but those people I ignored.

But my first virtual assistant was absolutely terrible.

Not to throw her *too* far under the bus, but before I hired her I didn't do enough due diligence. Not only was she located in India—which made communicating across time zones difficult—she was unreliable, took forever to learn new tasks, and I'm pretty sure she relied heavily on Google Translate to speak English. Since most of the tasks I gave her were digital, the time zone issue didn't matter all that much. But because she didn't speak English well and took so long to train even for the smallest tasks, I would have saved time and attention if I had simply done the work myself.

MY SECOND ASSISTANT

Thankfully, a few months later—after working with a couple of other VAs on and off—Luise came along.

When I gave a TEDx talk about my productivity project, Luise Jørgensen—a VA from Denmark—fortuitously stumbled upon my talk and decided to write a blog post about it. After I stumbled upon what she had written, it didn't take me long to ask if she had time to help me out. In a way, her blog post had carved out a desire path that led her directly to my project.

As I quickly discovered, Luise was the opposite of my other, inexpensive virtual assistants in pretty much every way. She was wicked smart, able to quickly learn pretty much anything, and had a ton of experience both with the kind of tasks I sent her way *and* productivity in general. She's still working for me today, while she studies in Thailand.

At first, I hired Luise simply to arrange calls and load up blog posts and email newsletters. But I soon also began to delegate other low-return tasks to her, like managing my calendar, booking appointments, researching and booking trips, and even doing website maintenance, or hiring and managing other contractors to do that maintenance.

I paid her $25/hour USD—substantially more than my first assistant—but she was easily worth it. It felt great to work on a project all day, hand it off to her in the evening, and have her work on it while I slept so I could be further ahead the next morning. Over the course of a month or so, as I began to trust Luise with more and more low-return tasks, I began to cross items off my to-do list and was able to free up more time and attention for bigger and better things.

I had finally discovered the benefits I'd hoped for with my first assistant. Here are the advantages of hiring a VA, in Luise's own words.

"It frees up time so you can focus on the activities that are at the core of your business and so that you can keep developing your business," she says. "The more a business grows, the more tasks there are on the to-do list, so it is very helpful to delegate some of the time-consuming tasks to a VA."

I found myself having more time to write, do research, read more books, and interview interesting people—my highest-return and most meaningful tasks. I also began to have much more attentional space to think deeply about my highest-return tasks, and do a much better job of them.

Is hiring a VA for everyone? And what do you look for? Again, Luise has some sage advice:

First, you should know what kind of skills you're looking for. Do you mainly need someone to take care of your administrative tasks? Or do you need someone who can take care of your correspondence with, say, clients or colleagues? By knowing the tasks you need taken care of, you can look for someone who has matching skills. I also think it's more

fruitful, easier, and enjoyable if you find someone that you can person-
ally connect with—this is why I always talk with a potential client
beforehand, to see if our working styles match. That way, in the end,
everyone is happier.

MISTAKES YOU SHOULDN'T MAKE

Even though I had to learn several lessons the hard way, I discovered a
few important things that are worth keeping in mind if you decide to
hire an assistant, a virtual assistant, an intern, or a team:

- **Don't be afraid to pay a bit more for someone who's much more
  qualified.** The less skilled someone is, the more time and attention you'll spend training and interfacing with the person on a
  daily basis—and that's a cost you should not overlook. For this
  reason, I recommend paying a bit more for someone more qualified, if you can. For example, expect a good virtual assistant to run
  you between $15 and $30 USD an hour.

- **Hiring someone in a different time zone can often be a good
  thing.** Depending on the nature of your work, and the type of
  tasks you intend to delegate, hiring someone in a different time
  zone can actually be advantageous for your work. For example, I
  have Luise load up a lot of blog articles and email newsletters, and
  because she's located overseas, I can finish a post in the evening,
  have her load it up overnight, and have it sent out for my review
  first thing in the morning. If you're hiring outside of your time
  zone, make sure whoever you're hiring is skilled, and that the person is someone you can trust implicitly.

- **Always check references.** Good virtual assistants will usually
  have references from people who are happy with their work. Don't
  be afraid to check someone's references—it can save you a *ton* of
  time in the end.

If you're not in the market for someone to support your work, consider outsourcing your work on a per-task basis when you have the flexibility or budget to do so.

Here are a few great websites I've discovered over the last few years, and a couple that friends of mine have recommended—whether you're looking for someone to work with you on a constant basis or on a per-task basis (I don't have an affiliation with any of them, and have used them all):

- Fancy Hands (FancyHands.com) for hiring virtual assistants
- Zirtual (Zirtual.com) for hiring virtual assistants
- eaHelp (Eahelp.com) for hiring virtual assistants
- Freelancer (Freelancer.com) for per-task hiring
- Upwork (Upwork.com) for per-task hiring
- Job postings at local colleges and universities to hire an intern
- "Help wanted" posts on Craigslist and Twitter for assistants

If you're in search of someone great to help you out—whether for specific tasks or on an ongoing basis—the preceding are some reputable websites that can give you the help you need.

THE MOST PRODUCTIVE WORD IN YOUR VOCABULARY

The most productive word in your vocabulary is one of the first words you learned as a toddler. It is also the fifty-sixth most common word in the English language: *No.*

When I realized I had bitten off more than I could chew as my project began to find its legs, I made a habit of deliberately saying no to low-return things every day. To me, it didn't matter whether they were large tasks, or small things, like listening to a podcast I wasn't interested in, responding to a mean email message, or reading the comment section on a news website. Making an effort to say no to things that weren't valuable, instead of accepting whatever came my way, saved me a great deal of time.

While it's one thing to eliminate, shrink, and delegate the tasks and commitments you already have, the number of tasks and commitments you take on is not static. It fluctuates over time. If you don't continually defend your time and attention against low-return tasks, projects, and commitments, your life can easily become flooded with low-return activities.

When Greg McKeown published his fantastic book *Essentialism* in 2014, a book about deliberately doing less, it struck a chord. When I asked Greg what it was about his book that connected with so many people, he put it simply: "everybody is in pain."

He continued: "People feel stretched too thin at work and at home. People feel busy but not productive. People feel constantly distracted and tripped by the trivial." Constantly trying to do more things—instead of the right things—leads to more stress, poorer quality of work, and lower productivity. The answer to this is to focus on the most essential tasks in your work and life.

Perhaps my favorite rule that Greg talks about for eliminating and saying no to tasks—Greg calls these types of tasks "nonessential"—is his 90 percent rule. He argues that we shouldn't just eliminate and say no to tasks that are pointless; we should also eliminate many of the "pretty good" tasks in our life and work when we can, because they take valuable time away from our most essential tasks. The 90 percent rule is simple: when you look at a new opportunity, rank it on a scale of 1-100 on how valuable or meaningful you think it is. If it isn't a 90 or above, don't do it.

As Greg put it, "your job isn't stuffing it all in; siphoning your energy into lots of good things. Your energy is best spent on the greatest things." Your energy is for working on what's most important—and most essential.

For every low-impact task, project, and commitment you say no to, you can say yes to working on your most valuable tasks.

This is, by the way, another great reason to work more deliberately instead of faster and harder. By working slower, you work with more awareness and mindfulness (page 190), and it's much easier to reflect on the return of the things that come your way.

In a similar way, the commitments and obligations you keep should be where your most important tasks and projects stem from.

Every commitment you make in your work and home life takes up some amount of time and attention. And each makes you less productive when it isn't high impact or meaningful to you. Take owning a home, for example. I'm lucky that at age twenty-six I can contemplate owning a home if I want to. But a few years ago I made the decision not to. It's not that I don't eventually want to own a house—I absolutely love the idea of owning a home, having a yard to barbecue in, and having my own space. But like with waking up at 5:30 every morning, the idea simply isn't worth the amount of time it would take in practice at this point in my life. In an apartment or condo, I don't have to mow the lawn, take out the trash, shovel show, or even repair my appliances when they break. Owning a home isn't a commitment I care enough about to sacrifice the time I can now spend on better things.

Examining the commitments you take on and reflecting on their return will let you simplify your work and life, and free up even more of your time and attentional space for commitments that are the most important to you. These commitments include things like the following:

- Full- and part-time jobs
- Industry associations you're a member of
- Owning and maintaining a home or a second home
- Educational commitments (e.g., attending university or college, or taking courses part-time)
- Relationships and friendships
- Clubs you're involved with
- Skills or hobbies you actively spend time on

I think a particularly powerful way to identify your commitments and obligations is to look at your low-impact tasks, and then think about which commitments they belong to. Every task or project you have stems from a larger commitment. By actively thinking about what commitment each task or project is affiliated with, you can identify the highest- and lowest-return commitments in your life relatively easily. Not every low-return task or project is part of a low-return commitment, but many of them will be.

I believe that one of the biggest reasons my productivity project began to find its legs was that I minimized how many other commitments I was involved with during that same time. When I started *AYOP*, I cut back on the number of commitments I took on and quit my part-time job (and declined other job offers). I even permanently deleted my Facebook account to free up time and attention for my project—which produced more benefits and was more meaningful to me. While it may sound on the surface like my life was less rich because I eliminated these commitments, the opposite was the case. To me my project was a much more meaningful and high-impact way to spend my time, and cutting down on the number of commitments I took on let me dive into it that much deeper.

Yo-Yo Ma didn't become the greatest cellist in the world by juggling cello lessons with soccer practice, salsa classes, and a couple of part-time jobs. He became a great cellist by investing as much of his time and attention in practicing the cello as he could, and it shows.

Similarly, one of the most productive and successful companies in the world is Apple. While other companies collect new product lineups like they're Pokémon cards, Apple has laserlike focus that has made it the most valuable company on the planet. The company has just four main product lines—the iPhone, iPad, Mac, and Apple Watch—and each line is just a few products deep and is updated only about once a year. At the time of writing, Apple is the world's largest company by market capitalization, yet every product the company makes would fit on a small table. Saying no is what got Apple there.

When you look around, you can find countless examples of how simplifying your commitments can make you more focused and productive. By doing this, you're able to better spend your time, attention, and energy on the select commitments that yield the most, are most meaningful to you, and create more time and attentional space for those valuable commitments.

The most productive people take the time to not only understand what's important, but also to simplify everything else.

THE DELEGATION CHALLENGE

Time required: 10 minutes
Energy/Focus Required: 8.5/10
Value: 7/10
Fun: 8.5/10
What you'll get out of it: A deeper understanding of exactly how much your time is worth, which will tell you your tolerance for delegating and outsourcing tasks in your work and home life.

My challenge for you in this chapter is to calculate the value of your time. Think deeply about how much you would pay to buy back an hour of your life—considering your income, how busy you are, and how valuable you find money and time to be—and then look at the cost of hiring someone to help you—a good assistant, a virtual assistant, an intern, or professional help in another area of your life.

It could be the most productive calculation you'll ever make.

And if you're looking to up your game even more, I challenge you to also

- consciously make an effort to say no to five things tomorrow, regardless of how large or small they are, and

- think about the commitments and obligations involving your lowest-return tasks, and ask how much value they add to your life. Should you consider eliminating some?

Of the three essential ingredients of productivity, your time is the most limited of them. It is worth spending as intelligently as possible.

Part Five

QUIET
YOUR MIND

15

EMPTYING YOUR BRAIN

Takeaway: Externalizing your tasks and writing them down is a powerful way to free up mental space and get organized. Performing a "brain dump" not only reduces stress and helps you focus, it also motivates you to action.

Estimated Reading Time: 16 minutes, 18 seconds

SNOWBALLING IDEAS

It's hard to imagine (for me, at least), but there was a time when books, newspapers, and the like didn't exist—when there wasn't a way to capture and then spread your ideas to other people.

With the advent of the printing press around 1440, books became civilization's first foray into externalizing knowledge and information on a large scale, which allowed humanity as a whole to become more productive. We no longer had to walk around carrying our collective knowledge in our heads. Instead, we could externalize it into a vast collection of books and then build upon those ideas to form newer and better ones.

There were, of course, those who thought this was a terrible thing—at least at first. Long before the printing press was invented, Socrates was averse to *writing*, arguing that it would destroy our memories and weaken our minds, even going so far as to argue that it was "inhuman." It's not uncommon to hear people saying the exact same thing today about Wikipedia and Google. But as powerful as our brains are, the latest neurological research shows that our brains are terrible at consciously processing more than a few thoughts at once. At best, our minds can only consciously hold on to a few ideas at one time—whether those include things we have to get done, emails we're remembering to send, or things we're waiting on. To summarize decades' worth of complex neurological research in one sentence, our brains are built for solving problems, connecting dots, and forming new ideas—not for holding on to information that we can simply externalize.

Here are a few examples:

- We can externalize tasks we have to do by putting them on a to-do list, so they don't take up space in our short-term memory or make us feel overwhelmed.
- We can put appointments and meetings in our calendar so we don't have to worry about them, and so we're reminded about them when the time is right.
- We can externalize things like our shopping list, so we don't forget half of what we need to buy the next time we're at the store, or realize when we're hunkering down on something important that we forgot to buy cantaloupe.

Just as the first books didn't weaken our minds, getting tasks, appointments, and information out of your head won't make your mind empty. It actually does the opposite by giving you more mental bandwidth. It frees up space so your brain can do what it's built for: forming new thoughts, ideas, and connections, and once you capture them all, snowballing them forward.

Your mind is an insanely powerful thinking machine, but it's the wrong place to store everything you have to get done, because it's simply not built for that purpose.

The more you get out of your head, the more clearly you'll think.

MY FIRST BRAIN DUMP

The very first productivity book I bought, about a decade ago, was David Allen's *Getting Things Done* (GTD). The premise of this book lies on the same principle: that your mind is not the best place to store everything you have to get done. Allen pioneered a system for getting all your tasks and projects out of your head into an external system—incredibly, before a wealth of research came out over the following decade that validated how powerful getting unresolved open loops outside of your head can be. As David Allen told me, "Your head is not for holding ideas—it's for having ideas."

I can hardly remember what I had for breakfast this morning, let alone the productivity books I read back in high school—but luckily some memories stick with me to this day. My first brain dump was one of them.

If you've ever created a to-do list, you're probably familiar with how great it feels to get everything you have to do out of your head. When I first cracked open *Getting Things Done*, this was one of the first activities David's canonical productivity book got me to do—but taken up several notches. I was in high school at the time so I didn't have nearly as many responsibilities and commitments as I do now, but per the book's suggestion, I sat down with just a pen and a notepad and listed every single thing that I had to get done that was floating around in my head. I still remember being stunned by how much I had on my plate; during my first brain dump, I captured probably about one hundred to-dos, projects I was in the middle of, things that slipped through the cracks that I had forgotten about, and more—all that I was storing in my head that I hadn't given the time or space to rise to the surface. Anything that was weighing on my mind, even slightly, I detailed in my notepad.

As Allen explains, "The first thing to do is to capture what's got your attention, then decide if it's actionable or not, and if it is, decide what the next action on it is, and do the action right then if you can."

The feeling I had after was, to put it very mildly, liberating: I felt as though a weight had been lifted from my shoulders.

My mind was finally clear.

As Allen writes in his book, "any 'would, could, should' commitment held only in the psyche creates irrational and unresolvable pressure, 24-7."

"What you need to do is take all of those things and one at a time, discipline yourself and ask yourself: is this something I'm actually going to do something about?" he explains. "If yes, then what's the very next thing you need to do to move that forward? That decision doesn't necessarily show up by itself. You have to think to decide what the next step is, whether it's to surf the web, make a phone call, draft a document on your computer. That granularity—getting it down to the next physical, visible action, is a really powerful thing to do."

This is a result of what Bluma Zeigarnik named the "Zeigarnik effect" in the late 1920s: incomplete or interrupted tasks weigh on our mind much more than completed tasks. After emptying my mind of everything that was weighing on it, I came to realize just how true this was as I experienced more space and clarity and felt less stress than I ever had before. My mind felt liberated—though it's worth noting that at this point I hadn't yet discovered girls, whiskey, or cosmology.

INCOMING!

But not only did David's book guide me to externalize the tasks in my head during that first mind dump, it also taught me how important it was to constantly capture tasks as they came up, especially if I wanted to maintain a clear mind. It's one thing to get every unresolved commitment you have out of your head and onto a task list, but fending off low-return tasks lets you maintain that clear mental space.

From then on, whenever I came up with an unrealized idea or thought, I added it in the notepad I carried around with me everywhere I went—which over time evolved into a smartphone. Whenever I thought of something to pick up at the store, I would write it down before the thought escaped me. And if I noticed even the smallest item weighing on my psyche, I would externalize it to create more attentional space for bigger and better things.

If that sounds obsessive, that's because it is. But except for meditation, nothing has helped me think more clearly.

Ten years later, almost every thought I have is new, because I make a note of anything important right away so I can deal with it or build on it later. Anyone can, and should, do the same. You'll be stunned at how many tasks, projects, and commitments you're keeping up there, and how clear your head will feel once you gather it all in one place. Your brain is much better at focusing on the task at hand when you have a clear mind.

THE SYSTEM I LOVE

Of course, merely making note of the tasks and projects on your plate isn't enough. If you don't do anything with what you've captured afterward, you won't clear up any mental space, because you'll go right back to stressing about what you still have to get done.

Over the last decade or so, and especially during my project, I experimented with using dozens of to-do list and task-management apps that deal with the tasks and projects I've captured, and although many of them have worked well, there isn't one I'd recommend above the others. In my experience, it doesn't matter how you organize your tasks and projects, as long as you find it helpful and user-friendly.

Today, I have a relatively simple way of capturing and organizing everything I have to get done. Throughout the day, as tasks, ideas, and other open loops grab at my attention, I put them in the notes app of whatever device is in front of me. (The notes app I use syncs between all my devices.) And every Monday, Wednesday, and Friday, after I check my email, I go through the notes I've compiled and add them to my to-do list or calendar.

My to-do list also couldn't be simpler: it's another note that I've pinned to the top of my list of notes that contains my three daily and weekly intentions at the top, and my task list underneath. I also maintain a calendar in which I try to schedule as little as possible.

After experimenting with every task-management app under the sun, the workflow I've fallen into is simple. Since my app syncs my notes between my devices, it's mindlessly easy to collect tasks, thoughts, and ideas whenever and wherever they come to me. When I'm away from my devices—like after my 8 p.m. shutoff ritual—I just carry a small pen and notepad around in my pocket. While the apps and devices I use change frequently, I also often revert back to using paper.

Regardless of how I've organized everything, though, my basic work-flow of capturing and then organizing the tasks on my plate has stayed the same for years, and the process has become seamless.

HOW TO ORGANIZE IT ALL

Because everyone's way of working is different, I won't recommend a specific organizational tool. It isn't about which method of organizing your tasks is best, but what's best for you. A large percentage of the most productive people I know use a pen and paper, and it's important to not discount this option. But if you're looking for a system, it's worth looking for something similar to what I've settled into, something that's almost invisible to you because it integrates so well with the way you work. It should also let you easily view, manage, and prioritize everything you have to get done, so that you can effortlessly pull together ideas, events, tasks, and projects.

As I experimented with corralling the open loops from my head, I discovered a number of other things that, in addition to to-dos and calendar events, are worth capturing. Two of these are straight out of *Getting Things Done*—a "Waiting For" list and "Projects" notes—and the rest are ideas I've experimented with myself with a lot of success.

Here are the best tools I've discovered to help you organize and deal with all your tasks and projects.

A "Waiting For" List

My absolute favorite golden nugget out of *Getting Things Done*, apart from the power of externalizing what's in your head, is the "Waiting For" list. I like to think of the Waiting For list as your to-do list's sexy, secret lover. It's pretty much what it sounds like: a list of everything you're waiting on, which—like a to-do list—you review on a regular basis to make sure nothing slips through the cracks.

Right now, I can say with near certainty that you're waiting on several things you're simply storing in your head, things that may slip through the cracks if you don't follow up on them. On a given week, my Waiting For list contains everything from packages I'm waiting for from Amazon, to important email responses I'm expecting, to money I'm owed, to important calls and letters I'm waiting for. I put pretty much everything on my list.

Because I schedule time to review my list three times a week (during my project, I also began to review my Waiting For list after I checked for new email), over the last several years, after I settled into a habit of capturing the things I have been waiting for, nothing has slipped through the cracks, and I worry way less about everything I have to manage. Once you capture something, you can immediately stop worrying about it. I also keep my Waiting For list in my notes app so everything is in one place, and group the items on the list by their context (i.e., Home, Owed, Email, Phone, etc.).

Another great way to capture what you're waiting for: After you send important emails that need responses, drag the message into a Waiting For folder. This also helps you catch any important email responses that might land in your Spam folder.

INDIVIDUAL PROJECT NOTES

Keeping separate notes about "Projects" is another golden nugget I love from *Getting Things Done*. While a simple task—like picking up a few things from the store after work—is a one-off thing, a project is anything that requires more than a few simple steps to complete and has an end or due date. In my notes app, I also keep a separate note for each project I'm tackling.

Right now, I have individual notes for trips I'm planning, speaking engagements I'm prepping for, and even one for writing this book. Every project note contains information about each project that I need to keep in mind to move the projects forward, and most important, the very next actions I need to take with each project. Having a separate note for each project not only lets me externalize the projects I'm in the middle of, but it also lets me logically plan out the next steps I need to take to move each project forward. The titles of all my project notes start with "PRO," so they're all in one place when I scroll through my list of notes in alphabetical order.

Every Maintenance Day, I scan through my lists of projects to define their next steps, and pull to-dos from them to add to my task list and the intentions I set for the week. Because of this, even though I'm often taking on dozens of projects at one time, I hardly ever think about them because I know that past Chris has taken care of things and captured everything that present Chris (and future Chris) needs to deal with at the start of every week.

A lot of projects take more attention than they do time; for example, if you have to give a thirty-minute presentation, even though it's only half an hour, if you're like me you'll spend hours thinking and worrying about the talk leading up to when you give it. Externalizing your projects helps you get them out of your head so you can move them forward every week, and when you're not planning, focus on what's in front of you.

A Worry List

One afternoon, between finishing university and starting my yearlong productivity project, I had a lot on my mind, worrying about everything from whether I should accept a full-time job or start *AYOP*, to what I was going to do for health insurance after graduating, to what my living situation would be. I created a project note for each decision (with next actions clearly defined), but I still couldn't stop worrying about them. So I externalized the very act of *worrying*.

To reclaim more attentional space, I made a list of everything I was worrying about—most of which I was blowing out of proportion, of course—and scheduled an hour every day to think through everything on the list. If I caught myself worrying about something throughout the day, I reminded myself that I had scheduled time to worry later, and if I started worrying about a new thing during the day, I captured it on the list so I could worry about it later, as well.

Most of the time I don't need this list, but if I ever feel like things are spiraling out of my control and want to clear some headspace, I create a list to clear my head.

An Inbox Review

When you look around, you quickly realize just how many "inboxes" you have.

I define an inbox as any place where you store the expectations other people have of you (such as responding to emails, tweets, Facebook messages, voicemails, LinkedIn invites, physical letters), or any place you store the expectations you have for yourself (such as listening to podcasts, sorting the papers on your desk, or going through research you've bookmarked). I'm a completionist at heart and like to stay on top of the messages people send me. But like many people, the number of inboxes I've built up over time is overwhelming.

That's why, on Maintenance Days, I completely review and empty all my inboxes that accumulate items over the course of the week. I also make sure to clear out the ideas and tasks I accumulated over the weekend in my notes app.

Potpourri

If you want to dive even further into externalizing the open loops in your head, here are a few more of my favorite ways to do so:

- **Notepads Everywhere:** I love capturing ideas as they come to me, but because I shut my phone off between 8 p.m. and 8 a.m., it's not always possible to capture them on my phone. For that reason I keep physical notepads *everywhere*. I keep a showerproof AquaNotes notepad in the shower for when ideas bubble up in the shower. I keep a notepad on my bedside table with a light-up pen (designed to be used by pilots) to write down any ideas that come up as I fall asleep or wake up. And when I head out without my phone, I carry around a notepad in my pocket to jot down ideas that come up. Ideas, tasks, and insights only have value when you capture and then act on them. Keeping notepads everywhere has helped me hold on to a ton of them.

- **Simpler Passwords:** Passwords are a pain to remember. I've solved this two ways: I have a password manager that stores all my passwords and fills them in automatically (I recommend either 1Password or LastPass). I also have a simple system for coming up with new passwords: my password for every website and service is simply the name of the website, but instead of typing the name of the website, I type the letter to the left of each letter of the website on my keyboard ("Google" turns into "Fiifkw") and then tack on a unique series of letters, numbers, and symbols at the end that are the same with every password ("8S5x8" to make "Fiifkw8S5x8"). This makes every password unique, impossible to guess, and best of all, impossible to forget.

- **Filing Emails:** Some things aren't worth keeping in your head—and that includes where you keep archived emails. A recent study by IBM compared email users who stored emails in folders and users who archived emails and searched for them later. On average, it took participants 66.07 seconds to search for an email, and *72.87 seconds* to find an email in a folder—and these times didn't take into account the time users spent sorting their email into folders in the first place! It's not worth your time or attention to file and retrieve emails. Search for them instead.

TAKING PRODUCTIVITY TOO FAR

Since being inspired by *Getting Things Done* a decade ago, I've found that there is a line that's relatively easy to cross, after which you begin to spend too much time managing and planning what you have to do instead of getting real work done. Working more deliberately is at the heart of productivity, but it's possible to take the idea too far. This is a trap I think a lot of people fall into when they become interested in productivity—and I include myself in this group.

From what I've found, the most productive people are the ones who strike a balance between the two extremes, who understand the power of capturing and organizing what they have to get done, but who also don't sacrifice real work in favor of being productive about productivity.

Research shows that the simple act of making a to-do list makes you less likely to get work done, because creating a task list *simulates* getting actual work done, even though it doesn't lead you to accomplish anything. To carve out more attentional space, I think it's crucial that you perform a brain dump of everything on your plate and capture open loops as they grab at your attention throughout the day. But it's also important you're mindful that you don't take things too far. Just because you feel productive doesn't mean you actually are—and this is something to keep in mind as you round up and organize everything on your plate.

Getting Things Done sits proudly on my bookshelf to this day, turned to face outward while only the spines of the other books I've acquired are exposed. I think it speaks volumes that over the last decade the system has become so integrated into the tapestry of my work and life that I don't notice that I'm practicing it.

That being said, I've never adopted it in its entirety. The system is pretty complex, and it's too easy to take it too far. To his credit, David has said many times that the crucial part about the *Getting Things Done* methodology isn't that you follow it to a T; it's that you externalize and organize everything you have to get done. You can take the parts that work for you, and leave the rest.

"Give yourself a couple of hours and literally grab every single thing that has your attention," he told me. "You don't have to go very far—just start to notice what has your attention."

The pros of externalizing everything on your plate outweigh the cons by a massive margin, but it's important to be mindful that you don't take this tactic—or any other tactic in this book—to the extreme. Productivity techniques exist to help you work smarter. But they're only useful when you still do the work.

THE CAPTURE CHALLENGE

Time required: 20–30 minutes
Energy/Focus Required: 9/10
Value: 9/10
Fun: 9.5/10

What you'll get out of it: Even though it might not look like it on the surface, this is perhaps the most fun and freeing challenge in the book. You'll clear up an incredible amount of attentional space to focus on important things throughout the day and become able to totally invest yourself in your work, feeling much calmer and confident that you're on top of your work and that nothing will slip through the cracks.

One of the biggest lessons I learned from my project, especially when it came to making changes to the way I lived and worked, was that the smaller the change I tried to make, the more likely I was to succeed at making it. Smaller changes are also far less intimidating, which makes them more likely to actually stick. This is why so many of these challenges are on the smaller side: not only does that make you more likely to actually do them, but after you do them, they're more likely to remain and help you become more productive. If you create a workout habit, and allow yourself to only work out for five minutes a day, you're going to be dying to do more by the end of the week.

This holds particularly true with externalizing the tasks, projects, and other open loops in your head. The value of capturing everything in your mind is immense, but it's also easy to dive in too deep and get discouraged, or dive in too deep and take things too far.

My challenge for you is to perform the brain dump ritual, the same ritual that got me hooked on productivity. Shut off all your devices, and sit down with only a notepad and a pen; capture everything in your mind that bubbles up to the surface and grabs at your attention, whether it includes tasks or projects you have to get done, things you're worrying about, things that have slipped through the cracks, or things you're waiting for.

Once you write down everything that is drawing your attention, I think you'll want to start managing everything in an external system—if only to make the good feeling last.

16

RISING UP

Takeaway: Doing a weekly review of your tasks and accomplishments not only gives you a better perspective on your wins and the areas you need to improve, it also gives you more control over your life. Adding in "hot spots" is a powerful addition to this technique that will keep you on the right path.

Estimated Reading Time: 9 minutes, 37 seconds

RISING UP

After I began to capture the tasks, projects, and concerns in my head, I found another unanticipated benefit.

In *Getting Things Done*, there is an important "Weekly Review" ritual, where you look over everything you've captured and organized throughout the week—including your projects, Waiting For list, and more. Seeing all your tasks, projects, and commitments from a bird's-eye view is exhilarating, not only because it lets you plan for the week ahead and make sure nothing slips through the cracks, but also because it gives you a new perspective on your life.

Whenever I scrolled through my list of tasks and projects, and everything else, I felt like I was in an airplane seeing the city I lived in quickly shrink beneath my feet. The tasks I was in the middle of—the cars on the streets below—became insects. I could see how much I was trying to do at once, and how much space I had carved out between them. The projects I was tackling—the buildings and parking garages below—also

shrank, and I could see how they fit together to make up the bigger picture of my life. And I could begin to think about the commitments I was
taking on—the neighborhoods that the cars and buildings were placed
in. It's crucial to rise up above your daily life every once in a while so you
can see it from a new, more distanced perspective. And doing so lets you
adjust course and make changes if you need to.

But it's possible to rise up even higher, and this is where the simple
idea of "hot spots" comes in.

PRODUCTIVITY AND CONTROL

What attracts a lot of folks to productivity books is their promise to help
them regain control over everything they have to get done.

I love feeling in control over what I'm responsible for. Every task,
project, and open loop I cleared from my conscience gave me a bit more
attention to focus on the task at hand, which gave me more control over
my work, which let me become more productive.

Today, even though I have more to do than ever before, I have more
control over my work than ever before.

When you step back and regain control over your work, you can work
smarter, more deliberately, and with more purpose, which makes it infinitely easier to become more productive.

The tactics I've written about so far have helped me reclaim an incredible amount of time and attention—which has given me more time,
attention, and energy to spend on what's actually important.

But of all the tactics we've discussed so far, no tactic will help you
feel more in control of your life than this one. Externalizing your tasks
and projects helps you focus more, worry less, and snowball your ideas
and projects forward—but believe it or not, you can take things up yet
another notch or two and feel even more in control over your work and
life after you capture your tasks and projects.

"Hot spots" is a fancy name for a very simple idea—an idea that let
me feel more in control of my work than I ever had before. Hot spots let
you see your work and life from ten thousand feet.

YOUR LIFE, BOILED DOWN TO ONE LIST

During my productivity project, I discovered something interesting about the different techniques that are supposed to help you organize or take control of your life: most of them aren't worth your time.

I think the return on any productivity method has to be *huge*, because for every minute you invest in your productivity, you lose one minute of doing actual work.

Luckily, hot spots fit the bill.

Your hot spots are the portfolio of your life. From a very high level, all your tasks, projects, and commitments can be categorized into one of seven basic "hot spots," a term that J. D. Meier coined.

According to J.D., we have seven areas in which we invest our time (and attention and energy) every day:

- Mind
- Body
- Emotions
- Career
- Finances
- Relationships
- Fun

Ninety percent of the people I've met fit their commitments into these seven life areas, even if they call them something else, such as Home, or Spiritual. What you name your hot spots doesn't matter as much as having a list of very high-level life areas that fit everything you're responsible for.

A simple list of your seven hot spots, of course, isn't all that powerful. But when you expand the areas—to list all the commitments you have in each part of your life—the list springs to life. For example, on my list of hot spots, I have expanded my "Mind" hot spot to hold all the commitments and responsibilities that fall under the heading the Mind:

- Learning (books, Instapaper, podcasts, audiobooks, RSS feeds)
- Meditation
- Reading
- Music
- Mindfulness
- Slowing down and working more deliberately
- Making more attentional space between work and life elements
- Stress relief (meditation, reading, listening to music)

The basic idea behind the technique is that once a week you review your list of hot spots, to think about how much time you spent in each one during the previous week, and to think about what to focus on and think about in the week ahead.

It took me a few weeks to collect all the commitments and responsibilities that I had under each hot spot, but once I did, I could look at the list and see my life expanded right there in front of me.

I would see "dental" under my Body hot spot, remember that I hadn't been to the dentist in a while, and book an appointment. I would see "my parents" listed under my Relationships hot spot, and remember to give them a call the next week. I would see "separating from work on weekends" under Fun, and realize that I had been working too hard. And I would see "mindfulness" under my Mind hot spot, and make an effort to be more mindful in the week ahead. Week after week, I collected tasks that would have otherwise fallen through the cracks and scheduled them the very next week.

Every week, as I pored over the list and thought a little about each item and what I needed to change in the week ahead, and evaluated how I did the previous week, I rose up above my tasks, projects, and commitments, as if I could see my life from ten thousand feet.

And best of all, I set the course for the week ahead.

TILTING

It's pretty much impossible to act deliberately 100 percent of the time. This is what makes productivity more of an art than a science.

After reflecting on my first log, I noticed how hard I was on myself because I could have been so much more productive than I was. But as I discovered through my interviews and experiments, no one acts deliberately or productively all the time.

What separates the most productive people from everyone else is that they make course corrections every week to gradually get better at everything they do.

And creating an expanded list of my life's hot spots is the best tool I've found to make course corrections every week. Every Maintenance Day, I look through the expanded areas of my life and ask myself a few questions—some from J.D., and some that I discovered during my year of productivity:

- What do I need to spend more time on next week?
- What did I spend too much time on last week?
- What do I need to schedule or do next week?
- What do I have to be mindful of next week?
- What are some unresolved issues I'm having in each area?
- What opportunities do I have in each of my hot spots next week?
- What obstacles will get in the way of my goals next week?
- Am I going in the right direction with all my commitments?
- Are there any commitments I need to add or remove? Expand or shrink?
- What did I knock out of the park last week?

To this day, this reflection helps me make course corrections and act more in accordance with my values and goals every week—without getting in my way too much.

While no one acts in accordance with their values all the time, the most productive people act in accordance with their values in the long run—and they do this by regularly making course corrections and finding what they need to improve on week after week. Even though in the short run, crises erupt and unimportant things eat into your time and attention, when you deliberately make adjustments every week, in the long run you will be able to act in accordance with what you care about.

I think the most productive people also spend some time thinking about which of their hot spots are the most important in their lives, and whether they need to "tilt" in the short run to focus on one more than the others. It's like spending more time on your career early on in adult life to ensure your advancement and give yourself the resources you can use later for other things. In my case, I "tilted" toward my Career hot spot by pouring a ton of time, attention, and energy into my year of productivity project, because I knew the long-term return on the work I did would be worth it.

Another great part about keeping a list of hot spots is that if one hot spot goes to hell, it doesn't take down your entire portfolio. For example, if you lose your job, the strengths of your Relationships, Finances, and Emotions hot spots will help to sustain you until you find another one.

Looking over my list of hot spots has become one of my favorite weekly rituals; nothing has helped me work and live more deliberately.

LAST LIST, I PROMISE

Scanning through your list of hot spots is a powerful ritual, but I found one additional cool use for the list.

The thing about your scannable list of hot spots is that it's relatively static. You'll never stop having commitments like visiting the dentist, phoning your parents, remembering to disconnect, or being mindful. But what *does* change on a weekly basis is what projects you take on—the elements of your work and life that have natural start and end dates and require more than a few simple steps to complete.

For years I had been keeping separate notes for the projects I was tackling so I could externalize them—but I had never created a master list of them all. There are hundreds of apps programmed around the *Getting Things Done* methodology that would have let me do this, but again, none of them stuck because so many of them got in the way of me actually doing good work.

Then I came up with the simple idea of creating a master list of my projects, with the projects grouped under each of my hot spots. (There's a sentence that would make zero sense if you flipped the book open to this page.) Much like creating a scannable list of hot spots, this list is refreshingly simple—but also amazingly powerful.

Under my Finances hot spot on this list I keep projects like:

- Pay off student loan.
- Do taxes.
- Spend less money on eating out and delivery.
- Create a budget for next year.
- Save up for a vacation in Ireland.

Just as my hot spot list lets me fly above my life, my master projects list, once I filled it out, quickly let me fly above all the work I had in progress, as well as every change I was trying to make in each area of my life. It also let me jog my memory for the projects I needed to focus on in the week ahead, as well as areas where I needed to improve. Keeping this list continually updated takes time, but I use my master projects list every week to rise above the areas of my life and think about the value of the projects I'm in the middle of, as well as other valuable projects I can start to become more productive.

To me, one of the biggest benefits to becoming more productive is having a better grasp of everything you're trying to do at one time, and the most difficult time to try to make sense of everything is when you're working at ground level. When you're working moment to moment, it's pretty hard to step back from what you're working on to think about how important it is—this is what makes setting intentions at the beginning of every day and week so important.

The same holds true for how you spend your time in general. When you're in the thick of things, it's hard to rise above your life to see what's important, and what you need to change.

Hot spots are the way to do exactly that.

THE HOT SPOT CHALLENGE

Time required: 10 minutes
Energy/Focus Required: 7/10
Value: 7/10
Fun: 9/10
What you'll get out of it: You'll see your life from a perspective you've never had before and be able to reflect on the importance of all the tasks, projects, and commitments you take on.

Once you externalize all the work on your plate, both in your work life and in your personal life, and capture any new tasks that come up, try scrolling through everything you've captured. Provided it's well organized, you should feel an incredible feeling of being able to envision every aspect of your life.

Creating a scannable list of hot spots is my favorite way to take this feeling even further; it's one of my favorite ways to work smarter instead of harder. After I scan through my projects, I pull tasks from them to adjust course for the week ahead.

When I first sat down to create a scannable list of hot spots, it took me about ten minutes to expand every area of my life; over the next few weeks as new hot spot elements came to me, I captured them in my notes app and added them to the list as I cleared my notes out a few times a week.

In this chapter, I challenge you to do the same. Take ten minutes, and think about the elements in seven areas of your life. If you've decided to start a Maintenance Day ritual, review your list at that time, thinking about where you want to improve the next week. When you don't act completely in accordance with what's important to you, don't be too hard on yourself—nobody is perfect. Just adjust course; in the long term, you'll get the exact balance you want.

MAKING ROOM

Takeaway: Letting your mind wander without distraction, such as when you're in the shower, is beneficial for brainstorming, problem solving, and becoming more creative.

Estimated Reading Time: 9 minutes, 53 seconds

THE NEUROLOGY OF A SHOWER

The last time you took a shower, you may have noticed that after a minute or two, something interesting began to happen: your mind started to wander, from what you had to do at work later in the day, to what you'd make for breakfast, to the fact you forgot to buy cantaloupe for that night's party. And occasionally during your shower, a brilliant idea or insight might even bubble to the surface.

This happens to pretty much everyone.

You may have also noticed that the opposite is the case when you mindlessly surf the internet or use your smartphone. While you may have the odd *Eureka* moment when you let your mind wander in the shower, chances are you rarely have a brilliant insight while you're on your smartphone.

There is a curious reason this phenomenon occurs in the shower and not when you use your smartphone: when you shower and let your mind wander, you carve out even more attentional space for yourself, which creates room for thoughts, ideas, and insights to bubble up to the surface from your unconscious mind and grab your attention.

Giving your mind the time and space to wander lets you carve out more attentional space, think more deeply about everything on your plate, and as many studies show, help you work smarter instead of just harder.

YOUR BRAIN'S TWO MODES

According to research, our mind seesaws between two modes throughout the day: a "wandering" mode, which we experience when we're taking a shower, and a "central executive" mode, which we experience when we're on our smartphones or focused intently on something.

You can't be in both modes at once, and most experts recommend spending time in both. As Daniel Levitin writes in his book *The Organized Mind*, "In the see-saw of attention, Western culture overvalues the central executive mode, and undervalues the daydreaming mode." And there are differences between the two that make spending time in both worthwhile. "The central executive approach to problem-solving is often diagnostic, analytic, and impatient, whereas the daydreaming approach is playful, intuitive, and relaxed," he explains. Some research even shows that your brain's mind-wandering mode can be beneficial when your work is complex or requires more creativity.

But with each passing year, letting your mind wander may seem to be a bit more difficult. More and more often, we seem to get sucked into using one more limbic-system stimulating device, like our computers, pads, and smartphones. And while they make us more connected, they can also prevent us from daydreaming, which makes it hard to step back from the decisions we have to make and problems we have to solve. In the average week today, the typical American spends *51.8 hours* staring at screens—that includes time in front of their smartphone, tablet, laptop, desktop computer, and TV—which averages out to 7 hours and 24 minutes of screen time *every day*. Assuming that you sleep for 7.7 hours every night (the national average), that means you spend 45 percent of your waking hours staring at shiny rectangular digital screens. Because your mind can't wander when you're focused on something, the productivity costs of being constantly connected can be massive.

One of the most memorable experiments I conducted during my project was to use my smartphone for only an hour a day for three months. After a while of walking around without my smartphone attached at my hip, I began to notice my mind wandering to new ideas and thoughts I wouldn't have arrived at otherwise. Not only did slashing my smartphone use give me more time to spend on higher-impact tasks, it also let me carve out more attentional space to think about them. Without my smartphone to focus on, my mind instinctively flipped into mind-wandering mode whenever I didn't have to focus on work, which created the space for ideas and thoughts to rise to my consciousness.

To this day, if I don't carve out at least thirty minutes of attentional space every day for my mind to wander, my productivity suffers.

YOUR BRAIN NEVER STOPS

The reason that *Eureka* moments seem to strike you from out of the blue when you carve out more attentional space for yourself is simple: your brain never stops thinking.

One of my favorite neurological studies was lead by Ap Dijksterhuis, at the University of Amsterdam. In the study, participants were given information about four cars and then were asked to pick which car they would buy. Researchers are usually a tricky bunch, and this study was no exception. They made one of the four cars significantly more attractive than the others, to see if participants could identify it as the best. They split the participants into two groups. The first group received information about 4 features per car, and the second received significantly more information—12 features per car—for a total of either 16 or 48 features in total.

Each of those groups was, again, split into two. Before participants were asked to pick a car, each of each group's participants were then either given four minutes to closely study the features of the car or given a series of totally unrelated word scramble puzzles to focus on for four minutes. This second group was seemingly at a disadvantage to figure out which car was the best, because they had no time to consciously think about which car was best.

So who fared better?

Here's where the study gets fascinating. With just four options per car, participants who could consciously think about their choices performed much better. That's not all that surprising: with just a few options, it was pretty easy for them to deduce which model is the best. But when participants had *twelve* options to consider for each of the four cars—forty-eight options to weigh in total—the group that could only unconsciously process the options *outperformed* the group who had four full minutes to think deeply about which car was best. And here's the kicker: they outperformed the conscious group by a massive margin; the conscious thought group picked the right car 23 percent of the time, while the unconscious thought group picked the right car *60 percent* of the time.

Several years after the experiment was conducted, a research team at Carnegie Mellon University performed a similar study again, but instead of having participants do word scramble puzzles, they had them memorize a sequence of numbers—while they scanned their brain activity inside an fMRI machine.

This team discovered something fascinating: while the brain regions responsible for memorizing numbers were (of course) fired up, so were the prefrontal cortices of the participants, which *continued to process the car problem* as they completely focused on memorizing the numbers. The unconscious minds of the participants wandered while they processed something unrelated to the task at hand.

Though there is some debate in the scientific community over how powerful our subconscious minds are, these studies illustrate something profound: that our minds never stop thinking. Even when we focus on something with our complete attention, our brain continues, like a computer, to have windows open in the background. And if a problem is particularly complex or requires a creative solution, our subconscious minds may even do a better job—especially when we give ourselves more attentional space to work on it.

MAKING ROOM

I began experimenting with more ways to shift into daydreaming mode during my project.

While I was planning my TEDx talk, I left my phone at home and wandered around Canada's National Gallery—just a short bus ride away from where I was living—with only a pen and notepad. To come up with new productivity experiments, I went on nature walks at lunchtime while I let my ideas germinate. On the weekend, I sat in a busy coffee shop with just a notepad to capture any thoughts that came to me.

In every instance in which I carved out time to let my mind wander, I made a point of keeping a notepad close by and shutting off the distractions around me to clear even more attentional space. And every time I captured at least a dozen thoughts, ideas, tasks, and people I should contact or catch up with. Without fail, whenever I carved out space for my mind to wander, countless thoughts would break through my attentional barrier, and I captured them in my notepad so I could deal with them later. In a way, my whole project was centered around connecting dots and coming up with creative ideas, and nothing helped me accomplish that more than carving out attentional space to do nothing.

Even today, in the middle of writing this book, I schedule more time for mind wandering than I ever have before, which has let me capture several hundred ideas for this book. As Steven Johnson so brilliantly put it in his six-part documentary *How We Got to Now*, "[new] ideas are fundamentally networks of other ideas." People who are paid big bucks in the knowledge economy are paid to solve problems and connect dots, which makes carving out time for mind wandering that much more important—particularly after you capture the unresolved things weighing on your psyche. Luckily, our brains are built for connecting dots, which makes them the perfect tool to use in the knowledge economy—provided we use them intelligently.*

---

* It also helped that I defined a structure for this book ahead of time, which, much like the car problem, gave my brain something concrete to chip away at in the background as I focused on other things.

Out of all the methods I tried in my project, though, nothing worked quite as well as simply sitting in a room with a pen and a sheet of paper. Every day or two I would set a timer, usually for fifteen minutes, and then simply give my mind permission to venture off and go wherever it wanted to go. In a way, it was the opposite of a planning session or brain dump—instead of staying in central executive mode, I shifted into daydreaming mode and captured the ideas and thoughts that would have gone unnoticed otherwise. I still use the same ritual today, and I'm almost always surprised at the ideas, thoughts, and even a few to-dos that come up when I create the attentional space for them to do so.

If this sounds strange, that's because it is. But your brain is also a peculiar machine, and sitting inside it right now are a ton of valuable thoughts, ideas, and insights it has been processing in the background that are waiting to be captured. A mind capture ritual is another great ritual to add to your Maintenance Day or perform when you feel overwhelmed and need to instantly create more attentional space for yourself.

The more attentional space you have, the calmer you'll feel, and the more productive you'll become.

MENTAL BLISS

During my year of the productivity project, I was able to secure almost as many insights with the other daydreaming techniques I tried, like visiting an art gallery or going for a nature walk. As long as they let me flip into mind-wandering mode and I had a notepad nearby, they worked. Generally speaking, the less attention the ritual required, the better. But even tactics like reading novels, which I thought required a lot of attention, often let me flip into daydreaming mode and capture new ideas. Whether knitting, gardening, yoga, going for a long

Your brain also continues to process and consolidate new information into memory as you sleep, which is why "sleeping on a problem" can work wonders, and why studying before bed will help you perform better on tests. This is also a great reason to define your three outcomes for the next day at the end of the previous day, or before you head to bed.

drive, walking somewhere without headphones, taking a candlelit bath, or visiting an art gallery works best for you, the key is that you take the time to shift your mind into wandering mode. Whenever Einstein had a difficult nut he was trying to crack, he would do much the same, and play the violin until the answer he was searching for seemingly struck him from out of the blue. The same can work for you, too.

> **Worth noting:** I devote an entire later chapter (page 255) to the importance of taking breaks and disconnecting from your work. Working insanely hard without recharging is a recipe for burnout. Since you rely on your brain so much at work, and likely face more pressure than ever before, breaks have never been more important.

The American Psychological Association (APA) recently named nine of the very best stress-relief strategies. Unlike quick fixes like shopping, gambling, drinking, and eating that don't actually reduce the cortisol levels in your body (the hormone your body produces in response to stress), the nine strategies the organization recommends all actually reduce your cortisol levels. Just as important, most of them also appear, at least on the surface, to flip your brain into mind-wandering mode, which makes them doubly valuable tasks to try when you're looking to carve out attentional space for yourself. They include:

- Exercising or playing sports
- Reading
- Meditation (page 201)
- Listening to music
- Investing in a creative hobby
- Praying
- Going for a nature walk
- Spending time with friends and family
- Going for a massage

Whatever your method of choice, taking the time to flip your mind into daydreaming mode can be one of the most productive things you do. Rest assured that when you take a break from your work, your brain will continue working in the background even though you might not be— and if you're trying to tackle a particularly creative or complex problem, it may even do a better job than your conscious prefrontal cortex will.

Your brain is a powerful machine. But you have to capitalize on its strengths and accommodate its weaknesses. Giving it space to slip into daydreaming mode, while externalizing the tasks, projects, and commitments you're working on, does exactly that.

Whenever you're in mind-wandering mode, again, make sure you capture what your brain comes up with, so that no great ideas slip through the cracks.

THE WANDERING CHALLENGE

Time required: 15 minutes
Energy/Focus Required: 2/10
Value: 7/10
Fun: 9/10
What you'll get out of it: A wealth of brand-new ideas that are residing in your brain, waiting to be harvested once you give them the necessary attentional space.

You probably saw this challenge coming from a mile away. My challenge for you this time is to let your mind wander for at least fifteen minutes tomorrow, and to capture any valuable thoughts, ideas, or things you have to do that break through your attentional barrier.

My favorite way to do this is to sit somewhere I won't be distracted or interrupted, with just a pen and notepad, and set a timer for fifteen minutes.

If you're like me, you'll be stunned at what comes to mind. You may even want to keep going for a longer period of time, say half an hour.

Part Six

THE ATTENTION MUSCLE

18

BECOMING MORE DELIBERATE

Takeaway: Research shows we only focus on what's in front of us 53 percent of the time. Developing a strong "attention muscle" is what makes it possible to focus more on the task at hand, which lets us spend our time and attention more efficiently in the moment.

Estimated Reading Time: 5 minutes, 8 seconds

TOO MUCH WANDERING

> *The successful warrior is the average man, with laser-like focus.*
> —BRUCE LEE

While carving out time to deliberately let your mind wander lets your brain form connections, relax, and think more creatively, when it comes time to do actual work, a wandering mind won't help you all that much.

Chances are your mind wanders more than you think. An interesting study conducted by Harvard psychologists Matthew Killingsworth and Daniel Gilbert found that we spend 47 percent of our waking hours (!!) in this daydreaming mode. In other words, throughout the day, while you're supposed to be focused on more important things, if you're like most people, you focus on something other than the task at hand *half* the time. You only bring 53 percent of your attention to the table.

It goes without saying that this has huge productivity costs, especially when you consider how intricately connected your time and attention are. The less attention you devote to a task, the more time you have to spend to complete it, because you work less efficiently. I try to use the word *efficiency* as little as possible, especially as far as productivity is concerned, since it reduces work down to something that feels cold and corporate. But there's no better word to use here: when you aren't giving your work your full focus, you simply aren't spending your time or attention efficiently. One hour of intense focus on your work is worth two or three hours of focusing on your work 53 percent of the time.

Time is the most limited productivity resource you have. By managing your attention intelligently—just like with intelligently managing your energy—you can spend it that much more wisely.

STOP . . . CHALLENGE TIME

Before we dive any deeper into this section of the book, I have a quick, early-chapter challenge for you.

As you read through this part of the book, I challenge you to break out a notepad or sheet of paper and jot down how many times your mind wanders against your will—how often it flips into daydreaming mode, resists reading on, begins to worry, tempts you to pick up your phone or do something else, or gets distracted. We'll tackle each of these roadblocks in turn, but as with managing your time and energy, it's helpful to know your starting point.

Whenever your mind wanders, don't worry; mind wandering is simply your brain's default mode. Even after years of meditating and doing my best to train my attention muscle, my mind frequently wanders, too. Simply make a note that your mind has wandered, and if you want, what it wandered off to focus on or think about, and then gently bring your attention back to, in this case, focusing on reading this book. (I use the word *gently* because it's pretty easy to be hard on yourself as you rein in your focus, even though mind wandering is 100 percent normal.)

This is also a cool hack to use when you're working hard on something important: just keep a notepad by your desk and make a note of every distraction or interruption that pops up and tempts you to interrupt what you are working on. Then get back to work. And if you need to, deal with the would-be interruptions after.

THE JOY OF BEING DELIBERATE

As I write these words, I'm sitting in a small tea shop in Ottawa. The Tea Store is located in the heart of Ottawa (it seats only about twenty people). I love coming here to read, write, and think. It's just a few steps from Canada's National Gallery, where I go to let my mind wander from time to time. The part I like most about the shop isn't the tea, though—it's the deliberate and thoughtful way they approach the tea ritual. After you choose one of the hundred-some teas on the wall of the shop, the staff will invite you to have a seat. Then they'll bring a small pot of the tea you choose to your table and light a candle under the pot to keep it warm. This shop has the best tea I've found in Ottawa—every variety is meticulously sourced or blended from scratch—and the care that goes into each variety is inspiring.

Since starting my project I've found myself oddly drawn to places like this; places that, in a world full of inexpensive tea and K-Cups, stand above the fray and are incredibly caring and methodical about the work they do. Like the scotch maker who spends years crafting his or her technique and recipe, or the owner of the winery who strives to craft the perfect vintage, or the accomplished musician who becomes a master of the guitar after tens of thousands of hours of practice;* these are people who invest time and energy into being deliberate in a world where working deliberately is hard.

These people take deliberateness further than most, but they've all homed in on a really powerful idea. Productivity isn't about doing more, faster—it's about doing the right things, deliberately and with intention. This is why carving out more time and attentional space around your tasks is so powerful: doing so gives you the room to work on higher-

---

* "It's not how many years you play; it's how many hours you play."

return tasks in the moment, fend off low-return tasks, and become more productive.

One of the reasons we make so many resolutions around New Year's is that during the holidays we can step back from our work and lives to think and reflect about other things. The same thing happens when you take the time to step back from your work and your life on a moment-to-moment basis: you'll plan more, come up with better ideas, and become able to work more deliberately.

If a tactic like separating your high-return tasks from your low-return tasks is a way of working more deliberately in general, and a tactic like the Rule of 3 is a way of working more deliberately on a weekly and daily basis, training your attention muscle lets you work deliberately in the moment. A strong attention muscle is what makes it possible to work deliberately and focus on your task at hand more than 53 percent of the time.

This is the final missing piece of working more deliberately—but it's also the toughest.

THE THREE PARTS OF YOUR ATTENTION MUSCLE

(Just checking in: has your mind wandered off yet?)

How we spend every moment makes or breaks our productivity. Technology and quick fixes provide us with more stimulation than tasks and projects that are meaningful. The faster we work, the harder it becomes to work deliberately. This is what makes staying focused and aware so hard—and this is what causes you to spend 47 percent of your time focusing on something other than the task at hand.

Thankfully, you can build up your attention muscle in a number of ways so you can focus better throughout the day—and all are backed up by a ton of research.

According to neuroscientists, our attention is made up of three parts:

- **Your Central Executive:** This is your thinking and planning brain that lives in your prefrontal cortex. So far, particularly in the procrastination section, I've done my best to write this book in a way that will fire up this part of your brain. It's mostly the other two parts of your attention muscle that I'll focus on in this section.

- **Focus:** This involves narrowing your attentional spotlight to focus on the task at hand, which helps you work more efficiently.

- **Awareness:** This means becoming aware of what's going on in your internal and external environments, which helps you work more mindfully and deliberately.

These three parts combine to make up your larger attention muscle. Training your attention muscle involves building up all three.

19

ATTENTION HIJACKERS

Takeaway: Dealing with distractions before they happen, like by shutting off alerts on your phone for new messages, helps you avoid attention-hijacking interruptions. It can take as many as twenty-five minutes to refocus on the task at hand after being interrupted.

Estimated Reading Time: 7 minutes, 25 seconds

BURSTING THE FOCUS BUBBLE

Tactics like setting daily intentions, externalizing your tasks, seeing your life as a collection of hot spots, and creating space for your mind to wander all help you see your work and life with more clarity and let you work on what's important every day.

But of course, not all distractions are internal. Just as it's important to build up your attention muscle, it's also important to protect it from external distractions that will derail your focus and productivity.

One of the things I noticed after I began to use my smartphone for just an hour a day—in addition to how much more mental clarity I began to have—was how infrequently I was interrupted. Instead of my attention being constantly hijacked, I was able to dive deeper into whatever I was working on, no matter how complicated it was, because I didn't have to constantly refocus my attention. Before the experiment, one text or interruption would instantly burst the focus bubble I was working inside of, and it took an incredible amount of time to work my way back into it. The more attention a task involved, the longer recovering from interruptions took.

Unnecessary alerts may not cost you a ton of time, but they cost you a ton of attention: every time you receive an alert for a new email, text message, Twitter mention, or Facebook notification, your attention is instantly hijacked, and this has huge productivity costs, particularly when you're working on something complex.

Since transitioning from the time economy to the knowledge economy, we no longer only trade our time for a paycheck. We also trade our attention for a paycheck, including when we're not in the office. In every nine-to-five job I've had, I was given a laptop so I could take my work home with me—and it was often expected that I would. Attention hijackers usually didn't exist after you went home from a day of working on an assembly line at a factory—when you punched out for the day, your attention was yours. Today, the opposite is the case. While it may be expected that you never disconnect, defending your attention from interruptions can produce great returns—whether you're at work or home.

Chances are you're interrupted more than you realize. Interruptions blend in so seamlessly with the tapestry of our work that it's often hard to notice them at all. However, according to RescueTime, a company that tracks exactly how people spend their time on the computer, the average knowledge worker opens his or her email program *fifty* times a day and uses instant messaging *seventy-seven* times a day. And according to research firm Basex, unnecessary interruptions from things like email and IM cost the U.S. economy *$650 billion* in lost productivity every year. It's clear that in the knowledge economy, our attention is worth quite a bit. (We'll get to the massive costs of multitasking in the next chapter, which can harm your productivity even more.)

Also according to Basex, "Interruptions and the requisite recovery time now consume 28 percent of a worker's day." And as Gloria Mark, an attention researcher at the University of California discovered, "each employee spent only 11 minutes on any given project before being interrupted," and it took the average employee **twenty-five minutes** to return to the initial task. That's a huge price to pay to tend to pointless interruptions, like emails and instant messages.

After my smartphone experiment, I began doing something relatively straightforward: I shut off every single notification on my smartphone and computer. Suddenly, whenever someone texted, tweeted, or emailed me, my attention was no longer derailed from what I was working on, and I could begin to tend to the new information that came in on my own schedule and terms.

Many people forget that their smartphone, computer, and other devices exist for their convenience—not the convenience of everyone who wants to interrupt them throughout the day. I don't own a watch, and so whenever I pull my smartphone out of my pocket to check the time—which happens a few times every hour—I also clear out any notifications that would have otherwise interrupted my more important work. Since my computer doesn't send me any notifications either, I clear those out at a time I prescheduled (page 127).

The only time my work is ever interrupted is when someone comes up to me in person, when I receive a phone call, or when I receive a reminder before a meeting is about to start. To me, these interruptions are worth it, and they save me time in the long run.

THE REASON YOU CAN'T REMEMBER ANYTHING

After I disabled pretty much every notification on my devices and began to disconnect from the internet, another curious thing began to happen: I started to remember a whole lot more.

The odd part about a lot of the best productivity tactics is that while they'll let you accomplish more every day, they often make you *feel* less productive. Tactics like stepping back from your work to plan, scheduling less time for tasks, and disconnecting from the internet all create the conditions for you to get more done—but they also make your work less stimulating, which creates the illusion that you're not accomplishing as much. Disabling distractions does the same thing. Even though pretty much every study on interruptions (and multitasking) shows that they hurt your productivity, your limbic system will tell you the opposite, and, just like when you procrastinate, it's hard not to listen to it. But at the end of the day, all evidence points to the fact that disabling attention hijackers will let you accomplish more, not less. Especially after you account for the fact that most interruptions cost you as much as twenty-five minutes of productivity, you quickly realize how detrimental most of them are.

But there's an equally large cost to being constantly stimulated and distracted: it affects your memory. When you repeatedly move your attentional spotlight from one thing to another, your brain gets overloaded. And when your brain is overloaded, it shifts its processing from your hippocampus (responsible for memory) to the area of your brain responsible for rote tasks, making it difficult to learn a new task or recall what you were doing before you were interrupted.

In his award-winning book *The Shallows*, Nicholas Carr uses a neat analogy to describe this effect: "Imagine filling a bathtub with a thimble; that's the challenge involved in transferring information from working memory into long-term memory. [. . .] When we read a book, the information faucet provides a steady drip, which we can control by the pace of our reading." While we read, we transfer information from our working memory to long-term memory one thimbleful at a time. The opposite happens when we use devices connected to the internet: we provide our limbic system with a delicious stream of distractions, which overloads our brain, making it difficult to transfer information from our working memory to long-term memory.

From the moment we wake up to the time we go to bed, we are plugged in; connected to a steady stream of attention hijackers that derail our focus, weaken our attention muscle, and cause us to remember less. Protecting your memory is yet another reason to disable as many attention hijackers in your work as possible.

I'll be honest with you: in my experience, disconnecting can be incredibly hard, especially after you grow accustomed to being steadily stimulated by distractions. As my yearlong project finished up, I was still nowhere close to perfect; after disabling almost every notification after my smartphone experiment, I was still tempted to check for new messages when I didn't have a steady stream of alerts coming in. But just like starting a new workout regimen, my attention muscle was weak at first, and then it got stronger as I began to regularly defend it against attention hijackers.

When you're on your deathbed, you're going to look back with satisfaction at all the cool and meaningful things you've accomplished, not that you stayed on top of your email.

Defending your attention muscle against interruptions will give you extra attention and focus to dive deeper into your work, to work more efficiently, and to become more productive.

> **While we're on the topic of distractions . . .** One of my favorite ways to tame the distractions around me (not interruptions or attention hijackers, but actual distractions) is by using the "20 Second Rule." Positive psychologists (like bestselling author Shawn Achor) suggest that twenty seconds is enough temporal distance to keep distractions at bay and out of your way, and this rule can be used to your advantage. During my year of productivity, I experimented with keeping negative distractions more than twenty seconds away with a lot of success. For example, I noticed that as soon as I moved unhealthy snacks to more than twenty seconds away from where I worked, I stopped impulsively snacking almost immediately. Some more examples of the rule in action include keeping your email client buried in nested folders so it takes more than twenty seconds to access, keeping your filing cabinet right next to your desk so it takes you less than twenty seconds to file something, keeping desserts at the bottom of your freezer, keeping your phone in the other room while you work, unplugging your internet modem, and setting a complicated, thirty-character password on your social media accounts.

THE NOTIFICATION CHALLENGE

Time required: 5–10 minutes, depending on how many devices you own
Energy/Focus Required: 3/10, depending on how tech-savvy you are. Notification settings are usually pretty easy to find.
Value: 8/10
Fun: 7.2/10
What you'll get out of it: You'll potentially reclaim hours of lost productivity every day because you'll no longer be interrupted by a barrage of alerts and notifications. You'll also remember quite a bit more and be able to focus more deeply on your work.

When every interruption costs you about half an hour in lost productivity, it's worth taming them.

If you're like me and the people I've met, you're interrupted a lot more than you realize—but thankfully, every device you own has settings to reduce and eliminate notifications. I challenge you to dive into the settings on your phone, computer, tablet, smartwatch, and every other device you own, and disable notification alerts on them all. Shut off buzzes, beeps, alert boxes, and anything else that hijacks your attention throughout the day. And be especially defensive of your attention during your Biological Prime Time; if you like to occasionally shut your office door but still like to remain accessible, your BPT is the best time to cordon yourself off to avoid your friends and coworkers. Any interruptions that aren't worth losing as much as twenty-five minutes of productivity over aren't worth keeping around.

Your limbic system may feel the loss of constant stimulation a bit at first as you adjust to not being interrupted, and you might even feel less productive because your brain isn't as stimulated, but when the day is done, you'll have a lot more attention to do meaningful and important work—not to mention remember the cool work that you do. And as far as productivity is concerned, that's what matters.

THE ART OF DOING ONE THING

Takeaway: Single tasking is one of the best ways to tame a wandering mind, because it helps you build up your "attention muscle" and carve out more attentional space around the task you are tackling in the moment. It is also a powerful tool for improving your memory. Just as working out in the gym builds the muscles in your body, continually drawing your attention back to your chosen task has been shown to build your attention muscle.

Estimated Reading Time: 14 minutes, 30 seconds

THE THING ABOUT MULTITASKING

To be everywhere is to be nowhere.
—SENECA

To kick off this chapter, I want to give you a quick refresher on a few ideas I've mentioned already that I think are especially relevant to this chapter:

- Busyness is no different from laziness when it doesn't lead you to accomplish anything.
- Productivity isn't about how busy or efficient you are—it's about how much you accomplish.
- Just because you *feel* productive doesn't mean you are—and the opposite is often true.

I know that by now I've repeated some of these concepts enough that your eyes may be starting to glaze over, but I think each of these statements contains a kernel of truth that's so profound that they are all worth repeating again, especially as far as multitasking is concerned.

Because here's the oddest thing about multitasking: although pretty much every study has shown that it's disastrous for your productivity, we all still strive to do it. Why? Because multitasking feels *amazing*.

THE PERKS OF BEING A MULTITASKER

Many of the books I researched during my year of productivity described how terrible multitasking is in terms of productivity. And indeed, pretty much every study ever done on multitasking has shown this is the case. But let's talk about the perks of doing more than one thing at once.

In my opinion, these studies neglect to mention that multitasking *feels incredible.* This is where, in my opinion, a lot of productivity books miss the boat. If every decision you made was perfectly rational, and your prefrontal cortex gained the upper hand over your limbic system 100 percent of the time, you wouldn't need this book. But assuming you're a thinking, feeling, loving, breathing human being, this is what makes productivity tactics like this one hard. Work is simply more fun and stimulating when you multitask—even though when you multitask you invariably accomplish less.

After I started *AYOP*, at first I ignored the research on multitasking, because I didn't feel like listening to it. Most days I accomplished what I intended to, and even though I wasn't focusing to the best of my ability, I was having a blast swimming in a sea of limbic-system-stimulating distractions. I knew that multitasking only created the illusion of productivity, but at the same time, multitasking made my work way more fun (and only slightly more stressful), and I felt like I was missing out on something when I tried to do just one thing at a time.

Near the start of my project I planned to experiment with single tasking, but I put off the experiment for quite a while because the idea of the experiment was so aversive to me. The busier I became, the guiltier I felt when I focused on only one thing at a time, and the more I dreaded the experiment.

I was addicted to the steady stream of distractions, and multitasking had become a habit.

SWITCHING TO AUTOPILOT

Habits are a powerful concept. If it weren't for them, and the fact that we perform many aspects of our life automatically, without thinking, we wouldn't be able to function in the world.

For example, you are now aware that in order to read, your eyes don't glance across a line of this book in one fluid motion. Instead, they jump to a few precise locations along each line to decipher these words.

You're also now aware that your jaw has weight and requires constant effort to hold up.

And if you think about it too much, you can no longer find a comfortable place in your mouth for your tongue.

By the way, have you noticed how your nose is always in your peripheral vision, and that now you can't stop noticing it?

And how every time you swallow, your ears click?

Studies show that 40–45 percent of everything we do happens automatically, and a lot of the time that's a good thing.* But some habits are counterproductive. Habits like sleeping in too late, binge-watching TV shows, smoking cigarettes, and eating too much pizza are often just as automatic, but usually counterproductive.

During my year of productivity project, I had the chance to chat with Charles Duhigg, the Pulitzer Prize–winning author of *The Power of Habit*. In his research and experimentation, he found that habits were quite simple, and that every habit was made up of three simple parts: a cue, routine, and a reward. "There's the cue, which is the trigger for an automatic behavior to start, and then the routine, which is the behavior itself, and then finally a reward." For example, when you wake up (cue),

---

* Have you yawned over the last few minutes? I hope you don't yawn. I'm trying to make this an exciting book, and yet I'm yawning as I type this sentence. Please don't yawn. I hope you don't yawn within the next thirty seconds or so.

you might immediately pick up your smartphone to bounce between a bunch of different apps (routine), which lets you feel caught up and connected with the world (reward). Or when you're trying to focus on an ugly task (cue), you might habitually open up your email (routine) to continue to feel productive even though you're really procrastinating (reward).

The more often you do a habit, the stronger the habit becomes. On a neurological level, a habit is simply a pathway in your brain that fires in response to a cue in your environment. As Charles put it, "[W]hen a cue and a behavior and a reward become neurologically intertwined, what's actually happening is a neural pathway is developing that links those three things together in our head." As Donald Hebb, a Canadian psychologist widely considered to be the founder of neuropsychology, put it, "Cells that fire together, wire together." Your smartphone and the other devices you multitask with are invisible to you because you use them habitually, without much thought—and you use them in response to cues that are embedded in your environment. This concept works in positive ways, too. Habits are also what let me work a new exercise and eating regimen into my life during my project (which I'll talk about in the next section).

According to Duhigg, cues that trigger habits fall into one of five categories: a specific time of day, a place, a feeling, the presence of certain people, or a preceding behavior that you have ritualized. This is why creating a productive daily routine is so powerful: you do the same thing every day, and when you ensure that your routine is genuinely rewarding to you, over time you solidify the neurological pathways in your brain until it becomes an automatic habit.

The reason habits are so powerful—and so difficult to break—is that your brain releases dopamine, a pleasure chemical, along with the reward at the end of each neurological pathway. Over time, the more often you fire up these neurological pathways, the stronger you link the cues, routines, and rewards that make up your habits because you reinforce the pathway that links them with that dopamine your brain loves so much. Much like repeatedly walking down a desire path, this makes your neurological pathways deeper, wider, and stronger.

Multitasking is a habit because you don't do it deliberately, by choice. If you left your phone at home for a day, and then walked around town without it in your pocket, chances are you would feel phantom vibrations in your leg or would automatically reach into your pocket for it even though it's not there. (I tried doing this toward the start of my smartphone experiment and found I reached into my pocket without thinking about five times a day.)

Since habits are, in their most basic form, a neurological pathway embedded in your brain, they're pretty much impossible to break overnight. This goes for multitasking, too; when your brain becomes accustomed to it, it's impossible to go from constantly multitasking to single tasking overnight.

Multitasking is something that you have to chip away at over time.

HOOKED ON DOPAMINE

Studies show that your brain releases steady hits of dopamine when you work on more than one thing at once. Neurochemically speaking, your brain rewards you more when you multitask, compared to when you do just one thing at a time. As Daniel Levitin puts it in *The Organized Mind*, "Multitasking creates a dopamine-addiction feedback loop, effectively rewarding the brain for losing focus for constantly searching for external stimulation."

But it's not just our limbic system that lusts after the sexy allure of multitasking. According to Daniel, "[t]o make matters worse, the prefrontal cortex has a novelty bias, meaning that its attention can be easily hijacked by something new—the proverbial shiny objects we use to entice infants, puppies, and kittens." No part of your brain is safe.

Unless you're doing totally mindless work and have attention to spare—like on your Maintenance Day—your brain is simply not built to focus on more than one thing at once. In fact, your brain *can't* focus on two things simultaneously—instead it rapidly switches between them, which creates the illusion that you're doing more than one thing at a time.

My favorite study on multitasking was conducted by Eyal Ophir,

Clifford Nass, and Anthony Wagner at Stanford. Leading up to the study, the prevailing research had established that people couldn't simultaneously process two things at once, so the team wanted to get to the bottom of exactly what made heavy multitaskers more productive—if anything.

First they tested whether multitaskers were better at ignoring irrelevant information. They weren't. When that failed, the researchers tested whether multitaskers were better at storing and organizing information or had better memories. They weren't, and didn't. Stumped, they conducted a *third* test to see if multitaskers were better at switching between tasks.

They weren't, and to make things worse, the light multitaskers in the study were better at *multitasking* than the heavy multitaskers! As Eyal put it, "We kept looking for what they're better at, and we didn't find it." The multitaskers perceived that they performed better, because their brains were more stimulated, but in every single study they performed worse.

Multitasking makes you less productive because it makes you more prone to errors, adds stress to your work, takes longer because it costs you time and attention to switch between tasks, and even affects your memory; much like being bombarded with interruptions and distractions, multitasking overloads your brain. This is why, when you watch a TV show or movie with your smartphone or tablet, you can't remember much of it. Multitasking even makes you more prone to experiencing boredom, anxiety, and depression.

If you think back to when you accomplished the most in a single sitting, you probably weren't tending to a million things at once. Chances are you were working with a crazy amount of focus and directing it all at just one thing.

When you multitask, you only skim the surface of your work because you scatter your attention in a million different directions. This prevents you from really getting into any one thing you have to get done. It's no wonder our brains wander 47 percent of the time.

When you do only one thing at a time, you give your work the attention it deserves.

DOING JUST ONE THING

> Time to check in again: How often has your mind wandered while you read this part of the book? The more your mind has trouble focusing, the more this chapter will help you out!

Of course, single tasking is easier said than done.

As I found during my project, much like doing algebra or assembling IKEA furniture, single tasking is one of those ideas that works incredibly well in theory but is insanely difficult to pull off in practice.

In my experience, a big reason single tasking makes you more productive is the same reason that simplifying the tasks you take on in general makes you more productive. When you simplify the tasks, projects, and commitments you take on, you spread your time, attention, and energy across fewer things—and invest more of each into everything you do. The same is true when you do only one thing in the moment: you invest all your time, attention, and energy into just one thing, which lets you accomplish more in the same amount of time.

While experimenting with single tasking during my project, I frequently fell off the wagon and went back to trying to do more than one thing at a time. The best solution I found was to start small—very small. At first, I would set a timer so I could single-task for a small amount of time, like twenty minutes, which I gradually increased as I began to build up my attention muscle. By the end of my project, I focused on only one thing at a time all day. Like most other tactics I discuss in this book, I'd be lying if I said I was perfect at it, but I did improve each week.

Something incredible happens when, over time, you push back against your wandering mind and continually bring your attention back to your most important work: you strengthen your ability to focus your attention on a task.

Research shows that when you repeatedly make a conscious effort to refocus on your work after your mind wanders, over time you heighten your executive control, harnessing the power your prefrontal cortex has over your limbic system, and ultimately, the control your brain has over itself. Every time you bring your attention back to a single task, you reinforce that habit, which gradually becomes stronger over time—particularly when you consciously fend off distractions and interruptions in the first place. Going from dedicating 53 percent of your attention to your work to 80 percent or 90 percent isn't a process that happens overnight, but it's well worth the effort, and it can produce incredible results—especially when you single-task on your most important tasks.

Here are a few of my favorite ways to practice single tasking and build up my attention muscle:

- **Work on Pomodoro Time:** The "Pomodoro Technique," developed by Francesco Cirillo in the 1980s, is a simple time-management technique that's also very powerful. With the technique, you work on only one task for twenty-five minutes, and then take a five-minute break. After four periods of working for twenty-five minutes, you take a longer break of fifteen minutes or more. I think this is one of the best ways to try single tasking on for size. After a few "pomodori," I think you'll be sold. (I don't find this technique to be effective all the time, but it's a great hack for dedicating a lot of energy and attention to high-return tasks.)

- **Conference Calls:** When on a conference call, try not to check for email or messages, and simply focus on bringing as much attention and value to the call as possible. Every time you're tempted to focus on something else, bring your attention back to the call, to perform one repetition of exercising your attention muscle. If you can't stop thinking of other things, question why you agreed to be on the call in the first place.

- **Listening:** When you actively listen to someone, you bring all your attention and focus to the conversation you're having without trying to think of what to say next, or thinking about or doing other things. Every time you bring your attention back to the conversation in front of you, you perform one repetition of exercising your attention muscle. This tactic takes practice, but over time it helps you better manage your attention, develop deeper and more meaningful relationships, and leads to fewer misunderstandings. While experimenting with active listening during my project, I found that almost everyone appreciated when I was able to bring my complete attention to the conversation. One of the first things I do when I meet up with someone is to shut my phone completely off so I create the conditions to focus just on the conversation in front of me. Productivity aside, this will also work wonders for your relationships.

- **Reading:** Like the challenge at the beginning of this section of the book, when you read, try to devote as much attention to what you're reading as you can. Notice when your mind begins to wander, and then rein it back in to perform another rep of your attention muscle. Also notice when your mind gets anxious and ahead of itself, like when it starts to turn the page before you're finished reading the current one.

- **Eating:** This is a fun one to try. It's a little hard to do when you're in the office, but it's a great way to work out your attention muscle at home. When was the last time you sat down to eat without doing anything else at the same time? When you slow down while drinking or eating something, you create attentional space around the flavors and textures of what you're eating so you can enjoy it that much more. This is a fun test to observe how often your brain naturally wanders. Simply set a timer for a few minutes, sit down somewhere quiet with a drink or food of your choice (this is especially fun when you pick something tasty), and focus on the flavors and textures of what you're eating. As with reading, be mindful that your mind doesn't get ahead of itself, that it doesn't think about or start to get the next bite ready before you're done with present one. My bet is you'll be surprised by two things: how frequently your mind wanders, and how delicious food can be when you slow down enough to taste it. (If you want to have even more fun with this one, try eating your food twice as slow—you'll get to enjoy it for twice as long.)

The key to all these tactics is to constantly bring your attention back to the task at hand when it wanders off. Every time you reengage your wandering mind with the task at hand, your attention muscle becomes that much stronger, and you'll heighten the amount of control you have over your mind so you can prevent it from wandering off in the future. This isn't easy, which is why I recommend starting out small—but it's well worth the effort.

I've found single tasking has a bunch of other benefits, too. After I began to single-task and work at a slower, more deliberate pace, I began to become much more aware of what I was working on, what habits I was doing automatically, the value of what I was working on, and even when I was procrastinating. Instead of my mind bouncing between the devices and apps I was using, I had the chance to reflect on the value of the work I was doing, which let me step back from my work in the moment to reflect on how to work smarter, and even more creatively. (Research shows that it's easier to think creatively when you're calm and unhurried.)

Single tasking also gave me the attentional space to become more compassionate, considerate, and happy. I'm a huge believer in being compassionate as you invest in your productivity—both to other people and to yourself. For example, compassion helps you behave less like a robot when you fend off low-impact tasks and projects. Doing just one thing at a time takes some adjustment, but in addition to helping you get more done, I think doing so will help you become a better human being, too.

I think this is the reason a lot of people want to become more productive in the first place. As Matthew Killingsworth and Daniel Gilbert, the two psychologists who conducted the 47 percent study put it, "[a] human mind is a wandering mind," and research shows that "a wandering mind is an unhappy mind." From an evolutionary standpoint, "[t]he ability to think about what is not happening is a cognitive achievement that comes at an emotional cost." You have a very limited amount of time; this is what makes productivity so important, but it's also why you should slow down and actually enjoy yourself as you invest in your productivity.

Single tasking is one of the best ways to tame a wandering mind and carve out more attentional space around your tasks in the moment—the final step to working deliberately and with intention.

THE SINGLE-TASKING CHALLENGE

Time required: 15–30 minutes
Energy/Focus Required: 9/10
Value: 10/10
Fun: 8/10
What you'll get out of it: You'll build up your attention muscle, so you can become able to devote more of your focus to the task at hand, which will let you get more done in the same amount of time.

My challenge for you this chapter is to spend between fifteen and thirty minutes tomorrow focusing on just one thing. (If the thought of this experiment puts you off, just shrink how long you'll single-task until you feel less resistance to it.) Whether you decide to dedicate all your attention to your work, a phone call, conversation, book, or piece of food you're eating, for fifteen to thirty minutes, focus on just the one thing. Naturally, the more important the task is, the more you'll get out of this challenge.

Whenever your mind wanders—and it will, especially at first—gently bring it back. Don't be too hard on yourself; simply redirect your focus when you notice your mind thinking about something other than the task at hand.

This is a simple challenge, but deceivingly so. Over time, the benefits of doing this will compound and blow you away.

21

THE MEDITATION CHAPTER

Takeaway: Practicing mindfulness and meditation makes you more productive because it makes your mind calmer, happier, and more focused. Meditation is also far less intimidating than you imagine.

Estimated Reading Time: 15 minutes, 15 seconds

A CONFESSION

I have a confession to make to you: that last chapter was a total sham. It wasn't about single tasking at all—it was about mindfulness.

Before you put down this book in disgust, and write me off forever, please give me a chance to explain.

Mindfulness has a massive PR problem. It's hard to overstate this point. When a lot of people hear the word *mindfulness*, or worse, *meditation*, their mind flashes to images of a skinny yogi sitting on a meditation cushion for hours on end in the middle of the sweltering heat of India. Or to a Buddhist monk who lives in a cave, eats beans and rice all day long, and lives in total silence. Like hearing about "mission statements," I think a lot of people immediately tune out when they hear the words—at least I sure did at first.

But the thing is, this isn't accurate. Mindfulness is simply the art of deliberately doing one thing at a time. And meditation is much the same, only instead of doing it alongside other tasks, you practice it by itself (I'll get to how to meditate—which is amazingly simple—in a bit).

If you wanted to, you could go through that last chapter, swap out every single mention of "single tasking" for "mindfulness," and it would still make sense. This is what that hippie mindfulness thing is all about: creating more attentional space around the present moment, so you can focus completely on what you're doing. That's pretty much it. It also means reflecting on how you're feeling about what you're doing, and what you think about what you're working on—which is important for a ton of productivity tactics, like the ones that help you beat procrastination.

When your attention is scattered all around you—like when you're multitasking—you simply aren't dedicating as much of yourself to the task at hand as you could be, which makes you less productive. Mindfulness and meditation are all about building up how much control you have over your attention, so you can direct more of it toward the task at hand.

On the surface, mindfulness and meditation seem like the antithesis of productivity. But in a world where productivity is about working smarter and more deliberately instead of doing more, faster, they have never been more relevant, or more important. On the assembly line, 53 percent of your attention was enough to do a great job. Today, your work benefits from all the attention you can dedicate to it.

THE HARD PART ABOUT PRODUCTIVITY

Just like a lot of people love the idea of waking up at 5:30 or running a marathon in theory, pretty much everyone loves the idea of getting more done.

But when it comes to working on the most productive things in the moment, the reality is that we usually have to make a lot of short-term sacrifices to accomplish more. In the long term, our planning, logical prefrontal cortex wants to have 10 percent body fat and become VP, but in the moment we'd rather be playing hooky and grabbing a cheeseburger. To get a sexy six-pack, you can't just decide to eat better. Every day you have to make a dozen small sacrifices to chip away at the body fat you have—which is infinitely more difficult than forming that original resolution to lose weight. The same holds true for when you try to single-task, work harder, or beat procrastination. It feels great to make resolutions, but making a million small sacrifices to achieve them is usually a lot less fun.

This is the hard part about productivity: while almost every single person on the planet wants to accomplish more, and usually knows at least one change to make to take a step in the right direction, in the moment, it's difficult to do what it takes to get there. (This is in part why I spent the entire first chapter talking about values: if you don't value the changes you're trying to make, or have a deep reason for why you want to accomplish more, you won't have the motivation in the moment to make short-term sacrifices to reach your long-term goals.)

This is where mindfulness comes in. Mindfulness is important because we value things differently in the moment than we do in the long term, and mindfulness gives us the attentional space we need to switch off autopilot and make more productive decisions in the moment. When we work automatically and lean too much on our habits, we have less attentional space for our prefrontal cortex to intervene to make the most productive decision. Mindfulness lets us carve out more attentional space in the moment to work smarter and more deliberately.

You'll still have to make the sacrifices, but mindfulness and meditation let you lay more productivity groundwork and create space around your tasks to make the best possible decisions in the moment.

BIT FLIPPING

When my meditation practice slipped toward the beginning of my project, and I picked it back up again, I quickly began to notice the profound benefits meditation had on my productivity—and every single one of those benefits orbited around having a stronger attention muscle.

Interestingly enough, some of the strongest advocates for meditation that I have met—aside from meditators themselves—were procrastination researchers. And this makes sense: the single best way to work out your attention muscle—the amount of control your prefrontal cortex has over your limbic system—is to meditate. In fact, when I interviewed Tim Pychyl, he was effusive in his praise for mindfulness and meditation and saw it as a powerful way to "direct our attention where it would be most useful to us." Mindfulness and meditation have also both been shown to help with impulsiveness, the character trait that contributes the most to procrastination.

After I resumed my meditation practice, I was immediately able to see the difference meditation made on my productivity. For one, I procrastinated less. Since meditation and mindfulness both build your attention muscle, I was able to focus on how I was feeling and what I was thinking about so I could step back and face my procrastination head-on. I also began to have much more impulse control, which helped me solidify my ritual of waking up at 5:30 every morning—and then reflect on how much I hated it. It gave me more attentional space, in a moment-by-moment basis, to step back, work deliberately, and see my work and life from ten thousand feet. It also made it easier to manage my energy throughout the day.

Meditation and mindfulness gave me the awareness I needed to step back from my work to become more productive.

FIVE MYTHS ABOUT MEDITATION AND PRODUCTIVITY

Before jumping in to how to meditate—which is *way* easier and far less mysterious than you think—I want to get a few quick meditation myths out of the way. I've had the chance to speak with a lot of people (especially businesspeople) about why they're resistant to the practice. Here are five of the most common meditation myths I've encountered, particularly as far as productivity is concerned.

I. Meditation makes you more passive

Don't worry, meditation won't turn you into a wimp. If anything, it'll help you become more resilient to the challenges you face. And at the same time, meditation changes how you relate to your experiences. Two people can experience the exact same thing and think about it completely differently. Meditation helps you see things more positively, but it also helps you become more resilient.

2. Meditation makes you less motivated

Au contraire, my friend. Meditation helps you focus more on your goals and on why you're doing them. You'll be more motivated to become more productive, if anything, because you'll have the clarity to see why you're doing what you're doing.

3. Meditation will make you care less about your work

Just as meditation won't make you more passive, it also won't make you care less about your work. If anything, it will help you see the deeper meaning behind what you do, which will make you care more about what's on your plate—assuming what you're working on is aligned to what you value. Meditation won't make you care less about your accomplishments; it will help you focus on them more.

4. Meditation takes too much time

I meditate for thirty minutes a day, but even *one* minute a day can make a profound difference. You can do pretty much anything for a minute.

5. It's too hard to get started

It's actually pretty easy. Here's how.

MEDITATION IS ACTUALLY INSANELY SIMPLE

Meditation is simple—almost stupidly so. The practice is like single tasking, only taken up a notch or two.

While single tasking (and mindfulness) are things you practice as you do something else, meditation is something you do by itself. They have the same benefits—though the benefits of meditation are more concentrated—with the main difference being when and where you practice them. Meditation and mindfulness are two sides of the same coin.

Here's how to meditate:

- Find somewhere quiet where you won't be distracted or interrupted.
- Sit upright. You don't have to buy a meditation mat or anything—a chair works fine for pretty much everyone. Sit upright so that the vertebrates in your back are stacked one on top of another. You shouldn't feel stiff—you should feel relaxed, but alert.
- You can close your eyes or not—up to you. Whatever helps you feel more alert is what you should do. I find if I meditate closer to bedtime, I need to keep my eyes open a bit so I can focus better.
- Set a timer for however long you want to meditate (I use my phone's clock app). I like to have my timer count upward in case I want to go for longer, but most people I know have their meditation timer count downward. Choose an amount of time you don't feel a ton of mental resistance to, however short that may be.
- After you set your timer for however long feels comfortable (I recommend starting with five minutes), focus on your breath. Observe all the sensations you feel as your breath flows in and out of your body; into your nose, down your esophagus, into your lungs, and then out again. Don't try to control your breath; simply observe it. Don't try to analyze it or anything—just notice its natural rhythms.
- And finally, here's the part that works out your attention muscle. When your attention wanders to focus on something else, and you notice that it has wandered (which can sometimes take a minute or two), bring your attention back to concentrate on your breath. You'll have to do this repeatedly while you meditate—this is normal, and this is what heightens your executive functioning. When thoughts or feelings come up, don't judge them; just notice them, as if they're cars on a highway, and you're on an overpass overlooking them. And remember, when your mind wanders—and it

will—that this is what your mind was programmed to do. When you approach meditation with a genuine curiosity of where your mind will wander off to, you'll get that much more out of it. I sometimes like to laugh when my mind wanders, which must look pretty weird to anyone watching.

This is all meditation is.

And mindfulness? Mindfulness is simply single tasking, so you can carve out space around tasks, which lets you become aware of what you're feeling and what you're thinking about. Meditation is mindfulness from concentrate.

To me, it seems almost comical that these practices are so simple and yet have so many benefits—but they do. Over the last several decades, a wealth of neurological research has shown just how beneficial the practices are. I think the most powerful finding, at least as far as productivity is concerned, is how the practice heightens your executive control and works out your attention muscle.

Sara Lazar, a neuroscientist at Harvard Medical School, has studied this effect firsthand, and she found that long-term meditators have lower brain activity in their posterior cingulate cortex (PCC)—the part of the brain responsible for mind wandering. According to Lazar, "[B]etter control over the PCC can help you catch your mind in the act of wandering and nudge it gently back on task." Meditation helps you regain control over your attention—and by extension, your brain—and prevent it from wandering when you don't want it to.

Both meditation and mindfulness are worth it for this reason alone. But you also experience a bunch of secondary benefits that make the practices doubly worthwhile.

There aren't enough pages in this book to lay out all the benefits of meditation. It reduces your cortisol levels, calms you down, increases blood flow to your brain, makes your brain age more slowly, and increases the amount of gray matter in your brain—the stuff responsible for muscle control, seeing, hearing, memory, emotions, and speech. Meditation has even been shown to boost your test scores. And if you have a team, the more mindful you are, the higher the performance of your team. All these effects—every one backed up by scores of neuro-scientific research—will help you boost your productivity.

In meditation, you'll observe firsthand your limbic system putting up a fight against your prefrontal cortex. It will tell you you're bored. Frustrated. Guilty. Worried. Restless. And you might even give into it once or twice when you first start meditating. Chances are it will also wander to something in your future, to a cringeworthy memory that happened in your past, and then to a crazy fantasy with Mila Kunis or Brad Pitt. This is just the brain operating at its regular pace, and every time you bring it back, you'll have performed one rep of your attention muscle. Just like when you battle procrastination, this will light your brain on fire.

If you're anything like the version of me that was put off by the idea of meditation before trying out my very first yoga class, my guess is that right now, your limbic system is resisting the idea of meditation—maybe quite a bit. But here's the thing: this is exactly what makes meditation worthwhile.

In my opinion, for every minute you meditate, you gain back ten minutes of productivity. Meditation helps you focus better, waste less time, work more intentionally, and also makes it easier to identify high-return tasks and, over time, resist your brain's limbic system. Focus and awareness are two of the largest parts of your attention muscle—and there is no better way to work them out than to single-task and meditate.

MICROINTENTIONS

If you asked me to name a city that isn't mindful or deliberate, I would almost immediately say New York. At least in my experience, New York is the least calm, patient, and mindful city I've been in. But that hasn't stopped Sharon Salzberg from making the city her home.

Sharon is an incredible woman. After a turbulent childhood (she lived with five different families by the age of sixteen), Sharon became enamored with Buddhism while learning about it in an Asian philosophy course in college. That motivated her to travel to India to delve into the practice.

Today, many years later, she is widely credited with bringing Buddhism and meditation to the West in the 1970s, after she returned from India and then founded the Insight Meditation Society with Joseph Goldstein and Jack Kornfield. Sharon is also the author of a number of bestselling books, including *Real Happiness at Work*, where she talks about how to bring mindfulness to work, without compromising your performance or productivity.

To interview Sharon, I flew to New York City and met her at her apartment—a five-minute walk from Union Square—one of the last places on Earth you'd expect to find a meditation teacher. But once you meet her, the whole thing starts to make a lot more sense. Sharon speaks like a regular New Yorker—though you get the feeling that she has all the time in the world for you. And despite living a calm and mindful life, she blends in well with the fabric of the city. She walks a little more mindfully than most, but aside from that, she blended in perfectly. You wouldn't be able to pick her out of a crowd as a meditation teacher.

Despite her history with meditation and Buddhism, Sharon doesn't have any illusions about how difficult it is to live mindfully in this day and age. She doesn't think meditation has to be tied to a particular belief system, or that you have to "be in a pretzel-like pose in order to do it." She also doesn't have any unrealistic ideas about how much time we have for the practice. In our chat, she referenced research that five or ten minutes a day is enough to rewire your brain and completely change the way you see your work and your life. Sharon takes a practical approach to meditation and considers it a way of living more deliberately, getting in touch with yourself, and living a happier life—not a path to ditching all your possessions to live in a monastery trying to achieve enlightenment.

Perhaps the most interesting nugget she mentioned during our chat, though, is the idea of integrating mindfulness into your day, which lets you carve out even more attentional space around your work, and even set tiny intentions for what you want to accomplish. When contemplating how she could help people practice mindfulness every day, much like Charles Duhigg, she discovered that we already have a lot of cues embedded in our work environment—different events that occur regularly that can serve as triggers for us to practice mindfulness—where we can take a few seconds to step back, observe our breath and how we're feeling, and calm down throughout the day. This can be as simple as letting a phone ring until the third ring instead of the first, so we can take a few seconds to slow down and be with ourselves. Or waiting a few seconds before hitting "Send" on an email—and instead taking a breath or two and reading over the email again. Or using the time it takes to walk from one room to another to simply walk and be present.

Mindfulness lets you work deliberately in the moment, because it lets you actually take a step back to think about what you want to accomplish, how you're feeling, and what you're thinking about. According to Sharon, the opportunities to do this throughout the day are endless. "Before a conversation, before a meeting, before an encounter of any kind, step back, and see if you can check in with yourself to see what your intention is. What do you most want to see come out of a conversation? Then work toward that, instead of getting caught up in what you're feeling." Mindfulness lets you set microintentions throughout the day, which accumulate by the end of the day to make you a lot more productive.

It's in this moment-to-moment deliberateness—where we step back from our work not just in general, but in the moment—that the heart of productivity lies. When you work on autopilot, it's hard to be deliberate and take control of your productivity. Habits no doubt have their place, and I'll talk about them in the very next section, but it is impossible to work deliberately without a solid amount of attentional space, or a strong attention muscle.

Mindfulness lets you step back and create space around your tasks in the moment so you can work more intentionally.

Partway through our chat, I noticed that on the desk behind Sharon was an iMac, iPad, and iPhone—and that as we spoke, she had a very steady stream of notifications flying in from every direction. While she could probably stand to shut a few of those off, I also couldn't help but notice that she wasn't phased by a single one of them, and that she wasn't tempted to check up on what was coming in while we were chatting. Even though she received a new email every minute or two, her focus wasn't swept up by the steady stream of limbic-jacking interruptions.

And in the cab ride on the way to her event, not once did she pull her iPhone out of her pocket, no matter how often her phone cried out for her attention.

In my eyes, Sharon is Exhibit A of the power of mindfulness and meditation. It's not easy to train your brain to become strong enough to overpower your limbic system at each turn, but she has done it. It's also, of course, not easy to go from traversing a tough childhood to writing nine bestselling books—but she's done that, too. And in New York there aren't many people as compassionate—or productive—as her.

The idea that mindfulness and meditation are concepts that need to remain within the confines of yoga studios and Lulu Lemon stores is over—and that moment was over the moment we moved from working in the time economy to working in the knowledge economy.

The most productive people are the ones who work deliberately—and there is no better way to work deliberately than developing and defending a strong attention muscle.

THE MEDITATION CHALLENGE

Time required: 5 minutes a day, for a week
Energy/Focus Required: 9/10
Value: 9/10
Fun: 7/10
What you'll get out of it: You'll build up your attention muscle even more than with single tasking, which will let you keep your long-term goals in mind in the moment, and act much more deliberately.

My challenge for you is to work out your attention muscle for five minutes every day for the next seven days, either by meditating or integrating mindfulness into your day.

If your brain is resisting this challenge more than the others in this book, that's normal. Since meditation and mindfulness are ways of training your mind to overpower your brain's instinctual limbic system, your limbic system is going to put up a fight when you first sit down to meditate. But every time you bring your wandering mind back to focus on your breath, your attention muscle will become stronger, and you will be able to work more deliberately.

It's normal for your brain to resist a challenge like this one, so let's make it a bit more fun. I challenge you to give this experiment a shot for just a few days, and simply observe what happens, especially how different you think and feel afterward. You can do pretty much anything for five minutes.

I also challenge you to, right now, plant one microintention into your work tomorrow. Whether that trigger is to be mindful of what you want to accomplish before attending a meeting, starting a task or project, checking your smartphone, or opening up your email inbox, right now, think about a trigger that you will use tomorrow to step back from your work, and reflect on how you're feeling, thinking, and what you intend to accomplish.

It's not easy to train your attention muscle, but that's what makes the process worthwhile.

It's an incredible thing when you train your brain to conquer itself.

Part Seven

TAKING PRODUCTIVITY TO THE NEXT LEVEL

22

REFUELING

Takeaway: The power of incremental improvements lies in the fact that although they're not significant by themselves, week after week, month after month, they add up to produce results in the long term that will blow you away. Small changes lead to big results, especially when food is involved.

Estimated Reading Time: 13 minutes, 16 seconds

SUFFERING THROUGH SOYLENT

There was only one productivity experiment I conducted that I completely and utterly failed at. It wasn't my experiment to live in total isolation for ten days—though that one was pretty rough, and I'll get to it in the next part. It was my experiment to eat only "soylent" for a week.

The idea behind soylent is actually pretty cool. It is a powdered food substitute that contains everything your body nutritionally needs over the course of the day. You just mix the powder with water, and then drink up the concoction a few times a day. It tastes like thick oat water, but not entirely in a bad way. Over the course of the day, you don't need to eat anything else. For the experiment I elected to formulate my own recipe for the stuff, following a recipe that had been posted online that was very similar to one a company by the same name sold. The recipe contained ingredients like oat flour for carbohydrates, pea protein powder for protein, ground flax for fiber, brown sugar for flavor and carbs, crushed up multivitamins for vitamins and minerals, and even olive oil for fat, which I added whenever I mixed the powder with water.

The great part about soylent is that you can modify the recipe to meet your exact dietary needs. Need a bit more protein? Great—just up the ratio of protein to carbs in the recipe. Need some extra vitamin D to help you beat the winter blues? Just crush up a few more tablets and add them to the recipe.

The idea behind soylent is awesome: it saves you time, since you can prepare it in bulk and it requires no additional prep time. It saves you attention, because you can continue focusing on work, instead of stopping to prepare food. And it saves you money—during the experiment I calculated that, even with the extra protein powder I added, it cost me a paltry $7.98 to live off the stuff every day. Without the extra protein powder, it would have cost me under $5 a day.

FOR THE LOVE OF FOOD

But while the soylent met all my nutritional needs, it didn't address my deep and abiding love of food.

I can honestly say that I remember pretty much every meal I've eaten from nicer restaurants and even from takeout. So far I haven't lifted any words from my blog in this book, but I'm going to cheat a bit here. I think I encapsulated my love of food pretty well in the post I wrote up about my soylent experiment:

> . . . *after my first year of university, I hopped on a plane to run around Europe on a solo trip. I don't remember much from that trip* [note from future Chris: Could it have been all the smartphone usage?], *even though it was just a few years ago—but I remember the food. I remember the tender rabbit I ate at a Michelin-starred restaurant in the central town square in Krakow, Poland. I remember walking down a side street of Paris, massive baguette in hand, breaking off and scarfing down chunks of the loaf as I walked by people I couldn't speak to or understand. I remember what I ate for breakfast today (oat flour pancakes and an apple), for lunch (rice and homemade chili), and for dinner*

(vegetables, pita, hummus, and more chili and rice). I also remember what I ate yesterday and the day before that.

. . . Take, for example, something as simple as the texture of food. I love the feeling of biting into a fresh stick of celery; feeling the fiber-rich framework of the vegetable crumble like a stone castle under the weight of my teeth. To me, food is poetry; the very tapestry that my day threads in and out of and around. If I'm excited on a given day, more often than not I'm excited about something I'm going to eat . . .

By the second day of the soylent experiment, I missed food—badly. While the first day was a challenge to slog through, on the second day, when I woke up and realized that I wouldn't be able to make myself a fancy breakfast and instead had to drink the oat-flavored smoothie concoction all day long, I wanted to curl up and hibernate for a week. That afternoon, while busing home from a speaking event, I recall looking longingly out the window, thinking about all the meals I would eat once the experiment was finished. It was in that moment that I decided to end the experiment. I didn't care how much cooking or prep time soylent would save me, how much more energy it would give me relative to when I didn't eat 100 percent right, or even how much money I would save, despite how cash strapped I was at the time. I was willing to do a lot to become more productive but I chose not to follow through with this experiment. I valued saving myself a week of hell more than I did my productivity.

On the bus ride back home, just as the sun was beginning to set, I got off the bus a stop early, walked to Burger King, and ordered the biggest Whopper they had, with jumbo-sized everything.

There were no survivors.

ENERGY AND PRODUCTIVITY

On the surface, it could seem like things that affect your energy—like what you eat, whether or not you exercise, and how much sleep you get—don't seem to have much of an impact on how much you accomplish. But as I learned from a few of my experiments, much like with single tasking or meditating, this isn't true at all. Energy is the fuel you burn throughout the day in order to be productive, and without it, your productivity is toast.

Especially on a neurological level, having lasting energy is critical. Your brain cells consume *double* the energy that the other cells in your body consume; even though your brain makes up just 2–3 percent of your body mass, it burns *20 percent* of the calories you take in. As you invest in your productivity, having a strong mental function becomes crucial—as does having a lot of energy. This is especially important in the knowledge economy, when so many of our tasks require just as much attention and energy as they do time.

Apart from my soylent experiment, the only other productivity experiment I (at least partially) failed was my experiment to lower my body fat from 17 percent to 10 percent. In practice the experiment was actually pretty similar to the soylent experiment because it involved cutting foods out of my diet that I really wanted to eat in order to try to reach 10 percent body fat. I designed the experiment in two parts: lowering my body fat from 17 percent to 10 percent, and gaining ten pounds of lean muscle. By the end of my project I gained almost fifteen pounds of muscle, which I'll talk about two chapters from now, but instead of reaching 10 percent body fat, by the end of my project my body fat still hovered around 15 percent.

In hindsight, I realize that although getting to 10 percent body fat was a noble goal, I executed it terribly. As soon as my initial motivation for the experiments wore off, I hated the fact that I had to continue to go on. Because I tried to make drastic changes so I could achieve my goals more quickly, it wasn't realistic. Past Chris wasn't realistic when he designed the experiments for future Chris to follow and didn't account for how difficult he would find the changes in practice.

Much like with my soylent experiment, I simply loved food too much.

CHIPPING AWAY

This is a pretty good illustration of just how hard productivity can be to achieve in practice. As I mentioned in the last chapter, to accomplish more, you often have to make sacrifices that are tough in the short term but rewarding in the long term. And let's be honest: although it would be great if you could make every sacrifice I've written about so far, not every sacrifice will be worth it to you. The key is to recognize which changes are worth your time and effort, and which ones aren't.

To me, a great meal is one of the most pleasurable things there is. At the end of the day, I value productivity a tad more than the pleasure food gives me—but they're close. It may be worth the sacrifice, but I know that if I try to make changes that are too big in the short term, they simply won't stick—especially when my habits around food are so firmly ensconced. (I know I'm not the only one who gets great pleasure out of food; research shows that your brain releases about as much dopamine when you eat two cheeseburgers as when you have an orgasm.)

As I write these words about a year after the end of my project, I'm now hovering at around 13 percent body fat, and I'm in the best shape of my life. But getting down to 13 percent body fat didn't happen overnight. It has involved making tiny, incremental improvements to the way I eat; changes that have been small enough to not pose too much of a burden when I make them, but large enough so that they add up to make a meaningful difference over time. There is absolutely nothing wrong with having huge ambitions—I think you should—but the more radical the changes you try to make to achieve them, the less likely they are to stick.

For example, one week toward the end of my project I started drinking my coffee black instead of with two creams and two sugars (we call this a "double double" when you order at Tim Hortons in Canada); a week or two after that, I began to put spinach and other vegetables in my breakfast omelette instead of sausage. By themselves these changes are incremental enough that they're hardly worth writing about. But over time they have compounded, and I gradually made enough of them to lower my body fat to that 13 percent level—and that percentage is steadily dropping as I continue to make incremental improvements. Small changes and habits add up over time.

When you try to completely overhaul the way you eat overnight, your initial excitement and motivation will wear off, and the changes you tried to make will eventually become too large and intimidating for you to continue with them for the long term. The opposite is true for small, incremental changes: since small changes aren't scary, and don't impose too great a burden, in the long run they'll actually stick. And as they add up, you'll become motivated to make more of them.

One of my favorite ideas is that of compound interest. If you put $100 in an investment account today and received 8 percent interest on that money every year, by the ninth year you'd be playing with the house's money—your money will have more than doubled to $205. And if you didn't touch the account for twenty-five years, by the end of that time your original $100 will have grown seven times, to *$734*. And it will only go up from there.

The exact same thing is true with the incremental changes you make with your habits. The best way to lose weight fast is to hop on a fad diet. But once your initial motivation wears off (which it almost always does), chances are you'll revert to the habits you had before and gain all that weight back. Not many people write books on the power of making tiny, incremental changes to the way you live and work, probably because the idea isn't all that sexy. But it works better than anything else I have tried. Like with interest at the bank, as you begin to make incremental improvements with every hot spot that makes up the portfolio of your life, your habits will compound and pay incredible dividends with time.*

And best of all, they'll actually stick.

EATING FOR ENERGY

The odd part about writing a chapter like this one is that you really don't need this book—or any diet book—to tell you how to eat better. While it's nice to be guided in the right direction every once in a while, chances are you know at least one improvement you can make to your diet to get more energy.

Over the year of doing my project, as I charted my energy levels

---

* Compound interest is also what makes reading books and investing in your learning so powerful.

around what I ate, I found that eating for energy—and productivity—is actually very simple.

While this chapter explores food from an energy (and productivity) standpoint rather than a health standpoint, in this case, the two are one and the same. The more I have lived by these two rules, the more energy I have had. The rules can be difficult in practice, particularly if you love food as much as I do, but the more you chip away at your habits and live by these two rules, the more energy you'll have.

Here are the rules:

1. Eat more unprocessed foods that take longer to digest.
2. Notice when you're full, and then stop eating.

These rules are way easier to talk about than to practice, of course—but from my experience they will provide you with more lasting energy than anything else. They're worth chipping away at over time.

Food provides you with energy because your body converts whatever you eat into glucose—a simple sugar your body (and brain) burn for energy. Just as an oil refinery turns crude oil into gasoline for your car, your digestive system turns what you eat and drink into glucose for your body. On a neurological level, you have mental energy when you have glucose in your brain. When you feel tired or fatigued, more often than not it's either because your brain has too much or not enough glucose to convert into mental energy. Research has shown that the optimal amount of glucose to have in your bloodstream is around 25 grams—about the amount of glucose in a banana. This exact number isn't all that important, but what is important is that your glucose levels can be either too high or too low.

Since unprocessed foods (in general) take longer to digest, your body converts them into glucose at a slower rate, which provides you with a steady drip of glucose (and energy) over the day—instead of a big hit of energy followed by a crash. In a way, processed foods are predigested for you by machines. This is why your body converts them into glucose so fast, and why a donut doesn't provide you with nearly as much *lasting* energy as an apple.

There is also something called the "glycemic index" (GI), which tracks how foods affect your glucose levels on a scale from 0 to 100. The lower a food is on the scale, the better it is for your productivity, because your body burns the food at a slower rate and doesn't release all its energy at once. While the index is informative, and if you want to take your energy levels up a notch or two you should take a look at it, I've found the list a bit tedious to reference in practice. I know some health nuts will take issue with this, but I'm a fan of rules and systems that are easy to follow in practice. Sure, there are a few unprocessed foods that have a high GI, like baked potatoes and white rice, but most of the foods low on the index are unprocessed, like vegetables, fruits, nuts/seeds, beans/legumes, grains, seafood, and meat. Although not every single unprocessed food is great for you, most of them are. I've had a lot of energy eating fewer processed foods than with anything else.

The second rule—notice when you're full, and then stop eating—has a similar effect. It provides you with more energy because you're not overloading your body with food to process, and you provide your brain and body with a steady drip of glucose over the course of the day, so you don't spike your glucose levels all at once. This is why you feel tired or groggy when you overeat—because you ingested too much food for your body to process. You'll have lasting energy when you provide your body with a steady stream of glucose—not a massive hit of it all at once.

During my meditation experiment, not only did I practice sitting and walking meditation, I also ate a few meals mindfully. One morning, while slowly and mindfully eating an omelette, I noticed something curious: when I devoted more of my attention to what I was eating, it became a lot easier for me to notice when I was feeling full, and I could stop eating before I ate too much. (I also enjoyed what I was eating that much more: when I ate twice as slow, I enjoyed what I was eating for twice as long, and got twice the enjoyment out of it, especially when I didn't focus on other things at the same time.) The more I practiced mindful eating during and after this experiment, the more enjoyment

I got out of food, and the more I learned to respect how full I was and was able to stop myself from eating too much. Studies show that it takes your stomach at least fifteen minutes to tell your brain that it's full. The more attention you pay to eating, the better your odds of stopping before you're full, and having more energy throughout the day.

These two rules gave me more mental and physical energy than I'd had in a long time. And the smaller the changes I've made to what and how I ate, the more they've stuck and compounded.

As far as your productivity is concerned, it's worth keeping these two rules in mind.

THE "LAMEST DIET IN THE WORLD" CHALLENGE

Time required: 2 minutes
Energy/Focus Required: 2/10
Value: 8/10
Fun: 7/10
What you'll get out of it: Your energy levels will be more constant, because you will provide your body and brain with a steady amount of glucose, which it burns off as energy throughout the day.

The best diet in the world is the exact one you already have, with one small, incremental improvement. Although this diet won't help you drop inches from your waist overnight, you'll actually stick with it in the long term. That's what matters. And you will lose weight over time.

My challenge for you is to make one small incremental improvement around how you eat, a change that will cause you to either eat more unprocessed foods or become more mindful of how much you're eating, and notice when you're full.

Whether that improvement is not taking any sugar in your morning coffee, snacking on a plate of vegetables instead of chips during the game, no longer eating in front of your computer so you can notice when you're full, or eating dinner with your family instead of in front of the TV so you devote more attention to eating—simply make one small, lasting change to the way you eat that won't be impossible for you to keep once your initial motivation to eat for more energy dies off.

When you review your list of hot spots a week or month from now, you can use that as a reminder to make another incremental improvement to your diet, so you can level up even further.

If you're like me, by that point you will be dying to make bigger or more changes to the way you eat—and that's the point. Small changes last because they don't suck up all your willpower, which gives you the energy you need to make further incremental improvements when the time comes.

The power of incremental improvements lies in the fact that while they're not significant by themselves, week after week, month after month, they add up to produce long-term results that will blow you away.

23

DRINKING FOR ENERGY

Takeaway: Luckily, what is good for your brain is good for your body. To drink for energy, drink fewer alcoholic and sugary drinks, drink more water (which is incredible for your brain health), and learn to drink caffeine strategically, when you'll actually benefit from the energy boost—not habitually.

Estimated Reading Time: 13 minutes, 7 seconds

ONLY WATER

As another productivity experiment, I drank only water for an entire month, cutting out all caffeine, alcohol, and sugary drinks from my diet. It's incredible just how many ingrained habits you have around what you drink over the course of the month, and I wanted to get to the bottom of how all the stuff I drank impacted my productivity—if at all.

Not only did this save me a ton of money—I spend way more on coffee and alcohol every month than I think—I also learned a lot about just how profoundly what I drank affected my productivity. While eating no processed foods and stopping when you're full are great ways to increase your energy, drinking for energy is more difficult to figure out—especially when common beverages like caffeine and alcohol hardly make a dent on your glucose levels.

A SIDE NOTE ON SUGARY DRINKS

Every day the average person consumes a whopping *356* calories through what he or she drinks—and *44 percent* of those calories come from sugary drinks that give the consumer a huge glucose rush and then crash afterward. I didn't have the chance to play around with sugary drinks during this experiment—though I drink the occasional smoothie, I've never had a habit of drinking sugary drinks. I've always tried to get as many of my calories from actual food as possible. There are also zero productivity benefits to drinking sugary drinks, so I've always steered clear of them. Even fruit juices that seem amazingly healthy for you on the surface spike glucose levels to crazy-high levels, and then cause an energy crash afterward.

I mostly experimented with cutting out caffeine and alcohol from my diet during the experiment.

BORROWING ENERGY FROM TOMORROW

Before starting the experiment, I didn't consume an excess of coffee or alcohol; most days I had a cup or two of green tea (which contains about 20 percent of the caffeine in a cup of coffee), and every week I had a cup or two of coffee. I also only drank a few alcoholic drinks a week, usually socially or while watching a hockey game. Before the water experiment, I wasn't deliberate about when and what I drank, but that quickly began to change as I had the chance to step back to reflect on how both alcohol and caffeine either helped or hindered my productivity.

Something is considered a "drug" when it has a physiological effect on your body, and caffeine and alcohol are no exception to this rule. As an example, both boost how much dopamine—a main pleasure chemical in your brain—the neural pathways in your brain produce, essentially rewarding you for consuming caffeine and alcohol. (Dopamine isn't entirely a bad thing, and it would be hard to become motivated without it, but it does make certain substances more rewarding than others.)

While I didn't experience any withdrawal when cutting out drinking caffeine or alcohol, I did notice something intriguing: by the end of the month, I began to have an *insane* amount of energy, particularly on weekends. Not only that, but the amount of energy I had (again, especially over the weekend) was incredibly stable and didn't fluctuate nearly as much as when I consumed a few or more drinks every week.

After I noticed these effects and conducted some research to dive deeper into them, I began to realize, much like sugar, alcohol isn't worth consuming for productivity reasons. (Drinking alcohol, unlike the tactics on page 174, also doesn't even make a dent on reducing the stress hormones in your body.) Alcohol may provide you with a bit more energy or creativity as you drink it, but it will also almost always provide you with a net loss in energy and productivity and make it much more difficult to accomplish what you intend to—especially after you come down off the buzz the drug gives you. I see drinking alcohol as a way of borrowing energy from tomorrow. But in the morning you have to pay interest on that energy loan. This leaves you with a net loss in energy. And mixing alcohol with either sugar or caffeine only exacerbates that crash.

Of course, this is a cost a lot of people are willing to pay, and this gets to my point at the beginning of the book about making changes that are meaningful to you. Every once in a while I'm willing to put up with those costs. When I'm out with friends, I sometimes have a few drinks—but only after I consider the energy costs that they will have, and mentally assess whether those costs are worth it. If you intend to have a wild and crazy night, then do—all the more power to you. But do consider the costs. Since my water experiment, I've begun to account for the fact that I will have a net energy loss when I have a drink or two, and I will usually drink more water that night and the next day to dampen their effects. Since discovering just how much energy I had when I didn't drink, I've cut my alcohol consumption in half. This isn't saying a lot since I didn't drink heavily to begin with. But I would encourage you to think about the fact that alcohol can have a significant impact on your energy levels and productivity when you decide whether or not to have a drink or two (or three).

A lot of the productivity and diet books I've read suggest cutting alcohol completely out of your diet. But I think for most people that is either too draconian to stick with in the long term or something they just don't want to do. At least by understanding the costs of drinking on your energy levels and productivity you are aware of the impact of your decisions. Then you can decide if you wish to change your habits, accordingly.

ADAPTING TO COFFEE

Just as drinking alcohol is a way of borrowing energy from tomorrow, drinking caffeine is a way of borrowing energy from later in the day.

If there were a way of consuming caffeine without crashing afterward, it would be an absolute no-brainer as far as productivity is concerned. This unfortunately isn't

If you're a fan of having a "nightcap" before you head to bed to help you sleep, watch out: while alcohol has been shown to help you fall asleep faster, it compromises your overall sleep quality, particularly toward the end of your sleep session.

the case. Eight to fourteen hours after you consume caffeine, your body metabolizes it out of your system, which causes an energy crash (though this exact number varies from person to person). There is a chemical in your body and brain called "adenosine," which tells your brain when it's tired. Caffeine prevents your brain from absorbing this chemical, which prevents your brain from knowing it's tired. But here's the thing: while caffeine blocks your brain from absorbing adenosine, the chemical continues to build up until caffeine eventually lets your brain absorb it again. Your body and brain then absorb a whole whack of this tired chemical at once, which causes your energy levels to plummet. There are a few ways to lessen these effects (which we'll get to), but there isn't a way to prevent them.

At the same time, though, while you invariably crash after consuming anything with caffeine in it, caffeine can be a powerful tool to have at your disposal as far as your productivity is concerned—when you begin to drink it deliberately instead of habitually. (Sense a theme?)

Let's say you have a ritual of preparing yourself a fresh, steaming cup of coffee every morning. Although this ritual is a romantic one, and a graceful way to ease into the day, it isn't all that great for your energy levels. Since drinking coffee is a way of borrowing energy from later in the day, having a daily cup of coffee in the morning simply causes your energy levels to dip at the same time every afternoon. Since it takes your body eight to fourteen hours to metabolize caffeine, if you have a cup after you wake up, this means you'll crash at the same time every day in the late afternoon—when you'll have to choose to either slog through a wave of low energy or drink another cup, which may compromise your sleep, since your body will only begin to metabolize the caffeine a couple of hours before you head to bed. This is a downward spiral more than a few people fall into.

But there is another downside to drinking coffee habitually that's easy to overlook: your body adapts to how much caffeine you consume. In other words, if you have one cup of coffee every morning, your body slowly gets used to that amount until it becomes your new "normal." In fact, your brain even begins to *grow new adenosine receptors* as it acclimates to how much caffeine you consume. At first, when you go from drinking no coffee to drinking one cup of coffee, you get a huge burst of energy and productivity, and this feedback is immediate, which reinforces your new coffee habit. But once your body gets used to that amount of coffee, to reach a comparable caffeine high, you need to drink *two* cups of coffee every morning because your body has adapted to only drinking one. If you simply continue drinking only one cup every morning, the science shows that you're no better off than when you started.

During my experiment to drink only water for a month, I didn't experience any caffeine withdrawal, but I quickly began to miss the stuff at the times I used to drink it—when I ran across cues in my work environment that triggered my habit of having a cup of tea or coffee—things like attending an important meeting, working on a high-return task, or visiting the gym. That's when I realized just how powerful becoming deliberate about when you consume caffeine can be. When you consume caffeine habitually, your productivity eventually flatlines after your body adapts to how much caffeine you consume. But when you drink caffeine *strategically*, your productivity takes off, because you'll begin to benefit from bringing more energy and attention to tasks that require a large amount of energy, focus, or both.

THE MOST PRODUCTIVE WAY TO DRINK CAFFEINE

As I write these words, it's 10:30 a.m. and I'm sitting in a small coffee shop close to home, sipping on a medium black coffee. While I don't have a habit of drinking a lot of coffee, on days like today I like to. Doing so is letting me bring even more energy and focus to writing this book, and in my view is worth the cost later on. There are certain periods of the day when having extra energy will help you out the most, and for me this is one of them.

Making the jump from drinking caffeine habitually to strategically is a tough one to make, but it's worth chipping away at. If you're hooked on coffee and drink two cups every day, for example, you can begin by filling each cup up with a quarter of decaf coffee. You'll likely not notice much of a difference.

The great thing is, something magical happens as you begin to drink caffeine strategically instead of habitually: you suddenly have access to a large reservoir of energy that you can summon whenever you need it the most. The more demanding a task is, the more having that extra energy will benefit you when it comes time to work on it. During my project, and particularly after my water experiment, I began to consume caffeine before doing tasks like:

- Giving an important presentation
- Writing a big article
- Working on one of my daily intentions (see Chapter 3)
- Diving into a complicated research paper
- A big workout (caffeine has been shown to positively affect athletic performance)

In addition to drinking caffeine at more strategic times, here are a few suggestions for drinking caffeine strategically in general:

- Don't drink any sugary or alcoholic caffeinated drinks. They'll only cause you to crash quicker and harder.
- Be careful about drinking caffeine before working on a creative task, because caffeine has been shown to hurt your performance with tasks that involve creativity.
- Be mindful that you don't consume caffeine less than eight to fourteen hours before bed, so it doesn't affect your sleep.
- If it makes sense for your productivity, consume caffeine between 9:30 and 11:30 a.m. (if you wake up between 6 and 8 a.m.). This is when caffeine will have the greatest impact on your energy levels, because you naturally have less energy then, when your cortisol levels are lower. Caffeine also has a bigger effect between 1:30 and 5:30 p.m., but because it needs eight to fourteen hours to leave your system, it's likely not worth the impact it will have on your sleep.
- Find a better caffeine delivery system, like green tea or matcha. Green tea and matcha are my favorite caffeine vehicles, because they're chock-full of antioxidants and L-theanine, which ease the caffeine crash afterward. Matcha is a tad more expensive than tea and coffee, but I think it's well worth the price; for a few extra

A quick note for you if you're an introvert:
Caffeine has been shown to make introverts perform poorer on tasks that are quantitative and done under time pressure, whereas it has been found to have the opposite effect for extroverts. This is because introverts are more stimulated by their environment by default, and that extra caffeine can push them over the edge. As an ambivert I fall somewhere in between (maybe even a little on the introverted side) and have found that a moderate amount of caffeine positively impacts my performance in nearly all situations.

bucks you essentially buy back some energy that you will be able to use later in the day. When you consider how your energy levels can have such a huge impact on how much you accomplish, it's often worth the extra cost.

- Use an energy *crash* strategically. I often like to drink a big cup of coffee twelve hours before an overnight flight, so I crash just in time to sleep all the way through the flight. And when I travel overseas, I like to drink coffee a few hours after I wake up so I have a ton of energy throughout the day, and crash in time for my new bedtime.

The productivity possibilities are endless when you step back to consume caffeine strategically.

This is yet another reason why becoming more deliberate is so powerful.

FOR THE LOVE OF WATER

While my original intention with the water experiment was to observe how removing caffeine and alcohol from my diet would affect my productivity, I should have guessed how much more energy I would have when I consumed only water all month.

Water is like meditation; so simple, but so pure and so powerful. As far as drinks go, it's by far the most basic, but after this experiment, it's become my clear favorite, and I've had a bottle of water by my side ever since. Every morning, the very first thing I do after waking up is to drink a liter of water. And on most days I don't stop drinking water until I go to bed. An innumerable number of studies back up just how great water is for your health and productivity.

One study found that drinking water first thing in the morning fires up your metabolism, making it 24 percent faster. (Plus, you're usually dehydrated when you wake up, because you just went eight hours without drinking anything.) Another discovered that participants who drank a glass of water before every meal lost 4.5 pounds over three months. Why? Because water partly fills your stomach before you eat and acts as a calorie-free appetite suppressant. Water also helps you think more clearly (your brain tissue is made up of 75% water), clears up your complexion, and significantly reduces your risk of many diseases and ailments. Drinking more water will even save you money. I'm a huge fan of living frugally—I see saving money as a way of buying back my own time in the future—and so every glass of water I drink is one glass of something costly that I don't drink. Drinking water for a month saved me *$150* because I didn't allow myself to buy other, more expensive, less healthy drinks.

Yes, water is boring as far as drinks go (unless you're a total badass and mix things up by drinking carbonated or flavored water), but don't overlook it. Unlike alcohol or sugary drinks that rob you of energy later on, or caffeine, which can wreak havoc on your energy levels when you don't drink it deliberately, water invariably leaves you with more energy than you started with. And when you drink three liters a day (if you're a woman) or four liters a day (if you're a man), I think you'll be surprised at how much energy you have, particularly if you aren't hydrated enough already. (I've found that I need more than the recommended eight cups [2 L] a day to perform at an optimal level. Many organizations, including the U.S. Institute of Medicine, have found the same.) Not getting enough water can cause fatigue, sleepiness, and anxiety and make it difficult to concentrate—all of which will hurt your productivity. After my water experiment finished up, I went out and bought a one-liter water bottle that I carry with me everywhere. I fill it four times a day.

Drinking more water, and fewer energy-hijacking drinks, is a simple tactic, but getting enough H2O will help you keep kicking ass all day long. Just as many people could eat half of what they already do and not be hungry, a lot of people could double their water intake and feel that much better.

THE WATER CHALLENGE

Time required: 2 minutes
Energy/Focus Required: 2/10
Value: 7/10
Fun: 7/10
What you'll get out of it: You'll experience far fewer energy crashes throughout the day and have much more overall energy throughout the week. Energy is the fuel that you burn in order to be productive. Drinking more water and fewer alcoholic, sugary, and even caffeinated beverages will give you more to burn over the course of the day and week.

My challenge for you is to, this week, make one small incremental improvement to what you drink.

It's almost impossible to completely overhaul what you drink overnight, if you want the changes to stick. Here are a few ideas of habits you can work on:

- **Consume fewer sugary drinks.** Sugary drinks spike your glucose levels and cause a huge energy crash later on. For productivity reasons alone, they aren't worth drinking. And sugary drinks that contain caffeine or alcohol can wreak havoc on your energy levels.

- **Reduce your caffeine tolerance.** Over time, this will help you drink caffeine strategically. (Reducing how much caffeine you drink is especially helpful when you drink multiple cups every day, which can cause adrenal exhaustion over time and stress you out.)

- **Drink caffeine strategically**, like before hunkering down on a pressing task, or when you need the energy the most, such as between 9:30 and 11:30 a.m. for most people.

- **Drink less alcohol.** Yes, alcohol is fun, and that enjoyment is often worth the cost. But when you chip away at how much alcohol you drink over time, you'll be surprised by just how much more energy you have.

Luckily, what is good for your brain is good for your body. Becoming more productive is a process of learning to live and work more deliberately, and when what you eat and drink has such a profound effect on your energy levels, I think both are worth taking a second look at, especially if your energy levels fluctuate quite a bit over the course of the day.

24

THE EXERCISE PILL

Takeaway: The amount of energy and focus that exercise provides you with in return for your time is incredible, and easily worth the challenge of integrating an exercise routine into your life. After you feel how much of an impact exercise has on your brain, I think you'll want to continue with a routine, if only to make the feeling last.

Estimated Reading Time: 11 minutes, 11 seconds

DIY BRAIN SURGERY

As far as productivity is concerned, habits are insanely powerful. At their most elemental level, habits are made up of neurological pathways that automatically fire in response to different cues in your environment. Although habits are not always easy to form, when you establish the right habits for the right reasons, they're worth the effort in the end.

Every habit takes willpower and perseverance to create; if it didn't, we could simply decide to make huge changes to how we work to become more productive than we ever have been. Because you have a limited amount of willpower to draw from every day, you have to use your willpower sparingly and intelligently. That's why these tactics are so important. To show the effort new habits require, I put together a graph of how much willpower you expend as you implement new habits into your life (see next page).

It takes effort to get to the end of the chart, but the right habits are worth the willpower you'll spend on them.

Every tactic in this book—from the Rule of 3 to meditation—can

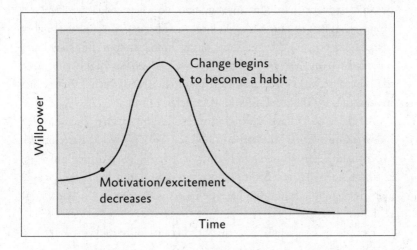

become a habit when you practice it enough. This is especially true when you understand the three elements that make up the habit loop, define a few cues that trigger you to do the tactics (a time, place, emotion, people, or preceding behavior), start small, and overcome your resistance to the change by battling procrastination and shrinking the change on a daily basis. Studies show that the amount of willpower you have is steadily depleted as you expend it over the day. Being smart about making new habits by following these techniques will let you make habits that actually stick.

Because forming new habits is a way of carving out new neurological pathways in your brain, when you take the effort to form new habits, in a way you perform brain surgery on yourself, on a microscopic level. This isn't easy, and it takes effort to carve out those pathways, but as soon as you do, you won't need to expend any more willpower on them. You'll become more productive automatically.

EXERCISING FOR PRODUCTIVITY

Much of the reason why it's so difficult to be productive today has to do with the fact that the working world has evolved much faster than our brain. We procrastinate because our prefrontal cortex hasn't evolved to become stronger than our limbic system, which is seduced by the un-productive tasks in our work. We find the internet and multitasking so stimulating because they're candy for our limbic system. But they harm our productivity. We feel tempted to overeat and eat highly processed foods because we evolved to stockpile fat to live off of during those times we had to go without food for long stretches of time.

All these traits have allowed us to evolve and survive. But since the industrial revolution, the structure of our working world has changed faster than the structure of our brain, which has made it difficult to adapt at times. Forming new habit pathways in our brain is hard enough—let alone reshaping our brain to become more productive in the knowledge economy.

Exercise is no exception to this. It's because of our evolutionary history that the productivity benefits of getting more exercise—especially aerobic exercise—can be so profound. It's an unfortunate fact that most jobs in the knowledge economy don't involve a lot of physical activity. Today, the amount of physical activity we get has never been lower; one recent study by the Physical Activity Council found that 28 percent of the U.S. population did not get *any* physical activity in the entire 2014 calendar year. This is terrible not just from a health standpoint, but also from a productivity standpoint. While our brains have evolved a bit since the Stone Age—2.5 million years ago—our bodies haven't. Our bodies are built to walk five to nine miles every day to hunt and gather food, not to spend fifty-two hours staring at screens every week.

This affects our work performance because of how our brain deals with stress. Today we are not only less active than we have ever been, we also have more distractions, demands, and deadlines in a typical day than we've ever had. Not to mention that we evolved to deal with stress that was short-lived, not lasting for days on end.

You've probably heard of the "fight or flight" concept before. This refers to how your body and brain respond to stressful situations; if you were to come face-to-face with a saber-toothed tiger, for example, you would instinctually decide whether to fight the tiger or flee from it. When you start to exercise—and this is especially the case with aerobic exercise—your brain sees it as a fight-or-flight situation, which causes your brain to release a concoction of chemicals that prepare you to fight the treadmill. These chemicals have a ton of neurological benefits, especially as far as stress relief is concerned. Biochemically speaking, exercise allows your brain to fight stress in a productive and controlled way.

But exercise doesn't only help you release stress—it also has a plethora of other benefits that will let you accomplish more. Exercise increases how much blood flows to your brain, which increases your mental performance and creativity. It combats fatigue, in addition to stress, and helps you bring more focus to your work. And studies show that in addition to bulking up your muscles, exercise quite literally bulks up your brain. When you exercise, your brain releases BDNF (brain-derived neurotrophic factor), a chemical that helps you create new brain cells. A lot of this growth happens in the hippocampus—the part of your brain responsible for memory. Exercise has even been shown to boost your mood and build cells in brain regions damaged by depression.

FIFTEEN POUNDS

Pretty much everyone has come across a stat or two about how great exercise is for your body and brain and how it releases "endorphins" and other wonderful things. When I started my project, I had heard about many of the stats I just named and had felt a few of the benefits firsthand, but these studies didn't move me much—even though I knew they were scientifically true. My rational, geeky prefrontal cortex ate the stats up, but they didn't motivate my limbic system to actually care enough about exercising in the long run to do it. This disconnect is what motivated me to experiment with how exercise impacted my productivity.

To experiment with exercise and productivity, as I mentioned earlier, I designed a productivity experiment to gain ten pounds of lean muscle, while lowering my body fat from 17 percent to 10 percent. Looking back, there was nothing wrong with the goal of the experiment. But the changes I tried to make to get there were too ambitious to stick with for the long haul. The experiments were also far too difficult, ambiguous, and unstructured, which didn't help. Indeed, I didn't stick with it and only lowered my body fat to about 15 percent by the end of my project.

But while I struggled to make drastic changes to how I ate, I was able to stick to my daily exercise ritual almost immediately.

To make the experiment more realistic, I forced myself to work out outside of regular working hours instead of in the middle of the day (when a lot of people don't have the flexibility to do so). I folded the ritual into my habit of waking up ultra early every morning. I'll talk about this a bit in the next chapter, but I really believe that if it weren't for my exercise ritual, I would have ended my experiment to wake up at 5:30 every morning much sooner.

As a pretty geeky guy, I've usually spent more time at the library than at the gym, though I have worked out off and on for as long as I can remember. When I ramped up this experiment, not having experienced the rush that came along with intense exercise that often, I almost instantly felt incredible.

Every morning for several months I settled into a routine of waking up at 5:30, walking over to my office, drinking a caffeine-based pre-workout drink, and then walking over to the gym, which was about a ten-minute walk from where I lived. Once there, still disconnected because of my daily shutoff ritual, I would listen to a podcast, audiobook, or Taylor Swift's latest album while doing thirty minutes of cardio, and then lift weights for about forty-five minutes. I started with going for just a half hour in the morning, but quickly ramped up the ritual once I felt less and less resistance to it and found a few friends to work out with every morning. Starting small was what got me going, but the benefits of exercise gave me the motivation to continue.

Looking back at my exercise habit—which I still follow, only later on in the day—it turns out that I had designed the perfect ritual for me, even though I didn't realize it at the time. I started small, at a level I was comfortable with—thirty minutes in the morning—and ratcheted that up over time as I felt less and less resistance to the habit. And I had almost every habit cue under the sun: a time (6 a.m.), place (the same gym every morning), emotion (feeling energized after having my preworkout drink or coffee), the presence of people I knew (my workout buddies), and a preceding behavior (waking up early).

I didn't feel a lot of resistance to the habit and made the habit more fun by listening to audiobooks and podcasts, which helped a ton. Contrary to what a lot of people say, there isn't a set number of days that it takes to integrate a new habit into your life. If you want to form a new habit of eating a chocolate bar every morning, for example, I bet it would take you just a day or two—and the opposite would be the case if you tried to form a new habit of walking on glass. For me, going to the gym felt exhilarating, especially considering almost every other element of my project involved almost zero physical activity and involved a lot of mental lifting. I believe that getting consistent exercise regularly is one of the reasons I was so productive during my project (I wrote 216,897 words by the time it was over).

Best of all, as soon as I settled into a regular workout routine (I worked out three to five days every week), my stress melted away, which resulted in a much more productive version of myself. I no longer experienced mental fatigue, and ironically enough, the more energy I seemed to expend at the gym, the more energy I had while working the rest of the day. Throughout the winter months, I was a lot happier and more upbeat (my mood usually dips along with the cold Canadian winter). And the challenges in my work didn't phase me one bit; I had more resiliency to face any crises that arose. Like with meditation, exercise changed how I related to what I experienced. Every morning I left my stress at the gym and was able to gain more energy throughout the day and become more productive.

As the months went by, my incremental changes added up, and I slowly gained more and more muscle mass, until, as I mentioned earlier, at the end of my project I had gained fifteen pounds of muscle—50 percent more than I had intended to. (Picture fifteen pounds of lean meat at the grocery store—only as muscle on a person.)

THE TIME COST

There is, of course, one problem with exercising for productivity reasons: the time you spend exercising has to come from somewhere, and for most people that time comes from commitments that may feel more important.

I've written about diet, exercise, and in the next chapter, sleep, because I think they are worth your time. But this is the challenge with the tactics in this part, and a couple of other tactics in this book, like meditation: when the average person looks at the choice between doing an extra thirty minutes of work and getting in thirty minutes of aerobic exercise (or more sleep, better meals, meditation, and so on), the better choice, at least as far as productivity is concerned, appears to be to work for thirty minutes longer. Doing extra work is easier and more stimulating than exercising, and you feel less guilty doing it.

But in practice, while in the short run you may get some extra work done in those thirty minutes, in the long run you accomplish more by nurturing your energy levels—not, as our friend Tim Pychyl would say, by giving in to feel good.

Nurturing your energy levels will ultimately *save* you time, because you'll be able to bring more energy and focus to your work, and get the same amount accomplished in less time. Like with every other tactic in this book, exercise lets you spend your time more efficiently. The same thing holds true for the time you spend eating better and getting enough sleep: all three activities provide you with a net gain in time and productivity, despite how hard they may be to do in the moment.

That's not to say they'll be worth it 100 percent of the time—there will be some days when you will (and should) value working an extra hour over eating well or hitting the gym, and others where you might value going out to have fun over getting a full night's sleep. But overall, as you make course corrections and incremental improvements with each passing week to become more productive, I think you'll find they are well worth your time.

Since my exercise experiment, and even since the end of my project, a few times I've been seduced by the idea of working longer hours instead of hitting the gym—I've fallen off the wagon. But every single time I've fallen I got right back on—not because I felt guilty about not living up to what I wrote about on my blog, but because I accomplished less and had less energy in the tank to do good work when I did.

In his book *Spark: The Revolutionary New Science of Exercise and the Brain*, John Ratey writes that exercise "is the single most powerful tool you have to optimize your brain function." He even goes so far as to say: "If exercise came in pill form, it would be plastered across the front page, hailed as the blockbuster drug of the century." I wholeheartedly agree. Exercise is worth your time and is one of the best things you can do to become more productive.

The more active you are, the more energy you'll have to burn.

THE HEART RATE CHALLENGE

Time required: 15 minutes
Energy/Focus Required: 7/10
Value: 7/10
Fun: 9/10
What you'll get out of it: You experience the incredible neurological benefits of exercise, including having more energy, focus, stamina, resilience, and memory, and less stress and fatigue. Exercise is worth your time.

My challenge for you this chapter is to elevate your heart rate for fifteen minutes tomorrow—either by walking, jogging, hopping on the elliptical machine, or doing any other form of aerobic exercise that gets your blood pumping faster than it normally does. (If you feel a lot of mental resistance to working out for fifteen minutes, shrink how long you'll work out until you no longer feel resistance to the challenge.)

This challenge is designed especially for people who get a limited amount of physical activity right now, or who have fallen off the wagon in terms of exercise. If you already have a regular workout habit, I challenge you to up your game even further and make one small incremental improvement to your workout regimen.

The key to making lasting changes to your behavior is to make changes to your habits that are small enough to not intimidate you when your initial motivation wears out. This is especially important with exercise. Exercising can be a beast of a challenge, especially as motivation and procrastination—which are opposite sides of the same coin—are concerned. For many people, exercising is boring, frustrating, difficult, ambiguous, *and* unstructured. No wonder people put it off. This is why starting small (and then continuing incrementally) is key. Making incremental improvements will help you sustain your momentum and motivation.

After you do the challenge, ask yourself: How do I feel? Is your head clearer? Do you have more energy? Do you feel less stressed out? Less fatigued?

When you feel how much of an effect exercise has on your brain, I think you'll want to continue the routine and make an effort to turn exercise into a habit. The increased energy and focus exercise provides you in return for your time and willpower are well worth it.

25

SLEEPING YOUR WAY TO PRODUCTIVITY

Takeaway: Although cutting back on sleep saves you time, any amount of sleep you lose below the amount your body requires is not worth the productivity cost. For every hour of sleep you miss out on, you lose at least two hours of productivity—the costs associated with not getting enough sleep are that great.

Estimated Reading Time: 10 minutes, 50 seconds

THE APOCALYPSE IS NIGH

Believe it or not, there is a zombie apocalypse happening right now. If you look outside your window, you'll see people who are the walking dead; they can't concentrate, remember much, drive safely, or get through the day with enough energy or focus. They drone through the day mindlessly on autopilot; this phenomenon is becoming so rampant that the Centers for Disease Control and Prevention has labeled it an "epidemic." These zombies even cause eighty thousand automobile accidents every year—all right under our noses.

You might even be one of them.

But unlike the zombies from the movies, these zombies don't hunger for human flesh.* They hunger for something that's much more precious to them: sleep.

In the United States, about *half* the population is walking around right now with some form of sleep deprivation. According to Gallup,

---

* Well, some of them might—who am I to judge?

40 percent of Americans get less than the recommended seven to nine hours every night. The Centers for Disease Control and Prevention have labeled this lack of sleep a "public health epidemic" because of the huge health and performance costs associated with not getting enough sleep. Sleep deprivation costs these zombies dearly, especially when you look at the connection between sleep and productivity.

Although the connection between nutrition and exercise and productivity is complex, the connection between productivity and sleep is simple. Sleep is a way of exchanging your time for energy. The more sleep you get, up to the recommended seven to nine hours, the more energy you'll have the next day. And the exchange rate is pretty damn good.

I probably don't have to go too deep into the science behind the reason skimping on sleep affects performance: chances are you have already experienced them firsthand at some point in your life. Not getting enough sleep—or getting poor-quality sleep—leads you to make more mistakes. It affects your mood, ability to focus, and how you tackle problems, learn, and remember. And it negatively impacts your concentration, working memory, and mathematical reasoning abilities. This chapter belongs in one of the focus sections of the book as much as it belongs in this one—the costs of not getting enough sleep are that significant.

Lacking sleep can also speed up the downward energy spiral I mentioned in the water/coffee chapter. When you miss out on sleep, you work less efficiently and with less energy, so tasks take longer, which means you have even less time for sleep the following night. When you add a bad diet and little exercise into the mix, your energy levels—and productivity—can spiral out of control pretty quickly.

During my project, I came up with a simple rule to live by for sleep and productivity: **for every hour of sleep I missed out on, I lost two hours of productivity.** This rule has no scientific backing whatsoever—from what I experienced, the negative effects can be even greater—but as far as pseudoscientific rules go, I think this is a pretty good one. Everyone is wired differently, requires a different amount of sleep, responds differently to sleep deprivation, and is motivated differently when they are sleep deprived. But from what I've found, two hours might even be on the conservative side.

UP AT 5:30

In hindsight, it's almost kind of funny how so many of my productivity experiments involved putting myself through hell in the name of understanding productivity. There were a few really fun experiments, like becoming a total slob for a week, watching seventy hours of TED talks, and taking a three-hour-long afternoon "siesta" every day, but at the same time, so many of the others were experiments I had to slog through.

It took only twenty-five chapters, but I finally get to talk about the most unpleasant experiment of the bunch: waking up at 5:30 every morning.

When I first set out to wake up at 5:30 every morning, I tried to shoehorn the habit into my life at the start of my project and really had no idea what the heck I was doing. For starters, I didn't plan how I would make the change in the slightest. Instead of chipping away at the bundle of habits that surrounded when I woke up and went to bed, I used up all my willpower trying to make a huge change in my life. And I fell flat on my face.

I failed to reward myself when I woke up early, define any cues to wake up early, or work to overcome the resistance I had to the ritual—all essential for making changes to habits. And maybe most important, I didn't approach the ritual with an ounce of deliberateness. Because of this, I failed—repeatedly. I even wrote an article about a month into my project titled "So far, I've mostly failed at waking up at 5:30," which chronicled my struggles in detail. Things were looking pretty bad.

But then I took a step back to approach the ritual with more deliberateness and made a plan for how to work it into my life.

As strange as this might sound coming from me, at first I didn't look at any articles or research on how I could work the habit into my life or plan how I could be smart about it. I simply forced myself to wake up at 5:30 every morning, which meant I would often miss out on an hour or more of sleep, which seriously affected my productivity the next day. A lot of days I wouldn't even make it to noon without needing a nap, and many mornings I presented myself with a tough choice: either sleep in and fail, or get up and not have enough energy and focus to get through the day. I often chose the latter, and the experiment became pretty tough to sustain in the long term. It's hard to form new habit pathways when you punish your brain for making them.

About a month into the experiment, I became fed up with failing at the experiment. That's when I finally stepped back to consider what I was doing wrong.

CHIPPING AWAY—ONCE AGAIN

When I stepped back to make a plan for how to work the habit into my life, I realized what time I woke up didn't matter one bit. What mattered was what time I went to bed, and that was the thing I had to chip away at.

This is something important to keep in mind when it comes to getting enough sleep. The key to getting enough sleep isn't to sleep in. Not many people have the luxury of being able to wake up whenever they want, and though it would be nice if we were all entrepreneurs who had control over our schedules, most of us have a relatively set routine of arriving at work. What we do have control over is what time we head to bed. To get enough sleep, going to bed at the right time is the key.

It took another two months to work at my nighttime routine and integrate the habit into my life, but after I finally realized that trying to force the routine into my life wasn't working, I made a plan to make enough incremental improvements to my routine to solidify an early-morning wake-up ritual. Setting aside the fact that I wasn't programmed to be an early riser, these will work for you regardless of when you're built to wake up, since they all revolve around getting to bed at a decent time. Here's what I found worked better than anything else:

✓ **Create a nighttime ritual.** If your target bedtime is 9 p.m., like mine was, it's pretty hard to force yourself to start getting ready for bed at 8:45 when you're in the middle of something. Creating a nighttime ritual will help you plan and become more deliberate about getting a good night's sleep. I recommend picking a very specific time to head to bed and planning out when you'll start your ritual to ease out of the day. Don't be afraid to have some fun with it: your nighttime routine should be custom-built to be both relaxing and meaningful to you, and let you ease out of the day and into the next one. I worked meditation, reflection time, and more into mine.

✓ **Expose yourself to less blue light.** Believe it or not (I found this hard to believe at first), the more "blue light" you expose yourself to before you sleep, the worse your sleep quality will be. Light that sits in the blue wavelength has been proven to inhibit melatonin production, a chemical in your body and brain that helps you sleep. To combat this, I recommend a nightly electronics shutoff ritual, where you shut off your electronics two to three hours before bed (this also helps you switch off your autopilot switch and begin slowing down). I also own a pair of blue-blocking sunglasses, which I wear whenever I make an exception and use electronics late at night, and I've surprisingly found them to make a big difference in my sleep quality. So has science—one study found participants who wore the glasses slept 50 percent better and were 40 percent happier when they woke up! You can also download an app named "f.lux" on your computer that color-shifts your computer display to blast less blue light at you (justgetflux.com). Things might look a bit funny at first, but you'll sleep way better. Exposing yourself to more natural light during the day has also been shown to help you sleep—and also boost your productivity. One study found that when call center employees sat near a window, they processed calls 12 percent faster than everyone else!

✓ **Don't be afraid to nap!** One of the more fun experiments I did— even though I didn't learn as much from it—was taking a three-hour-long Spanish-style afternoon siesta for three weeks, where I took a long break in the afternoon to nap, eat, and socialize before working again later into the evening. Surprisingly, in addition to seeing the importance of taking breaks (which I'll get to in the next chapter), I discovered the profound productivity benefits of napping. Like sleep, napping has been shown to boost your focus, accuracy, creativity, decision-making skills, and ultimately your productivity. For the amount of time it takes you to walk to the coffee shop and back, you can get the same energy boost with a nap, without the crash afterward. Napping at work can be a bit strange (though I've had some coworkers in the past who managed to make it work), but if I ever work in a traditional office environment again, you bet I'll do all I can to grab a bit of shut-eye whenever I need a mental boost. If you have the freedom to do so, taking a nap in the middle of the workday is one of the best ways to get a quick jolt of energy—and productivity.

✔ **Stop drinking caffeine eight to fourteen hours before you sleep.** Again, caffeine takes about eight to fourteen hours to begin to leave your system and can severely hurt your sleep quality and productivity the next day when you don't plan to stop drinking it in time.

✔ **Think of your bedroom as a cave.** The American Academy of Sleep Medicine recommends "thinking of a bedroom as a cave: It should be cool, quiet, and dark." But above all else, it should be "thermally neutral," meaning that your body "doesn't have to do anything to create heat (shiver) or shed heat (sweat) to compensate for being too cold or warm."

I value my time more than most people, but sleep is something I simply won't compromise on. And since my early wake-up experiment, I haven't. Compromising sleep so you have more time to get more work done simply isn't worth the productivity cost. And you won't even have a net gain in productivity, because your tasks will take longer when you're sleep deprived—you'll have less energy and focus to bring to them, and you'll make more mistakes that will take more time to fix. When you cut back on sleep, you always lose more time than you gain.

IT DOESN'T MATTER WHEN YOU WAKE UP

Over the course of my project, I stumbled upon a number of articles written by "productivity gurus" about why waking up early is fantastic for your productivity. But the truth is that this simply isn't true. Studies show that what time you wake up has no impact whatsoever on your socioeconomic standing, cognitive performance, *or* health. As far as your productivity is concerned, it's what you do with your time after you wake up, and whether you got enough sleep in the first place, that makes the difference.

Looking back, I realized that waking up early is one of those pieces of urban myth productivity advice that is simply flat-out wrong. That's not to say that it won't work for you, because it might—but everyone's wired differently. If you have a family and rising early lets you have some quiet planning time before their day starts, or you're wired to be an early riser, the ritual may be for you. But there are just as many people who won't benefit from an early wake-up ritual. It's not that there's a perfect wake-up time—it's about what the best wake-up time is for you.

ENERGY

A lot of people find themselves with more tasks on their list than they have time for. One of the first things they compromise is their energy. To free up time to try to get more done, they begin to order more takeout, caffeinate to insane levels, cut back on exercise, or work later hours and compromise on sleep—all short-term sacrifices that lead to more productivity in the short run, but less productivity in the long run. I've fallen into most of these traps—a couple even during my project.

The truth is that I value my time and productivity so much that I would have dropped the tactics I've covered here a long time ago if they didn't work. They're hard, and they take valuable time and willpower away from other things. But they pay off in the end.

When you eat properly, you'll have enough glucose in your brain to bring more energy and focus to your work. When you drink caffeinated, alcoholic, and sugary beverages intelligently (or not at all), your energy levels won't roller-coaster throughout the day, and your productivity will stay steady. When you exercise more, you'll have more energy and focus to do good work and feel less stressed out. And when you get enough sleep, you'll work far more efficiently and won't feel like a zombie all day.

Sleep is one of the best and simplest ways of exchanging your time for energy.

THE SLEEPING CHALLENGE

Time required: 5 minutes
Energy/Focus Required: 7/10
Value: 9/10
Fun: 9/10
What you'll get out of it: You'll save time, because you'll be able to expend more energy (instead of time) on your work, which will let you work more efficiently. You'll also experience more mental clarity, concentration, short-term memory, and problem-solving skills, and make fewer mistakes.

My challenge for you this chapter is to reflect on whether you're getting enough sleep each night, and if you're not, make a plan to rectify that. A good place to start is to ask yourself whether you feel the need to catch up on sleep over the weekend. If you do, chances are you aren't getting enough sleep during the week, and you need to invest in a bedtime ritual to head to bed by a reasonable time.

As far as challenges go, this one is small—but the productivity costs of not getting enough sleep can be massive.

If you need to form a new bedtime ritual, it helps to pick a very specific target time you want to be in bed, and then work backward from that time to plan your bedtime ritual. Watch out for how much unnatural blue light you expose yourself to, how much caffeine you drink up to ten hours before heading to bed, and whether your sleeping environment is cool and comfortable.

Although cutting back on sleep saves you time, any time you save below the amount your body requires is not worth the productivity cost. Remember: for every hour of sleep you miss out on, you lose at least two hours of productivity.

Part Eight

THE FINAL STEP

26

THE FINAL STEP

TAKING IT EASY

Over the course of my project, I discovered something curious whenever I pushed myself to get more done: it was almost impossible to push myself to become more productive without being hard on myself at the same time.

Frankly, this is the downside to working on your productivity. When you do it wrong (and I have), and you're hard on yourself in the process, you end up less happy than when you started. When most of us invest in our productivity to increase our sense of well-being, odds are that goes against why you want to be more productive in the first place.

Investing in your productivity is a worthwhile goal, but life is too short to not be kind to yourself in the process.

But there is good news: research shows that productivity and happiness are in sync. In fact, the happier you are, the more productive you will become. According to psychologist and happiness researcher Shawn Achor, who wrote the bestselling book *The Happiness Advantage*, when your brain is happier, it "performs significantly better than it does at negative, neutral, or stressed. Your intelligence rises, your creativity rises, [and] your energy levels rise." In fact, in his research he's found that happier people are *31 percent more productive*, have 37 percent better sales figures, have better, more secure jobs, are also better at keeping their jobs, are more resilient, and have less burnout.

His research illustrates a profound idea: investing in your happiness and being kind to yourself can have a huge impact on your productivity.

So far, I've done my best to give you ways of being kind to yourself as you invest in your productivity—in fact, many of the tactics in this book *themselves* are ways of being kind to yourself as you strive to get more done. When you set daily and weekly intentions that are realistic and not too hard to achieve, you'll be motivated to achieve them. When you accommodate the way your brain operates, it becomes infinitely easier to beat procrastination and quit wasting time. When you consider your future self when making decisions, you don't burden the future you with responsibilities that you won't be able to handle. When you clear attentional space to think, you give yourself more clarity and feel less pressure. Making small, incremental improvements, rewarding yourself, finding your resistance level, working mindfully, and cultivating your focus and energy levels are all ways of taking it easy on yourself and having fun as you invest in your productivity.

Over the course of my project, I discovered a number of fun ways to take it easy on myself as I invested in my productivity, often after unnecessarily beating myself up for not accomplishing the goals I set. Oddly enough, you may *feel* less productive—or if you're like me, even guilty—as you become kinder to yourself. But doing so will allow you to accomplish more at the end of the day because you'll continue to stay motivated.

These tactics serve as the perfect chaser to the last twenty-five chapters, and I can't think of a better way to end *The Productivity Project*. If you care about productivity, being kind to yourself is crucial. Here are nine of the best ways I've found to be kind to yourself in the process.

I. Disconnect from productivity more often

As a general rule, you should be taking more breaks than you are now—that includes breaks throughout the day, and breaks from work in general. I've listed this one first because it's easily the most important of the bunch: taking too few breaks can absolutely shatter your productivity. The more breaks I took during my project, the more energy and focus I had, and the less often I became fatigued. The benefits are innumerable and incredible: breaks help you work more mindfully and deliberately, come up with new ideas, flip into mind-wandering mode, reflect on your work, see the meaning in what you do, and ultimately make you more productive. One study found that the ideal break length for productivity is seventeen minutes for every fifty-two minutes you work, and while I don't buy that number completely—everyone is programmed differently—I buy the idea behind it. You should take breaks a lot more frequently than you do now.

One study from the University of Toronto looked at the link between breaks and productivity; it found that when we feel low on energy, it's because we have a limited amount of physiological energy in our brain. According to John Trougakos, the study's coauthor, "All efforts to control behavior, to perform and to focus draw on that pool of psychological energy. Once that energy source is depleted, we become less effective at everything that we do." Completely separating from your work—whether throughout the day or in general—helps you replenish that pool of energy. I break for at least fifteen minutes every hour, because when I don't, I notice a drop in how much energy and focus I have.

For a few great break activities, flip to page 174, where I've listed the best stress-relief activities. They let you recharge, destress, and have fun as you take a step back from being productive.

2. Recall three things you're grateful for

In his research, Shawn Achor has encountered a number of ways you can actually train your brain to think happier. In addition to meditation and exercise—which Shawn is a huge advocate for—my favorite two tactics of his are recalling three things you're grateful for, and journaling one positive experience you had at the end of each day. As Shawn told me, recalling three things you're grateful for every day is powerful because "as you consciously practice scanning for positives, your brain gets better at it and it retains the new pattern of unconsciously continually scanning the world for the good." It's not the gratitude as much as it is "the ability to scan your [life] for positives that makes the habit so effective." Every night, even after the toughest days, I write down the three biggest things I'm grateful for from that day, or if that's too hard, three things I'm grateful for in general. For something that takes only a minute or two, I've found the effects of this tactic to be absolutely profound.

3. Journal about a positive experience you had

According to Shawn, neurologically speaking, when you journal—or if journaling isn't your thing, talk about—a positive experience you had at the end of each day, "your brain stamps it as meaningful." Over time, doing this helps you train your brain to think happier by letting you recall the most positive and meaningful parts of your day. But perhaps most important, as Shawn put it, "the brain can't tell much difference between visualization and actual experience, so you just doubled the most meaningful experience of your day. Done over time, your brain connects the dots and you realize you have a trajectory of meaning running throughout your life." To create lasting, long-term effects, Shawn recommends giving these tactics a few weeks to train your brain to think happier and become habits.

4. Break tasks down

There is a reason video games seem so much more rewarding than work: video games provide you with a rapid succession of milestones, goals, and rewards, whereas most jobs are far more ambiguous and unstructured.

Creating subgoals for larger projects, spending more time planning out projects to add structure to them, and keeping a running list of things you have to get done for each of your projects will make your work more structured, rewarding, and engaging. Research has shown this also makes you more likely to achieve a "flow" state, that magical feeling where you're so engrossed in your work that time seems to not exist at all.

5. Ask yourself for advice

One of my favorite ways to become more productive when I'm facing a challenge is to ask myself for advice. I value the opinions of my friends and family, but I always ask myself for advice at the same time. The next time you're facing a challenge and are looking around for someone to lean on, try leaning on yourself. What advice would you give yourself in your situation? (This tactic also works wonders for firing up your prefrontal cortex when you're resisting aversive tasks.)

6. Reward yourself

I've talked about rewarding yourself throughout this book, but it's so important that it's worth mentioning again. Whether that means spending fifteen minutes on Facebook after each long workout, transferring a dollar into a frivolous spending account for every day you don't bite your nails, or treating yourself to a fancy steak dinner when you finish a big work project, rewarding yourself works wonders not only for solidifying habits, but also for having fun as you invest in your productivity.

7. Know You Can Grow

According to research conducted by Stanford psychologist Carol Dweck, the author of *Mindset*, the main thing that separates successful people from unsuccessful people is whether or not they feel their intelligence and abilities are fixed.

People who have a growth mindset believe that through hard work and persistence, they can accomplish more. They embrace obstacles as challenges to be overcome, instead of seeing them as roadblocks, and they see working hard as the only way of mastering a skill. If you think your intelligence and abilities are set in stone, you are wrong. Reminding yourself that you can always grow and that your intelligence and abilities aren't fixed is a great way to challenge yourself to become more productive.

8. Create an Accomplishments List

For the last few years, I've maintained an Accomplishments List that I've reviewed and added to every Maintenance Day. It's a simple list, so it doesn't take long to review, but every week it lets me step back from my work and life, pat myself on the back, and recognize the achievements my increased productivity leads to.

Before keeping the list, I had invested in productivity without actually taking the time to reflect on what I accomplished. Reviewing the list at the end of each week propels me into the week ahead and motivates me to accomplish more—especially when I'm working on longer-term projects where the results aren't immediately apparent.

9. Look at pictures of cute baby animals

Not only can looking at cute baby animals make you go "awwwwww," it can also boost your cognitive and motor performance. One study analyzed the cognitive and motor performance of participants who looked at cute baby animals (as well as other cute images, which didn't have the same effect). They found that cute baby animals had a positive effect on how participants managed their attention, and that "viewing cute things improves subsequent performance in tasks that require behavioral carefulness, possibly by narrowing the breadth of attentional focus." This tactic may be a bit of a stretch, but there's no denying that it's fun.

BROKEN

I've always been a fan of taking vacations from my work for productivity reasons: to let my mind wander, take it easy on myself, let thoughts and ideas percolate, and to give myself space to make connections and think about the ideas I'm juggling.

Three months after I started this book, I was ahead of schedule, so I decided to treat myself to a weeklong vacation to clear my head. I found a deal on a flight to Dublin and jumped at it. For my weeklong trip, I elected to stay in Howth, a small fishing town of about eight thousand people that sits on the outskirts of Dublin. Most days I walked out of the Airbnb I was staying at without my cell phone or laptop in tow, only carrying around a notepad while I toured the Irish seaside. I let my mind wander and captured any interesting thoughts or connections that came up on paper. It was February and the nights were chilly, but even though it was "winter" in Ireland, it felt pretty damn warm during the day to me. (The average high in February in Dublin is a solid 5°C (41°F), thirty to forty degrees warmer than Ottawa that time of year.)

But less than two days into my trip, everything went to hell.

While walking home from a friend's place shortly after midnight, I fell down a steep, slick cobblestone sidewalk. After the seemingly innocuous fall, I tried to get up—but realized that I couldn't. When I transferred my weight from my right leg to my left, the pain—even after a pint or two of Guinness—was unbearable, and I crumbled back down to the ground. I pulled my cell phone out of my pocket, but it was dead. I tried shouting for help, but I was out in the Howth countryside and there weren't any people around—or if there were, they weren't awake. It was cold, and after the first hour of lying there, I started shivering so uncontrollably that I had to curl up into a ball to keep myself warm. A couple of times I tried to hop on one foot, but the pain was too great, and I fell back down again.

After about three hours, a couple of people finally heard me yelling for help. An ambulance rushed me to the hospital, just as the sun was beginning to rise. I was in a good deal of pain, and all I wanted to do was fly back home to Canada. But I couldn't, because with a shattered ankle and leg bone, I wasn't allowed to fly.

It's amazing how much damage you can do when you fall the exact wrong way.

After a long reconstructive surgery that left me with a pin, plate, and footlong incision in my left leg, I lay in a hospital bed for three days, exhausted. To add insult to injury, I wasn't even sure the surgery would be covered by the travel insurance I had purchased for the trip and had to live with that uncertainty for a while as well. (It turned out it was covered—whew.)

Unable to get up out of the hospital bed without assistance—even a couple of days after my surgery—I remember lying helplessly while emails, phone messages, and more piled up on my smartphone. I didn't have the energy or focus to deal with any of what was coming in and wouldn't have enough energy for *weeks*. When I asked the surgeon how long it would take me to recover from the injury, his answer crushed me: because the fracture was severe, it would take about *six months* to fully recover, and I would need six months of physiotherapy. As I write this, I still have to walk around town with a cane and can't run or jump. (That said, the cane is pretty badass.)

Making the deadline for this book in time—let alone doing a good job of it—would have been hard *without* my injury, never mind while being in recovery for six months. I was burned out, with no energy left to think or to handle anything else I had on my plate. I wished I could fast-forward six months until the cast was off and the book was in, and I was home again, surrounded by the people I loved—instead of being stranded and alone, five thousand kilometers away.

Every day, all day, each of us talks to ourselves—and this is perfectly normal. Everyone has an internal dialogue that runs through their head throughout the day; psychologists often call this an "internal monologue," or "self-talk." Of all the people you talk to regularly, there isn't one person you talk to more than yourself.

If you've tried out the tactics I've written about in *The Productivity Project*, chances are you've experienced this self-talk firsthand. Perhaps when you've become aware that you were procrastinating, as you observed your limbic system and prefrontal cortex battling, you also noticed your self-talk increase. Tim Pychyl told me recently that when you procrastinate, your "self-talk goes through the roof." Maybe you noticed your brain having a heated dialogue with itself while you were meditating. Or perhaps you noticed this self-talk flare up when you were considering whether or not you should tackle some of the challenges at the end of the chapters in this book—especially the ones you were the most resistant to.

I experienced this self-talk during my project, too, and if anything, it increased as the project went on. Curiously though, most of it was negative—and I don't consider myself to be a negative person. After I made the decision to decline those jobs to start *AYOP*, my mind was full of excitement, nervousness, doubt, fear, and anxiety—and self-talk. Whenever I would put off reading an intimidating research paper, my negative self-talk went through the roof. When I stopped meditating toward the start of my project and began working faster and harder instead of deliberately and with intention, my self-talk went up right along with the pace I was working at. After I kept my first time log, my negative self-talk exploded as I came down on myself for procrastinating for six hours a week. When I failed to lower my body fat to 10 percent, I was again needlessly hard on myself. I expected myself to be able to lower my body fat seemingly overnight—when in reality I loved butter chicken too much. When I worked twenty-hour weeks, I was needlessly hard on myself again because I wasn't working as long as I felt I should.

Even at the peaks of my project—such as after the *New York Times* published an interview with me, or after getting the deal to write this book, I was needlessly hard on myself. I remember calling myself a "fraud" and feeling a pretty strong case of "imposter's syndrome."

About midway through the yearlong project, I stumbled upon an incredible fact that lifted a thousand pounds off my shoulders. Negative self-talk is absolutely, completely *normal*. One psychologist, Shad Helmstetter, has found that "*seventy-seven percent* of everything we think is negative, counterproductive, and works against us." Another study conducted on business students found that "somewhere *between 60 and 70 percent* of the average students' spontaneously occurring thoughts are negative."

Self-talk is naturally hard to measure—after all, how do you analyze what's going on in someone's head? But I think these stats confirm an idea that's profound. Having a negative dialogue in your head isn't just average, it's *human*.

Have you experienced that phenomenon where you receive fifty emails, forty-nine of them positive and one of them negative? I'll bet you remember that one damned email more than the other forty-nine put together. This is simply the way we're programmed. Just as we have evolved to walk five to nine miles every day, we have evolved to perceive threats in our environment. That's why that email sticks out, and that's in part why your monologue can be so negative.

Over the course of a few months, I collected all the negative thoughts that popped into my head, most of which seemed to come out of nowhere. Here are a few of the more interesting ones:

- I'm way out of my element.
- I'll never get better at this.
- I'm no good.
- I know they'll say no.
- I'm a fraud.
- I have nothing valuable to say.
- I'm not good enough.
- I know no one else feels this way.
- I can't do this.
- I can't do anything right.
- Why did I say that?!
- I'm pretty sure I'm the only one that doesn't get this.
- They're not going to like me.
- They're going to laugh.
- I doubt anyone's as lost as I am.

These are harsh words, and if I talked to my friends the way I talked to myself, I doubt I'd have any friends left. But as soon as I became aware that this is simply the result of how my brain was programmed, I felt as if another thousand pounds had been lifted off my shoulders.

Suddenly, I could start to step back and observe this dialogue, instead of becoming caught up in it. And I found I could challenge any thoughts that were B.S.—which roughly 60–77 percent of them were.

———

As I slowly started to become coherent after my surgery, it hit me that I would likely miss the deadline for this book. Here I was, writing a book about productivity, "the most productive man you could ever hope to meet," and I would miss my own book deadline. Ha!

In that moment I was back in the city bus riding home after my soylent experiment, ready once again to throw in the towel. I remember saying to myself a phrase I hadn't recalled using up to that point: *I give up.*

But shortly after that thought came to me, I started laughing. Not maniacally or anything like that—after all, I didn't transfer to the psych ward—just a small chuckle, as if my mind had wandered off during a meditation session. Because in a way, it had: instead of simply being in the present moment, my mind had wandered off to where it was programmed to go—to a place that was negative.

It was hard overcoming my negative self-talk, but a part of me knew that somehow, at the end of the day, I would be all right.

Ever since my project one of the very first things I've done after waking up has been to define the three things I wanted to accomplish over the course of the day. Old neurological pathways die hard, and after a day or two of lying in the hospital bed, as I slowly regained some energy and focus, I began to flip back into "productivity mode" and define three simple things I wanted to accomplish each day.

Productivity is often a process of understanding your constraints. The first day after the operation, I simply made an intention to do a couple of laps around the ward with my newfangled metal-framed walker. As I sat back down again, I felt exhilarated. I had achieved exactly what I intended to—taking into account the physical and mental limitations I faced. For the first few days I made one or two simple intentions—to read a book, type an important email or two, coordinate stuff with my assistant, or get in touch with friends and loved ones back home. And each day, as I reflected on how much time, attention, and energy I had,

I adapted my intentions accordingly, and most days accomplished everything I set out to.

By that point, I had laid enough productivity groundwork that I was able to get right back up on my feet—even though I wasn't allowed to bear any weight on the left one for at least a couple of months. I knew which tasks were the most important to me at the time, which gave me a guiding light when I found it hard to focus. I had a habit of forming daily and weekly intentions to accomplish what was important. I had worked hard and was ahead of schedule, so I could be kind to my future self. I had simplified my work and delegated many of my lowest-return tasks to my assistant so I could focus on what was essential, instead of struggling to keep my head above water. I wasn't storing my task list in my head, but rather on paper and on my devices, which helped when my mental capacity was reduced. And I had built up habits, like disconnecting from the internet, taming the distractions around me, single tasking, eating well, and getting enough sleep, that propelled me further and let me make good use of my limited energy.

I also took the time to meditate, even if just for a few minutes every day. This didn't change any of what I was experiencing, but it completely changed how I related to what I was experiencing. It made me see the good in it, and it made me more resilient. In just a short day or two, particularly after my nightly gratefulness ritual, I became grateful that even though the people I loved were thousands of miles away, I could still talk to them every day, that I was covered for health insurance, and that I could probably even turn the injury into a interesting story someday.

You're reading this book because of the productivity groundwork I had laid. In a weird way, this book is a product of the productivity research I was doing.

Three and a half months after breaking my ankle, I sent the manuscript of this book to my editor. I'm still not fully recovered—that will take another few months—but I finished the book, on time.

Actually, that's not true. I shipped it six weeks ahead of schedule.

TEN DAYS IN ISOLATION

One of the questions I get the most often about my year of productivity is which productivity experiment I've learned the most from. Early on when I was asked, I'd usually be stumped by the question, but eventually the answer became very clear. The experiment I learned the most from was living in total isolation for ten days.

My intention behind most of my experiments was to take an element of my work or life that I figured either contributed to or detracted from my productivity and intensely focus on it for a period of time to think about and research how it influenced my performance. Meditating for thirty-five hours let me step back and observe the connection between meditation and productivity; using my smartphone for an hour let me think about technology and the internet; and eating only soylent let me think about food (even more than I regularly did).

When I set out to live in total isolation for ten days, my intention was to observe how people (and to a smaller extent, since I was living in a room without windows—sunlight) impacted my productivity. We can sometimes take people for granted, or settle into less than ideal relationships: we don't often give ourselves space to step back from our relationships, or take the time to think about how much meaning they add to our lives.

But partway into my project, I hit a roadblock: when my girlfriend and I crunched the numbers and budgeted our finances through to the end of my project, they simply didn't work. I wouldn't have enough money to make it through my year of productivity. At the least I would have to take on a part-time job, or take out a loan to finish the year. (I had no ads or sponsorships on my site, because my intention with the site wasn't to make money.)

Even though the idea for the productivity project has only publicly existed as a website, *A Year of Productivity* was always more than just a blog to me. The yearlong project was a way of exploring every single one of my curiosities and connecting as many of them as I could—whether through experiments, by diving into research, or by talking to experts—and then sharing everything I learned to help out other people.

So when we realized that the numbers didn't add up, we came up with another option that is a bit embarrassing to write about. That option was for the two of us to move back home, into her dad's house. After six years of living on our own, the thought of Ardyn and me moving in with her dad, even if only until the project was finished, felt like taking a thousand steps backward—especially for me, after declining two well-paying jobs to start the project. My negative self-talk was through the roof. But after letting the idea stew, a part of us felt that it was the right decision to make. (It's worth noting that Ardyn didn't have to move back home; she had more than enough cash in the bank, and she would be moving back to stay with me.)

The instant we moved in, I decided to double-down on my project. Why do anything if you're not going to do it right? The sacrifices I was making would have to be worth it.

Just a few short weeks later, I decided to run my experiment to spend ten days in isolation, and to reflect on the relationships in my life.

When I stepped back from the relationships in my life—from my relationships with family, friends, my girlfriend, and even strangers on the street—it quickly became clear to me just how important people are to productivity. Without people around me, my motivation to get work done plummeted. The research backs this up; two studies found that deeper office friendships boost your job satisfaction by about 50 percent, and that you are *seven times as likely* to be highly engaged at work when your best friend works at the same place. When I asked Shawn what the most interesting thing he discovered in his research has been, he talked about how "the greatest predictor of long-term happiness is social connection," and how "social connection is as predictive of how long you will live as obesity, high blood pressure, or smoking"—only in the opposite direction, of course. Deeper friendships and relationships provide us with the drive to accomplish more at work—and make us happier, to boot.

But more important, outside of work, relationships give us purpose and meaning. This is the lesson that struck me the hardest during the whole of my project, and it struck me from out of the blue: without people, productivity is meaningless.

As hellish as that basement was, I quickly realized how lucky I was to be down there, exploring my passion in my own weird way. Just a few days in, I became overwhelmed with gratitude for everyone who had helped me get there. Without my girlfriend and her dad, I wouldn't have been able to continue with the project and would have had to accept a job working somewhere that had almost no meaning to me. Without the people who followed me, reading my site, the words I wrote wouldn't have helped others. Without a loving family, I would have felt far less confident in my work. And without loving friends, I wouldn't have had a support net to constantly fall into when I first started my project. It was the people around me—who supported me, helped me, believed in me, and loved me—that motivated me and gave me purpose. I quickly realized that the people around me weren't just the reason my project existed—they were who my project existed for. People are what gave my work meaning, and in every job I had up to that point, people are what gave those jobs meaning, too.

People are why we do what we do, and why we push ourselves to accomplish more. Surrounding ourselves with people has been shown to make us happier and more engaged and makes us want to be more productive, too.

People are the reason for productivity.

PRODUCTIVITY AND HAPPINESS

Happiness and productivity go hand in hand. But in a rather odd way, the desire to invest in your productivity implies, at least to some extent, that you're not entirely satisfied with where you're at right now. For me, this is one of those conflicts that forced me more than once to step back and consider the place that becoming more productive deserved to have in my life.

On the one hand, the Buddhist in me believes that happiness is nothing more than coming to terms with how things change. On the other hand, the driven part of me has always been uncomfortable with where I'm at, and for whatever reason has always wanted to accomplish more.

But I came to realize that it's a *good* thing to never feel fully satisfied—as long as I found ways to continually cultivate my happiness along the way.

The reason humans have survived and evolved for millions of years is that we, as a species, have never truly been content with where we are. We have always wanted to build bigger inventions, buildings, ideas, and movements. The fact that we have, for millions of years, constantly been motivated to advance ourselves as well as one another is a good thing and is the reason you're reading these words today. Without the printing press, there would be no way of spreading these ideas and eighty thousand words to people like you. Without the internet, I wouldn't have been able to reach millions of people with my blog. Without language, I wouldn't have a way of expressing the dots I have connected, or the strings I've pulled on over the last decade. Without your own desire to become better, you wouldn't have picked up this book. While never truly being satisfied has had consequences (like supersized everything at fast-food restaurants), I think they're worth the cost a hundred times over. This unsettledness is the reason we've evolved to be around today.

Over the course of my project, I found that the best attitude to have with productivity is an odd one: to never be satisfied—but to continually find ways to cultivate happiness. Luckily, productivity, when done right, isn't only one of the keys to happiness—happiness is one of the keys to productivity.

The kinder you are to yourself as you become more productive, the more productive you will become.

AFTERWORD: ONE YEAR LATER

Estimated Reading Time:
2 minutes, 14 seconds

Whenever I watch a cooking show where a celebrity chef like Gordon Ramsay visits a struggling restaurant to make over the place and its menu, I'm always a little disappointed when the show doesn't revisit the same restaurant a year or two after the episode is shot.

In the shows that do, it's usually hit or miss.* About half the time the restaurant thrives, and the other half of the time it either reverts to the way it operated before or goes under. Although the transformation always makes for good television, it often doesn't last.

My yearlong experiment finished up on May 1, 2014, and I'm writing these words on May 20, 2015—more than a full year after it ended. If I was reading a book like this one, I would ask the same question that I do after a cheesy cooking show: Did the changes stick? Or did this productivity guy simply go back to the way he worked before?

The answer, put simply, is, the changes stuck. Every single one of them.

---

* I watch the Food Network *a lot*.

My favorite part of my yearlong productivity project was how I actually got to experiment with everything I read about, to filter out what worked from what didn't. To put it bluntly, about half of the quick tips and productivity hacks I encountered didn't work—and as you might have guessed, those usually didn't make it into the book. Pretty much everyone wants to get more done every day and have more time to do things that are meaningful and impactful. Quick productivity hacks are sexy, but they're the fad diets of the workplace. While you may lose a bit of water weight in the first few weeks, you won't accomplish anything real over the long haul. That takes work.

While some of the tactics in this book are on the easier side, most of them take more time, attention, and energy than a simple productivity hack. But they work—and because I value my productivity so much, I've stuck with them.

They will work for you, too. But you have to step up. I'm not some self-help guru by any stretch of anyone's imagination. But this much is inescapable: if you want to make the jump from the romantic idea of being more productive to actually accomplishing more on a daily basis, you have to put in the effort.

As I've done my best to make clear, productivity is made up of three things: time, attention, and energy. And I believe strongly that the greatest leaders in the knowledge economy will be the ones who combine all three better than anyone else. People like Marie Curie, Thomas Edison, Albert Einstein, Jane Goodall, and Steve Jobs all willed into existence some of the most brilliant ideas and inventions humanity has seen—and they had the exact same twenty-four hours every day that we do. The difference between them and everyone else—and between the corporate vice president and the employees who work for her—isn't how much time they have every day. It's that they know how to effectively manage their time, attention, and energy, and constantly make an effort to spend each more deliberately.

Just as this has been the case in the past, this will be the case in the future.

The future will be carved out by the people who combine all three ingredients of productivity to work more deliberately than everyone else.

ACKNOWLEDGMENTS

I have a confession to make: I hardly ever read the Acknowledgments section of books. But as I wrote *The Productivity Project*, I quickly realized how special the Acknowledgments section is. Over the last couple of years, an incredible number of people have been instrumental in making this book a reality. They deserve the gratitude of a thousand pages.

First, thank you to Roger Scholl, my editor, who believed in this book from the start and gave me the freedom to make a thousand changes along the way. When I started researching the book-writing process, I slightly freaked out about how difficult publishers and editors could be to work with. Every single person I worked with at Penguin Random House contradicted that—including Roger. Roger is one of the kindest people I've met; he put up with all of my annoying questions during the writing process, and made this book infinitely better. A huge thank you also to Ayelet Gruenspecht, Megan Perritt, Campbell Wharton, and Owen Haney for their hand in marketing this book, and to Tina Constable for publishing this book. I couldn't imagine a better team to work on this project with.

Of course, I didn't simply walk into the Random House Tower in New York and drop my book proposal down with a *clunk* on Roger's desk. My agent, Lucinda Blumenfeld, did that, and this book wouldn't exist without her, either. Lucinda was by my side on this project from its inception through its completion, and I couldn't have asked for a more helpful partner. Over the last couple of years, Lucinda has become more than just a trusted business partner; she's become someone who deeply cares about me and my career, and even more, a good friend. Thank you, Lucinda. (Also, sorry I wouldn't stop rambling on about how beautiful the universe is when you and David took me out for dinner.)

One of the questions my girlfriend, Ardyn, gets asked when her friends hear about my project is "How the heck did you put up with his weird experiments?" A lot of people thought I was crazy when I started my project, but Ardyn didn't, and she supported me from the very first day, even though she probably shouldn't have. I can say with certainty that my project and this book would not have happened without her. This book is hers as much as it is mine. Thank you, Ardyn.

To Victoria Klassen and Luise Jørgensen, for your help with the research process for this book. Thank you. Any mistakes in these pages are my own. I've included a few on purpose to see if you'll catch them.

To everyone who helped out with AYOP—usually for free, without asking for anything in return, because they wanted to help me create something neat. That includes Jim Reil, Chris O'Gorman, Todd Luckasavitch, and Phil Cole for helping me flesh out the initial idea for my project; Samuel Caron, Alexandre Desjardins, and Carlos Lopez of ETC Productions for creating the ending video for AYOP; Ryan Wang, Zack Lovatt, and Chris Sauve for helping me design, animate, and program my New Year's Resolutions Guidebook (alifeofproductivity.com/resolutions/); Beverley Mitchell and Ryan Wilfong for helping out with my site; Rachel Caven and Jenni Beharry for helping me with my body fat experiment; Erin Murphy for taking pictures for articles; and finally, to everyone who "pitched in" to my project. When I started my project, I had a feature on my site where readers could "pitch in" if they found what I made valuable. For those who did, thank you.

To everyone else who supported me on a personal level along the way, including my sister, Emily; my parents, Colleen and Glen; Dan Trevisanutto; Steve and Helene Nordstrom; Mary, Des, and Harry (in Dublin); Jon Krop; and Andrew Payeur. Thank you.

To you—for picking up this book, taking the time to read what I wrote, and for staying curious right to the very end. You're awesome, and I hope you never change.

And, finally, to everyone in my Camp Quality tribe—in particular Mathew Perkins, every single camper, and the camp counselors who return year after year, dedicating themselves to an incredible community of people without asking for a single thing in return. You inspire me, and I could not have written this book without that inspiration. This book is for you.

NOTES

INTRODUCTION

2   **According to the most recent American** Bureau of Labor Statistics, "American Time Use Survey," last modified September 30, 2014, http://www.bls.gov/tus/charts.

13   **Fifty years ago, about a third** Charles Kenny, "Factory Jobs Are Gone. Get Over It," *Bloomberg Business*, January 23, 2014, accessed June 1, 2015, http://www.bloomberg.com/bw/articles/2014-01-23/manufacturing-jobs-may-not-be-cure-for-unemployment-inequality.

PART ONE: LAYING THE GROUNDWORK

21   **It's what you do with your** Catherine Gale and Christopher Martyn, "Larks and Owls and Health, Wealth and Wisdom," *British Medical Journal* 317, no. 7174 (1998): 1675–1677.

34   **Brian, who has a similar view** Brian Tracy, *Eat That Frog* (San Francisco: Berrett-Koehler Publishers, 2007).

37   **Though the concept behind the idea** *Zenhabits Blog*, "Purpose Your Day: Most Important Task (MIT)," February 6, 2007, http://zenhabits.net/purpose-your-day-most-important-task; Gina Trapani, "Geek to Live: Control Your Work-day," *Lifehacker Blog*, July 14, 2006, http://lifehacker.com/187074/geek-to-live--control-your-workday.

42   **Studies show this makes acting out** Peter M. Gollwitzer, "Implementation Intentions, Strong Effects of Simple Plans," *American Psychologist* 54, no. 7 (1999): 493–503.

45   **Everyone is wired differently** Jeanne F. Duffy, David W. Rimmer, and Charles A. Czeisler, "Association of Intrinsic Circadian Period with Morningness–Eveningness, Usual Wake Time, and Circadian Phase," *Behavioral Neuroscience* 115, no. 4 (2001): 895–899.

46   **To me, it also feels incredible** B. J. Shannon et al., "Morning-Evening Variation in Human Brain Metabolism and Memory Circuits," *Journal of Neurophysiology* 109, no. 5 (2013): 1444–1456, accessed June 1, 2015, doi:10.1152/jn.00651.2012; Olga Khazan, "When Fatigue Boosts Creativity," *The Atlantic*, March 20, 2015, http://www.theatlantic.com/health/archive/2015/03/when-fatigue-boosts-creativity/388221/.

48   **Studies show that when you keep** Kaiser Permanente, "Keeping a Food Diary Doubles Diet Weight Loss, Study Suggests," *ScienceDaily*, July 8, 2008.

PART TWO: WASTING TIME

57   **Piers Steel, the author of** Piers Steel, *The Procrastination Equation: How to Stop Putting Things Off and Start Getting Stuff Done* (New York: HarperCollins Publishers, 2012), 11.

57   **According to a recent Salary.com survey** Aaron Gouveia, "2014 Wasting Time at Work Survey," accessed June 1, 2015, http://www.salary.com/2014-wasting -time-at-work/slide/2/.

59   **Assuming you live until eighty and** Nielsen, *An Era of Growth: The Cross-Platform Report Q4 2013*, March 5, 2014, http://www.nielsen.com/us/en/insights/ reports/2014/an-era-of-growth-the-cross-platform-report.html; Central Intelligence Agency, *The World Factbook*, accessed June 1, 2014, https://www.cia.gov/ library/publications/the-world-factbook/rankorder/2102rank.html.

60   **Evolutionarily speaking, the limbic is an** Peter M. Gollwitzer, "Implementation Intentions: Strong Effects of Simple Plans," *American Psychologist* 54, no. 7 (1999): 493–503.

61   **In a very general sense, though, your** Jonathan Haidt, *The Happiness Hypothesis* (New York: Basic Books, 2006), 11.

62   **The limbic system has evolved** J. A. Vilensky, G. W. Van Hoesen, and A. R. Damasio, "The Limbic System and Human Evolution," *Journal of Human Evolution* 11, no. 6 (1982): 447–60; Jonathan Haidt, "The New Synthesis in Moral Psychology," *The American Associaton for the Advancement of Science* 316, no. 5827 (2007): 998–1002.

63   **Igniting your prefrontal cortex** Ibid.

64   **Because doing taxes is such an** IBISWorld, "Tax Preparation Services in the US: Market Research Report," April 2015, http://www.ibisworld.com/industry/ default.aspx?indid=1399.

64   **According to Intuit—the makers of** *The Turbotax Blog*, April 11, 2013, http:// blog.turbotax.intuit.com/2013/04/11/turbotax-top-10-procrastinating-cities -infographic/.

66   **"The dread of doing a task** Rita Emmett, *The Procrastinator's Handbook: Mastering the Art of Doing It Now* (New York: Walker Publishing Company, 2000).

72   **After the experiment, he discovered** Hal E. Hershfield, Daniel G. Goldstein, William F. Sharpe, Jesse Fox, Leo Yeykelis, Laura L. Carstensen, and Jeremy N. Bailenson, "Increasing Saving Behavior Through Age-Progressed Renderings of the Future Self," *Journal of Marketing Research* 48, no. SPL (2011): S23–S37.

75   **Before getting in touch with your** Hal E. Hershfield, Taya R. Cohen, and Leigh Thompson, "Short Horizons and Tempting Situations: Lack of Continuity to Our Future Selves Leads to Unethical Decision Making and Behavior," *Organizational Behavior and Human Decision Processes* 112, no. 2 (2012): 298–310, doi:10.1016/j.obhdp.2011.11.002.

80   **(The runners-up: too many meetings** Aaron Gouveia, "2014 Wasting Time at

Work Survey," Salary.com, accessed June 1, 2015, http://www.salary.com/2014
-wasting-time-at-work/slide/6.

82   **(Piers Steel, who wrote *The Procrastination*** Piers Steel, *The Procrastination
Equation: How to Stop Putting Things Off and Start Getting Stuff Done* (New York:
HarperCollins Publishers, 2012): 50, 30.

PART THREE: THE END OF TIME MANAGEMENT

88   **In the Malay language** "Toujours Tingo: Weird Words and Bizarre Phrases,"
The Telegraph, December 18, 2008, http://www.telegraph.co.uk/news/news
topics/howaboutthat/3830559/Toujours-Tingo-Weird-words-and-bizarre
-phrases.html.

88   **That's when, in 1883** History.com, "Railroads Create the First Time Zones,"
accessed June 1, 2015, http://www.history.com/this-day-in-history/railroads
-create-the-first-time-zones.

90   **Over the last sixty years, manufacturing** Charles Kenny, "Factory Jobs Are
Gone. Get Over It," *Bloomberg Business*, January 23, 2014, accessed June 1, 2015,
http://www.bloomberg.com/bw/articles/2014-01-23/manufacturing-jobs-may
-not-be-cure-for-unemployment-inequality; Bureau of Economic Analysis, U.S.
Department of Commerce, "New Quarterly Statistics Detail Industries' Economic Performance. Statistics Span First Quarter of 2005 through Fourth Quarter of 2013 and Annual Results for 2013," April 25, 2014, http://www.bea.gov/
newsreleases/industry/gdpindustry/2014/pdf/gdpind413.pdf.

98   **In working ninety hours a week** Ben Hughes, "Why Crunch Mode Doesn't
Work," *InfoQ Blog*, January 10, 2008, http://www.igda.org/?page=crunchsix
lessons.

98   **One study found that when you** Sara Robinson, "Bring Back the 40-Hour Work
Week," *Salon News*, March 14, 2012, http://www.salon.com/2012/03/14/bring
_back_the_40_hour_work_week/.

98   **Yet another study found that your** Bob Sullivan, "Memo to Work Martyrs:
Long Hours Make You Less Productive," *Today*, January 26, 2015, http://www
.today.com/money/why-you-shouldnt-work-more-50-hours-week-2D80449508.

106   **You can block off several hours** "Maker's Schedule, Manager's Schedule," *Paul
Graham Blog*, July 2009, http://www.paulgraham.com/makersschedule.html.

106– **It might sound counterintuitive (and not** Winifred Gallagher, *Rapt: Attention
107   and the Focused Life* (New York: Penguin Books, 2010).

PART FOUR: THE ZEN OF PRODUCTIVITY

122   **It's how much space exists *between*** William Beaty, "The Physics Behind Traffic Jams," *SmartMotorist.com*, accessed June 1, 2015, http://www.smartmotorist
.com/traffic-and-safety-guideline/traffic-jams.html.

126   **Another (more scientific) study found** Karen Renaud, Judith Ramsay, and
Mario Hair, "'You've Got E-Mail!' . . . Shall I Deal with It Now? Electronic

Mail from the Recipient's Perspective," *International Journal of Human-Computer Interaction* 21, no. 3 (2006): 313–332.

128   **A survey of 150 senior executives** Verizon, "Meetings in America: A Study of Trends, Costs, and Attitudes Toward Business Travel and Teleconferencing, and Their Impact on Productivity," accessed June 1, 2015, https://e-meetings .verizonbusiness.com/global/en/meetingsinamerica/uswhitepaper.php; OfficeTeam, "Let's Not Meet," accessed June 1, 2015, http://officeteam.rhi .mediaroom.com/meetings.

130   **One illuminating study found that** Karen Renaud, Judith Ramsay, and Mario Hair, "'You've Got E-Mail!' . . . Shall I Deal with It Now? Electronic Mail From the Recipient's Perspective," *International Journal of Human-Computer Interaction* 21, no. 3 (2006): 313–332.

140   **It is also the fifty-sixth** Oxford Dictionaries, Oxford University Press, "The OEC: Facts about the Language," accessed June 1, 2015. http://www.oxford dictionaries.com/words/the-oec-facts-about-the-language.

PART FIVE: QUIET YOUR MIND

147   **Long before the printing press was** Thomas C. Brickhouse and Nicholas D. Smith, *Plato's Socrates* (New York: Oxford University Press, 1994); Walter J. Ong, *Orality and Literacy: The Technologizing of the Word* (New York: Routledge, 2002), http://dss-edit.com/prof-anon/sound/library/Ong_orality_and_literacy.pdf.

148   **At best, our minds can only** George A. Miller, "The Magical Number Seven, Plus or Minus Two. Some Limits on Our Capacity for Processing Information," *Psychological Review* 101, no. 2 (1994): 343–352.

150   **This is a result of what** Bluma Zeigarnik, "Das Behalten erledigter und uner-ledigter Handlungen," *Psychologische Forschung* 9 (1927): 1–85.

156   **Search for them instead** Steve Whittaker et al., "Am I Wasting My Time Or-ganizing Email? A Study of Email Refinding," IBM Research-Almaden, 2011, http://people.ucsc.edu/~swhittak/papers/chi2011_refinding_email_camera _ready.pdf.

157   **Research shows that the simple** Ayelet Fishbach and Ravi Dhar, "Goals as Ex-cuses or Guides: The Liberating Effect of Perceived Goal Progress on Choice," *Journal of Consumer Research* 32, no. 3 (2005): 370–377.

169   **In the average week today, the** Mary Meeker, "Internet Trends 2015 – Code Conference," Kleiner, Perkins, Caufield, Byers, 2015, http://www.kpcb.com/ internet-trends.

169–   **Assuming that you sleep for 7.7** Bureau of Labor Statistics, "American Time Use
170   Survey," last modified September 30, 2014, http://www.bls.gov/tus/charts.

170   **The first group received information about** Ap Dijksterhuis et al., "On Mak-ing the Right Choice: The Deliberation-Without-Attention Effect," *Science* 311, no. 5763 (2006): 1005–1007.

171   **Several years after the experiment was** J. David Creswell, James K. Bursley, and Ajay B. Satpute, "Neural Reactivation Links Unconscious Thought to Decision

Making Performance," *Social Cognitive and Affective Neuroscience* 8, no. 8 (2013): 863–869, doi:10.1093/scan/nst004.

173 **Your brain also continues to process** Jonathan Hasford, "Should I Think Carefully or Sleep on It?: Investigating the Moderating Role of Attribute Learning," *Journal of Experimental Social Psychology* 51 (2014): 51–55; J. D. Payne, M. A. Tucker, J. M. Ellenbogen, E. J. Wamsley, M. P. Walker, D. L. Schacter, et al., "Memory for Semantically Related and Unrelated Declarative Information: The Benefit of Sleep, the Cost of Wake," *PLoS ONE* 7, no. 3 (2012): e33079, doi:10.1371/journal.pone.0033079.

174 **Whenever Einstein had a difficult** Ronald W. Clark, *Einstein: The Life and Times* (New York: World Publishing, 1971), 106.

174 **The American Psychological Association** Kelly McGonigal, *The Willpower Instinct* (New York: Avery, 2012).

PART SIX: THE ATTENTION MUSCLE

179 **An interesting study conducted by Harvard** Matthew A. Killingsworth and Daniel T. Gilbert, "A Wandering Mind Is an Unhappy Mind," *Science* 330, no. 6006 (2010): 932.

182 **According to neuroscientists, our attention** Yi-Yuan Tang and Michael Posner, "Attention Training and Attention State Training," *Trends in Cognitive Sciences* 13, no. 5 (2009): 222–27.

185 **However, according to RescueTime** Matt Richtel, "Lost in E-Mail, Tech Firms Face Self-Made Beast," *New York Times*, June 14, 2008, accessed June 1, 2015, http://www.nytimes.com/2008/06/14/technology/14email.html.

185 **It's clear that in the knowledge** Steve Lohr, "Is Information Overload a $650 Billion Drag on the Economy?" *Bits Blog New York Times*, December 20, 2007, http://bits.blogs.nytimes.com/2007/12/20/is-information-overload-a-650 -billion-drag-on-the-economy/.

185 **Also according to Basex** Maggie Jackson, *Distracted* (Amherst, NY: Prometheus Books, 2008); Marci Alboher, "Fighting a War Against Distraction," *New York Times*, June 22, 2008, http://www.nytimes.com/2008/06/22/jobs/22shifting .html.

185– **And as Gloria Mark** Gloria Mark, Victor M. Gonzalez, and Justin Harris,
186 "No Task Left Behind? Examining the Nature of Fragmented Work." *Proceedings of the SIGCHI Conference on Human Factors in Computing Systems*, ACM, 2005.

187 **And when your brain is overloaded** Sam Anderson, "In Defense of Distraction," accessed June 1, 2015, *New York* magazine, http://nymag.com/news/ features/56793/.

188 **Positive psychologists (like bestselling author** Shawn Achor, *The Happiness Advantage: The Seven Principles of Positive Psychology That Fuel Success and Performance at Work* (New York: Random House, 2011).

193 **"Cells that fire together, wire together** D. O. Hebb, *The Organization of Behavior* (New York: Wiley & Sons, 1949).

193 **The reason habits are so powerful** "The Addicted Brain," Harvard Health Publication, June 9, 2009, http://www.health.harvard.edu/mind-and-mood/the _addicted_brain.

194 **"Multitasking creates a dopamine-addiction** Daniel Levitin, *The Organized Mind: Thinking Straight in the Age of Information Overload* (Westminster, London: Penguin UK, 2015).

194 **In fact, your brain** *can't* **focus** John Medina, *Brain Rules: 12 Principles for Surviving and Thriving at Work, Home, and School* (Edmunds, WA: Pear Press, 2008); Joshua Rubinstein, David Meyer, and Jeffrey Evans, "Executive Control of Cognitive Processes in Task Switching," *J Exp Psych* 27 (2001): 763–771; N. F. Ramsey, J. M. Jansma, G. Jager, T. Van Raalten, and R. S. Kahn, "Neurophysiological Factors in Human Information Processing Capacity," *Brain* 127 (2003): 517–525; Stephen Monsell and Jon Driver, *Control of Cognitive Processes: Attention and Performance XVIII* (Cambridge, MA: MIT Press, 2000).

194– **My favorite study on multitasking** Eyal Ophir, Clifford Nass, and Anthony D.
195 Wagner, "Cognitive Control in Media Multitaskers," *Proceedings of the National Academy of Sciences* 106, no. 37 (2009): 15583–15587.

195 **"We kept looking for what they're** Adam Gorlick, "Media Multitaskers Pay Mental Price, Stanford Study Shows," *Stanford Report*, August 24, 2009, http://news.stanford.edu/news/2009/august24/multitask-research-study-082409 .html.

195 **Multitasking even makes you more prone** Mark W. Becker, Reem Alzahabi, and Christopher J. Hopwood, "Media Multitasking Is Associated with Symptoms of Depression and Social Anxiety," *Cyberpsychology, Behavior, and Social Networking* 16, no. 2 (February 2013): 132–135, doi:10.1089/cyber.2012.0291.

199 **(Research shows that it's easier** Bill Breen, "The 6 Myths of Creativity," *Fast Company*, December 1, 2004, http://www.fastcompany.com/51559/6-myths -creativity.

199 **As Matthew Killingsworth and Daniel Gilbert** Matthew A. Killingsworth and Daniel T. Gilbert, "A Wandering Mind Is an Unhappy Mind," *Science* 330, no. 6006 (2010): 932.

199 **From an evolutionary standpoint** Ibid.

207 **Sara Lazar, a neuroscientist at Harvard** Sara W. Lazar et al., "Functional Brain Mapping of the Relaxation Response and Meditation," *Neuroreport* 11, no. 7 (2000): 1581–1585; Sara W. Lazar, "The Neurobiology of Mindfulness," in *Mindfulness and Psychotherapy*, ed. Christopher K. Germer, Ronald D. Siegel, and Paul R. Fulton (New York: Guilford, 2013), 282–295.

207 **According to Lazar** Caroline Williams, "Concentrate! How to Tame a Wandering Mind," BBC, October 16, 2014, http://www.bbc.com/future/story/20141015 -concentrate-how-to-focus-better.

208 **All these effects—every one backed** Daphne M. Davis and Jeffrey A. Hayes, "What Are the Benefits of Mindfulness?," *Monitor on Psychology* 43, no. 7 (2012), http://www.apa.org/monitor/2012/07-08/ce-corner.aspx; Sue McGreevey, "Eight Weeks to a Better Brain," *Harvard Gazette*, January 21, 2011, http://news.harvard.edu/gazette/story/2011/01/eight-weeks-to-a-better-brain;

Erik Dane and Bradley J. Brummel, "Examining Workplace Mindfulness and Its Relations to Job Performance and Turnover Intention," *Human Relations* 67, no. 1 (2013): 105–128, doi:10.1177/0018726713487753; Sara Lazer et al., "Meditation Experience Is Associated With Increased Cortical Thickness," *Neuroreporter* 16, no. 17 (2005): 1893-1897; Michael Mrazek et al., "Mindfulness Training Improves Working Memory Capacity and GRE Performance While Reducing Mind Wandering," *Psychological Science* 24, no. 5 (2013): 776–81.

PART SEVEN: TAKING PRODUCTIVITY TO THE NEXT LEVEL

218 **Your brain cells consume** Ferris Jabr, "Does Thinking Really Hard Burn More Calories?" *Scientific American*, July 18, 2012, https://www.scientificamerican.com/article/thinking-hard-calories.

219 **(I know I'm not the only** Richard A. Rawson, "Meth and the Brain," *Frontline*, February 14, 2006, http://www.pbs.org/wgbh/pages/frontline/meth/body/methbrainnoflash.html.

221 **Research has shown that the optimal** E. Leigh Gibson, "Carbohydrates and Mental Function: Feeding or Impeding the Brain?" *Nutrition Bulletin* 32, no. s1 (2007): 71–83; Michael Parsons, and Paul Gold, "Glucose Enhancement of Memory in Elderly Humans: An Inverted-U Dose–Response Curve," *Neurobiology of Aging* 13, no. 3 (1992): 401–404.

223 **Studies show that it takes your** "Guide to Behavior Change," National Heart, Blood and Lung Institute, accessed June 1, 2015, http://www.nhlbi.nih.gov/health/educational/lose_wt/behavior.htm.

226 **Every day the average person consumes** Liwei Chen et al., "Reduction in Consumption of Sugar-Sweetened Beverages Is Associated with Weight Loss," *American Journal of Clinical Nutrition* 89, no. 5 (2009): 1299-1306, http://www.ncbi.nlm.nih.gov/pmc/articles/PMC2676995/.

228 **If you're a fan of having** Irshaad O. Ebrahim et al., "Alcohol and Sleep I: Effects on Normal Sleep," *Alcoholism: Clinical and Experimental Research* 37, no. 4 (2013): 539–549.

228 **Eight to fourteen hours after** "Sleep and Caffeine," American Academy of Sleep Medicine, August 1, 2013, http://www.sleepeducation.com/news/2013/08/01/sleep-and-caffeine; David M. Mrazik, "Reconsidering Caffeine: An Awake and Alert New Look at America's Most Commonly Consumed Drug," 2004 Third Year Paper, http://nrs.harvard.edu/urn-3:HUL.InstRepos:8846793.

229 **In fact, your brain even begins** Joseph Stromberg, "This Is How Your Brain Becomes Addicted to Caffeine," Smithsonian.com, August 9, 2013, http://www.smithsonianmag.com/science-nature/this-is-how-your-brain-becomes-addicted-to-caffeine-26861037/?no-ist.

231 **As an ambivert I fall somewhere** Brian R. Little, *Me, Myself, and Us: The Science of Personality and the Art of Well-Being* (New York: PublicAffairs, 2014).

231 **Be careful about drinking caffeine before** Maria Konnikova, "How Caffeine Can Cramp Creativity," *The New Yorker*, June 17, 2013, http://www.newyorker.com/tech/elements/how-caffeine-can-cramp-creativity.

231 **Caffeine also has a bigger effect** Steven Miller, "The Best Time for Your Coffee," October 23, 2013, *The BrainFacts Blog*, http://blog.brainfacts.org/2013/10/the-best-time-for-your-coffee; Miguel Debono et al., "Modified-Release Hydrocortisone to Provide Circadian Cortisol Profiles," *Journal of Clinical Endocrinology & Metabolism* 94, no. 5 (2009): 1548–1554.

232 **One study found that drinking water** M. Boschmann et al., "Water Drinking Induces Thermogenesis Through Osmosensitive Mechanisms," *Journal of Clinical Endocrinology & Metabolism* 92, no. 8. (2007): 3334–3337, http://www.ncbi.nlm.nih.gov/pubmed/17519319.

232– **Because water partly fills your stomach** American Chemical Society, "Clinical
233 Trial Confirms Effectiveness of Simple Appetite Control Method," August 23, 2010, http://www.acs.org/content/acs/en/pressroom/newsreleases/2010/august/clinical-trial-confirms-effectiveness-of-simple-appetite-control-method.html.

233 **And when you drink three liters** The Institute of Medicine, "Dietary Reference Intakes: Water, Potassium, Sodium, Chloride, and Sulfate," February 11, 2004, https://www.iom.edu/Reports/2004/Dietary-Reference-Intakes-Water-Potassium-Sodium-Chloride-and-Sulfate.aspx.

233 **Not getting enough water can cause** Susan M. Shirreffs, Stuart J. Merson, Susan M. Fraser, and David T. Archer, "The Effects of Fluid Restriction on Hydration Status and Subjective Feelings in Man," *British Journal of Nutrition* 91 (2004): 951–958, doi:10.1079/BJN20041149.

238 **Today, the amount of physical activity** Sara Germano, "American Inactivity Level Is Highest Since 2007, Survey Finds," *Wall Street Journal*, http://www.wsj.com/articles/american-inactivity-level-is-highest-since-2007-survey-finds-1429796821.

238 **Our bodies are built to walk** Daniel Lieberman, *The Story of the Human Body: Evolution, Health and Disease* (Westminster, London: Penguin UK, 2013), 217.

239 **Exercise has even been shown to** Matthew T. Schmolesky, David L. Webb, and Rodney A. Hansen, "The Effects of Aerobic Exercise Intensity and Duration on Levels of Brain-Derived Neurotrophic Factor in Healthy Men," *Journal of Sports Science & Medicine* 12, no. 3 (2013): 502–511; Chris C. Streeter et al., "Effects of Yoga Versus Walking on Mood, Anxiety, and Brain GABA Levels: A Randomized Controlled MRS Study," *Journal of Alternative and Complementary Medicine* 16, no. 11 (2010): 1145–1152; M. Rottensteiner et al., "Physical Activity, Fitness, Glucose Homeostasis, and Brain Morphology in Twins," *Medicine & Science in Sports & Exercise* 47, no. 3 (2015): 509–518, doi:10.1249/MSS.0000000000000437.

245 **These zombies even cause eighty thousand** U.S. Department of Transportation, National Highway Traffic Safety Administration, National Center for Statistics and Analysis, "Drowsy Driving," March 2011, http://www-nrd.nhtsa.dot.gov/pubs/811449.pdf.

245– **According to Gallup, 40 percent** Jeffrey M. Jones, "In U.S., 40% Get Less Than
246 Recommended Amount of Sleep," Gallup, December 19, 2013, http://www.gallup.com/poll/166553/less-recommended-amount-sleep.aspx.

246 **The Centers for Disease Control** Centers for Disease Control and Prevention,

"Insufficient Sleep Is a Public Health Epidemic," last modified January 13, 2014, http://www.cdc.gov/features/dssleep.

246 **And it negatively impacts your concentration** Division of Sleep Medicine at Harvard Medical School, "Sleep, Performance, and Public Safety," last modified December 18, 2007, http://healthysleep.med.harvard.edu/healthy/matters/consequences/sleep-performance-and-public-safety.

246 **Everyone is wired differently, requires** Ibid.

249 **Light that sits in the blue** Harvard Health Publications, "Blue light has a dark side," May 1, 2012, http://www.health.harvard.edu/staying-healthy/blue-light-has-a-dark-side.

249 **So has science—one study found** K. Burkhart and J. R. Phelps, "Amber Lenses to Block Blue Light and Improve Sleep: A Randomized Trial," *Chronobiology International* 26, no. 8 (2009): 1602–1612, doi:10.3109/07420520903523719.

249 **One study found that when call** Derek Croome, *Creating the Productive Workplace* (London: E & FN Spon, 2000).

249 **Like sleep, napping has been shown** Catherine E. Milner and Kimberly A. Cote, "Benefits of Napping in Healthy Adults: Impact of Nap Length, Time of Day, Age, and Experience with Napping," *Journal of Sleep Research* 18, no. 2 (2009): 272–281, doi:10.1111/j.1365-2869.2008.00718.x.

250 **The American Academy of Sleep Medicine** WebMD, http://www.webmd.com/sleep-disorders/features/cant-sleep-adjust-the-temperature.

250 **But above all else, it should** Sleep Number, "How to Sleep at the Perfect Temperature," accessed June 1, 2015, http://www.sleepnumber.com/eng/individualNeeds/sleepTemperature.cfm.

251 **Studies show that what time you** Catherine Gale and Chistopher Martyn, "Larks and owls and health, wealth, and wisdom," *British Medical Journal* 317, no. 7174 (1998): 1675–1677.

PART EIGHT: THE FINAL STEP

256 **In fact, in his research he's** "Shawn Achor: The Happy Secret to Better Work," TED Talk, TEDxBloomington, 2011, http://www.ted.com/talks/shawn_achor_the_happy_secret_to_better_work?language=en; Shawn Achor, *The Happiness Advantage: The Seven Principles of Positive Psychology That Fuel Success and Performance at Work* (New York: Random House, 2011).

257 **You should take breaks a lot** Lisa Evans, "The Exact Amount of Time You Should Work Every Day," *Fast Company*, September 15, 2014, http://www.fastcompany.com/3035605/how-to-be-a-success-at-everything/the-exact-amount-of-time-you-should-work-every-day.

257 **Once that energy source is depleted** John P. Trougakos et al., "Making the Break Count: An Episodic Examination of Recovery Activities, Emotional Experiences, and Positive Affective Displays," *Academy of Management Journal* 51, no. 1 (2008): 131–146.

258– **Research has shown this also makes** Mihaly Csikszentmihalyi, *Flow* (Nether-
259 lands: Springer, 2014).

259   **According to research conducted by Stanford** Carol Dweck, *Mindset: The New Psychology of Success* (New York: Random House, 2006).

260   **They found that cute baby animals** Hiroshi Nittono et al., "The Power of Kawaii: Viewing Cute Images Promotes a Careful Behavior and Narrows Attentional Focus," *PLoS ONE* 7, no. 9 (2012): e46362.

263   **One psychologist, Shad Helmstetter, has found** Shad Helmstetter, *What to Say When You Talk to Your Self* (New York: Simon and Schuster, 1990).

263   **Another study conducted on business students** Raj Raghunathan, "How Negative Is Your 'Mental Chatter'?" *Psychology Today*, October 10, 2013, https://www.psychologytoday.com/blog/sapient-nature/201310/how-negative-is-your-mental-chatter.

268   **The research backs this up; two** Gallup, "State of the American Workplace," 2012, http://www.gallup.com/services/178514/state-american-workplace.aspx; Tom Rath, *Vital Friends: The People You Can't Afford to Live Without* (New York: Gallup Press, 2006).

INDEX

ABOUT THE AUTHOR

© CHRIS ROUSSAKIS

CHRIS BAILEY, a graduate of Carleton University in Ottawa, wrote over 216,000 words on the subject of productivity on his blog, *A Year of Productivity,* during a yearlong productivity project where he conducted intensive research, as well as dozens of productivity experiments on himself to discover how to become as productive as possible. He has written hundreds of articles on the subject and has garnered coverage in media as diverse as the *New York Times,* the *Huffington Post, New York* magazine, TED, *Fast Company,* and *Lifehacker.*

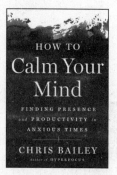